THE GREAT BOOK OF
PHILADELPHIA
SPORTS LISTS

Completely Revised and Updated

GLEN MACNOW & BIG DADDY GRAHAM

RUNNING PRESS
PHILADELPHIA

Running Press
Hachette Book Group
1290 Avenue of the Americas, New York, NY 10104
www.runningpress.com
@Running_Press

Printed in the United States of America

First Edition: November 2006
Revised and Updated Edition: October 2019

Published by Running Press, an imprint of Perseus Books, LLC, a subsidiary of Hachette Book Group, Inc. The Running Press name and logo is a trademark of the Hachette Book Group.

The Hachette Speakers Bureau provides a wide range of authors for speaking events. To find out more, go to www.hachettespeakersbureau.com or call (866) 376-6591.

The publisher is not responsible for websites (or their content) that are not owned by the publisher.

Additional credits information is on page 279.

Print book cover design by Joshua McDonnell.

Library of Congress Control Number: 2019938512

ISBNs: 978-0-7624-9608-2 (paperback), 978-0-7624-9607-5 (ebook)

LSC-C

10 9 8 7 6 5 4 3 2 1

To Carl and Benny. May all the stories in this book help make you into sports fans—loyal Philadelphia sports fans.

—Glen Macnow

To Jameson and Lucy, eat your dinner.

—Big Daddy Graham

Acknowledgments

Many of our friends contributed their expertise and opinions to this book. Special thanks to Ray Didinger, Kevin Keenan, Tom Kelly, Zack Hill, and Spike Eskin. Thanks also to all the friends and followers who contributed names and ideas on our radio shows and social media.

Contents

Introduction

When we first wrote this book in 2006, we figured we covered every important name, great moment, and crushing defeat in Philadelphia sports history. Our work was done.

Well, time moves on. New faces come in; new memories are created. And in reading our own book for the 437th time (hey, we have no lives), we realized there was nothing in it about Super Bowl LII. Or about the Phillies' great run from 2007 to 2011. Or Villanova's two national titles. Or, well, Ilya Bryzgalov.

Thirteen years produce a lot of great stories. So we decided it was time to update what we'd written before. We've added dozens of new lists here and updated many of the old ones with new personalities and highlights. And we called on some famous names to add their contributions: you'll read about Claude Giroux's top sports movies (page 223), Jay Wright's favorite days of the year (page 39), Scott Franzke's most memorable moments as a Phillies broadcaster (page 264), and Questlove's all-time favorite Philly athletes (page 18).

Overall, about 50 friends contributed their expert opinions. Alas, over 13 years, some passed away. We decided to honor some of our favorites from 2006 by rerunning their lists as a tribute to their lives. So you will find thoughts in this book from Tommy McDonald (page 174), Bill Campbell (page 170), Harry Kalas (page 262), Ed Snider (page 123), and Johnny Callison (page 89). We salute them all.

From the substantive (most inspirational people) to the silly (best bald guys), *The Great Book of Philadelphia Sports Lists* compiles the funniest, most awe-inspiring, and most heartbreaking times in our local sports history.

We've even tossed in some off-sports topics to add grist to the mill. Because, let's face it, when guys aren't debating sports, we're probably arguing about movies, music, food, and women—most often women.

Our lists are designed—in some cases—to be definitive. And in other cases, we hope they'll serve to start debate. Heck, the two main authors disagreed so often that we decided to face off in some head-to-head showdowns.

As we learned over all these years, the sports scene is constantly changing. Coaches we laud now may be fired before you finish reading the book. Players who are today's toast of the town could be tomorrow's stale crust. Records we cite may be broken. That's okay. Feel free to write your own revisions in the margins.

Enjoy this book on the beach, by your bed, or in the bathroom (yeah, we know our audience). And if you're a bartender in Philly, you better have a copy behind the bar, because it'll be sure to start many a great conversation—and resolve many a bet.

Big Daddy grew up in Southwest Philadelphia. I have lived in the Pennsylvania suburbs for more than 30 years. So we started a debate: Which area spawns more great athletes?

Of course, Big Daddy stood up for his hometown. I lobbied for the sticks. And we even involved a third party, who argues that the preeminent stars come from South Jersey.

Here are our lists. Let's start with mine, since it's the most impressive. But you be the judge.

Honorable mention: Jim Furyk, Rip Hamilton, Brendan Hansen, Joe Klecko, Jameer Nelson, Herb Pennock, Geoff Petrie, Lisa Raymond, Jay Sigel, Mickey Vernon, Johnny Weir.

10. Billy "White Shoes" Johnson.
A flamboyant 170-pound water bug out of Chichester High and Widener, he's also the choreographer of the best touchdown dance in history. Johnson made the NFL's 75th anniversary team as a punt returner. Hmmm, Big Daddy, I don't see any Philly natives on that all-time team.

9. Leroy Burrell.
As a high school kid from Lansdowne, Burrell long-jumped more than 24 feet and once scored more points in the state track meet than every member of the second-place team combined. Burrell set the world record for the 100-meter dash in 1991 and then broke that record in 1994. Is there any title cooler than "world's fastest human"?

8. Matt Ryan.
Our friend Ray Didinger recalls watching Ryan play as a 16-year-old at William Penn Charter and projecting him as a future NFL star. Ray was correct, as usual. "Matty Ice" and teammates may have historically collapsed during Super Bowl LI, but the 2016 NFL MVP continues to climb up the all-time leader charts. He's a lock to make the Pro Football Hall of Fame—which will give the burbs one more enshrined QB than the city.

7. Emlen Tunnell.
Speaking of the Hall, Tunnell is the first African American ever inducted into that shrine. Raised in Radnor, that famed breeding ground of football talent, Tunnell played 14 seasons (1948–1961), mostly for the Giants, and was referred to as "Offense on Defense." He retired as the NFL's all-time interception leader.

6. Jamie Moyer.
The lefty from Souderton High and St. Joe's started in the big leagues at age 23 and was still throwing 26 years later. Moyer won 269 Major League games, including 56 with the Phils at the end of his career. It was all the more impressive considering that his fastball couldn't break through tissue paper.

5. Eddie George.
An amazing athlete out of Abington who won the Heisman Trophy in 1995 by rushing for 1,927 yards and 24 TDs at Ohio State. He went on to rush for more than 10,000 yards in the NFL. A shame he never played for the Eagles. By my count, there are four Heisman winners from the area—George, Ron Dayne of Berlin, Mike Rozier of Camden, and John Cappelletti of Upper Darby. You got any from the city, Big Daddy?

4. Mike Richter. This isn't really a fair debate here, since you city guys only know how to play hockey on sneakers and with those orange Mylec balls. Richter, born in Abington and raised in Flourtown, won more than 300 games with the New York Rangers. He was a Stanley Cup winner, a four-time All-Star, and MVP of the 1996 World Cup, in which he led the United States to gold.

3. Mike Piazza. "The Pride of Norristown," as he was invariably called, although we always thought he was from Phoenixville. Piazza began as the 1,390th player taken in the Major League draft, chosen mostly as a favor to his dad, millionaire car dealer Vince Piazza. Mike finished his career as the best offensive catcher in Major League history, with 427 homers and a .922 OPS. The 12-time All-Star got to give his Cooperstown speech in 2016.

2. Reggie Jackson. You remember Mr. October, right, Big Daddy? Three homers on three pitches in the 1977 World Series. A 14-time All-Star, two-time World Series MVP, and American League MVP in 1973. He slammed 563 career homers and got into nearly as many scuffles with teammates and managers. And you know the funny thing? A friend of mine who played football with Reggie at Cheltenham High said Mr. Jackson was five times as good at running back as he was with a baseball bat.

1. Kobe Bryant. Folks in Philadelphia never liked him, largely because he's a product of Lower Merion. To be honest, we didn't much like him either out here in the hinterlands. But give the devil his due: Bryant retired in 2016 as the NBA's third all-time leading scorer (three notches above Wilt Chamberlain). He's the owner of five NBA championship rings, an MVP trophy, and two All-Star Game MVP awards. Boo him if you like, Big Daddy, but you can't beat him.

Ten Greatest Athletes from the Great City of Philadelphia (to Hell with the Suburbs!) :: Big Daddy

For the record, Glen, Eddie George lived two blocks from my mother in Southwest Philly, so I'm not sure if he should even be *on* your list. You can have Kobe; ain't no way he'd ever be on *any* city list. I'd take Dawn Staley over stinkin' Kobe any day of the week.

You see, city kids get tough by slugging it out for their next meal, not over who gets the keys to the Beemer. Athletes who didn't even *make* my list would *top* your suburban 10. Check these names out: the late, great Hank Gathers, John B. Kelly, Larry Cannon, Rich Gannon, Gene Banks, Clifford Anderson, Frank Reagan, Rasheed Wallace, Erik Williams, Ernie Beck, Del Ennis, Bo Kimble, and Kyle Lowry. Geez, I had to leave Guy Rodgers off the list, who's maybe the greatest player ever to lace them up in the Big 5, because he's not in the Hall of Fame.

Then I had a real dilemma. I had three amazing athletes who will all be in a Hall of Fame one day, yet I could only choose two. So let me just apologize to the legendary Bernard Hopkins—and start running! So eight here are already in a Hall, and the other two will be there any minute.

10. Dawn Staley. Okay, here we go. Three-time Olympic gold medal winner, two-time National Player of the Year at UVA, where she went to three straight Final Fours. Numerous world championships. North Philly's Dawn was part of that famous 1995–1996 national team that went 60–0. This Dobbins Tech grad has a seven-story mural at 8th and Market, for chrissakes (go see it and learn, Glen), and was voted by the US Olympic team (not just her basketball team) to carry the American flag into the Olympic stadium in 2004. We love you, Dawn.

9. Marvin Harrison. As much as it pains me as a West Catholic grad to add Marvin, let's face it—he smashed a ton of records. In fact, he and Peyton Manning teamed up for 114 TDs together, more than any QB-WR duo in NFL history. He's also a three-year letterman in basketball at Roman Catholic. Not surprisingly, there's a bust of him in Canton.

8. Paul Arizin. Now here's a story for you: Paul didn't even make his high school basketball team at La Salle. He went to Villanova without a scholarship. A year later, in '49, he set an NCAA record by scoring 85 points in a game. Are you kidding me? He was an All-American and the College Player of the Year his senior year and went on to a great 10-year NBA career with his hometown Warriors. When he retired he had the third-most points in NBA history. Enshrined in the Hall of Fame in '78, Paul was named one of the 50 Greatest NBA Players ever in 1996, and there's a certain other Philly boy on this list (I'll give you a hint—he once scored 100 points in one game) who cited Paul as one of the top five players he ever saw. So for all you young heads out there, keep your chin up if you ever get cut from a team.

7. Leroy Kelly. Quick, name me the player who replaced a legend like Jim Brown, as Leroy had to, and then went on himself to the Hall of Fame. A Simon Gratz grad, this NFL great was one of the top running backs of his time (and an awesome punt returner) who missed just four games in 10 seasons. That's pretty damned incredible, Glen.

6. Tom Gola. Yet another Warrior Hall of Famer, Tom is one of only two players in history to win an NIT (when it truly mattered), NCAA, *and* NBA championship. He was a four-time

All-American at La Salle College—and did I mention that he also won a City Championship at La Salle High? He not only bailed La Salle University out of an ugly mess as a coach, but as a city controller, he also helped the city out of many messes. City kids remain loyal.

5. Earl Monroe. Look, I could rattle off a bunch of fantastic stats, but the fact is the Pearl, a Bartram High grad, just might be the coolest man to walk the planet Earth. He should have played with a sax around his neck. By the way, I once *played* in a game with Earl Monroe. Got any Hall of Famers on *your* list, Glen, who *you* played with? Huh?

4. Roy Campanella. Another Simon Gratz alum, Roy was the starting National League All-Star catcher eight straight years. He made four appearances in the World Series with the Dodgers (unfortunately only one a win) and was a three-time MVP. He hit 40 homers in '53, a record for catchers that lasted for 43 years. Elected to the Hall of Fame in '69, Roy was paralyzed after a car accident in '58 yet continued to work for Major League Baseball up until his death in 1993, teaching and inspiring many.

3. Herb Adderley. Get ready for the numbers from this Northeast High Hall of Famer. He won six—yes, you're reading correctly—*six* NFL championships, including three Super Bowls. Three of his titles were with the Packers before there was a Bowl; then he won two Bowls with the Pack and another with the Cowgirls (and even got to *another* Bowl, losing to the Colts in '71 on a last-second field goal). Still living in the area, he calls into my show occasionally and once hit a home run off West Philly High's (and late WIP host) Steve Fredericks that Steve told me "still hasn't come down."

2. Joe Frazier. I originally wasn't going to have Smokin' Joe on this list because he didn't move to Philly until he was 15. But, Glen, you said if an athlete went to high school in Philly, he's eligible. Although Joe dropped out of school by that age, your qualifier still puts him at high school age, so he's in! And who's gonna knock him off this list? Not me. He was Heavyweight Champion of the World when that title truly meant something. Joe battled the greatest fighters around and, on March 8, 1971, defeated Muhammad Ali in what might be the single greatest event in the history of sports. He was elected to the Boxing Hall of Fame in '80. I met Joe—a truly gracious man—many times, and I even performed with him once at Resorts, when he used to sing with his band, the Knockouts. Smokin', Joe!

1. Wilt Chamberlain. Take every suburban lame-ass on your list, Glen; add them all up; and they still couldn't carry Wilt's jock.

Reuben Frank covers the Eagles for NBC Sports Philadelphia. He's also a part-time host on 94-WIP, a track and field announcer, and an obsessive concert attendee.

Nice lists, guys. So where's the varsity?

Hey, Philadelphia and the suburbs have produced some nice little athletes. Clap, clap, clap.

But consider this: Heisman Trophy winner Mike Rozier of Camden doesn't make the South Jersey list. Olympic track gold medalists Dennis Mitchell of Atco, English Gardner of Gibbsboro, and Lamont Smith of Willingboro couldn't sprint their way on. Haddonfield's three-time Olympic gold-medal swimmer Debbie Meyer couldn't freestyle her way on to this list.

Merchantville native George Dempsey, who starred on the Philadelphia Warriors' 1956 NBA championship team? Milt Wagner and Billy Thompson, who both came out of Camden and won an NCAA title at Louisville and an NBA title with the Lakers? NFL stars Lydell Mitchell of Salem, Art Still of Camden, and Dave Robinson of Moorestown? There's just no room.

Check out who *does* make the list.

10. Deron Cherry. One of the most improbable superstars in NFL history. He was a baseball star at Palmyra. A walk-on punter at Rutgers. An undrafted free agent with the Chiefs. The guy nobody wanted became the best free safety in football in the 1980s and is considered one of the greatest undrafted defensive players *ever*. Cherry finished his remarkable NFL career with 50 interceptions—with a record-tying four in one game. He made six consecutive Pro Bowl teams, five straight as a starter. He also received the Byron White Award in 1988 for his tireless humanitarian and charity work. He's now a part owner of the Jaguars.

9. Mel Sheppard. Okay, admit it. You've never heard of him. You've probably never even heard of his hometown, Almonesson. But that's what they called Deptford Township back before they built the mall. And in the 1908 Olympics in London, Sheppard won both the 800- and 1,500-meter runs, setting an Olympic record in the 800. He also won Olympic relay gold in both 1908 and 1912. Since Sheppard, no American has repeated that Olympic 800–1,500 double, and no American has won the Olympic 1,500. He's truly one of the all-time greats, even though nobody knows it.

8. Carli Lloyd. Lloyd grew up in Delran playing coed soccer as a kid and went on to become one of the most accomplished women players in US history. Lloyd starred at Rutgers and has played pro soccer for more than a decade, but she really made her mark playing for the US team, scoring an astounding 105 goals in 260 games as of early 2019. In the 2008 Beijing Olympics, her overtime goal against Brazil led the United States to a win in the gold medal game, and in the 2012 Olympics in London, she scored both goals in the 2–1 win over Japan in *that* gold-medal game. She remains the only person—male or female—to score game-winning goals in two separate Olympic gold-medal games.

7. Leon "Goose" Goslin. He grew up on a farm in remote Salem, but by his 21st birthday, Goslin was on his way to a brilliant Hall of Fame baseball career as a left-hand hitting outfielder. In 18 seasons with the Senators, Tigers, and Browns, Goslin amassed 2,735 hits, 248 home runs, and a .316 batting average. His .379 average led all of baseball in 1928, and he was inducted into Cooperstown in 1968. Goslin played in five World Series, winning one each with the Tigers and Senators. Anybody from Philly ever hit .379?

6. Jersey Joe Walcott. Walcott grew up in Merchantville and worked in the Camden shipyards while establishing a reputation as an indomitable local boxer in the 1940s. He lost his first four heavyweight title bouts and was 37 when he knocked out Ezzard Charles in seven rounds in Pittsburgh in 1948 to become the oldest heavyweight champ in history—a record that stood until George Foreman won the title in 1994 at 45. Walcott retained his belt until 1952, when he lost a 13-round KO to Rocky Marciano in what's considered by many the greatest heavyweight championship fight ever. After he retired, Walcott served as New Jersey's boxing commissioner and remained a revered figure in South Jersey until he died in 1994.

5. Orel Hershiser. He pitched for 18 years, won 204 games, threw 25 shutouts, received the 1988 Cy Young Award, and pitched in three World Series, winning once. But Hershiser will forever be remembered for his untouchable streak of 59 consecutive scoreless innings to end the 1988 season, a streak that broke Don Drysdale's record by a third of an inning. Hershiser, who grew up in Cherry Hill, extended the streak to 67 innings with eight scoreless innings to open the 1988 League Championship Series against the Mets. That's the equivalent of 7½ shutouts. In a row.

4. Ron Dayne. Forget everything you know about Ron Dayne, the NFL running back. An awful lot of people have carried the football in college, but—including in bowl games—none has rushed for more yards than Dayne, a Pine Hill native and Overbrook High graduate. Dayne rushed for 7,125 yards at Wisconsin, breaking the NCAA record of 6,592 set by Ricky Williams. He ranked ninth or better in the nation in rushing all four years in college and won the 1999 Heisman Trophy. *And* he was a national prep discus champ.

3. Mike Trout. The pride of Millville put up numbers in his first eight years that compare to legends like Hack Wilson, Lou Gehrig, and Willie Mays. In his first eight MLB seasons, Trout piled up 1,187 hits, 488 extra-base hits, 240 homers, 189 stolen bases, a .307 batting average, and .990 OPS. He's the only player in history to hit .300 with 240 homers and steal 180 bases in his first eight seasons—and he barely played as a rookie. Trout made seven All-Star teams before his 27th birthday and has been first or second in MVP voting *six times* in his first seven full seasons. He's led the AL at least once in runs scored, RBIs, stolen bases, walks, on-base percentage, and slugging percentage. He's an all-time great, and he's just reaching his prime.

2. Franco Harris. Harris was a reliable, durable, productive running back during the regular season. He was picked to nine Pro Bowl teams and still ranks 11th in NFL history with 12,120 rushing yards. But Harris was all about the postseason. His bruising cold-weather playoff performances helped the Steelers win four Super Bowls in a six-year period, and he remains the Super Bowl record holder with 354 rushing yards. He retired with NFL records of 1,556 playoff rushing yards and 16 touchdowns, marks since surpassed by Emmitt Smith. Harris was MVP of Super Bowl IX and was also on the receiving end of the greatest play in NFL history—the Immaculate Reception. Can any Philly guys say that?

1. Carl Lewis. Ten Olympic medals, nine of them gold. An unprecedented four consecutive Olympic long jump gold medals. A world record in the 100-meter dash. A 10-year undefeated streak in the long jump. Lewis, who grew up in Willingboro, is the greatest Olympic athlete ever and arguably the greatest American athlete ever. And he's from South Jersey. Not Montgomery County. Not Delaware County. Not the Northeast. South Jersey.

I win.

Peter Mucha once edited a magazine in Delaware—which qualifies him to write this list. Delaware is such a puny state, so we only let him name eight people.

Well, the definition of this chapter's title doesn't allow me to cite a trio of Diamond Staters who helped Philly score professional championships. We're talking Phils manager Dallas Green and owner Ruly Carpenter, along with Sixers GM Pat Williams. They weren't All-Star players, so I won't even mention them. (Okay, I just did.) Or Dave Raymond, the original Philly Phanatic.

And I won't count actress Teri Polo, even though polo is a sport and she had a role in *Sports Night.*

8. Valerie Bertinelli. Oops, I mean **Chris Short.** (Bertinelli just looked good in shorts.) Anybody who could win 17, 18, 19, and 20 games for the Phillies (1964–1968) must have, uh, been in a four-man rotation when relievers stayed in the bullpen playing cards.

7. Vicki Huber. Won US collegiate titles running for Villanova in the 1,500 meters, 3,000 meters, and cross-country. Set a college record for the 3,000 and a US road record for the 5K. She placed sixth in the 3,000 at the 1988 Olympics.

6. Johnny Weir. The Skating Club of Wilmington trained many world-class athletes. Okay, it's not fair to count Philly's gold medalist Tara Lipinski, who lived in Delaware for just two years. But Weir moved to Delaware at age 12 and went to Newark High. He was a US juniors champ, three-time national champ, and two-time Olympian.

5. Mike Hall. He won world super heavyweight powerlifting titles in 1986 and '89. Lots of US titles, too. Was known as the world's strongest drug-free man. Preferred shirt: Texas Tee, size XXXXXXL.

4. William "Judy" Johnson. Famous Negro League third baseman who was inducted into the Baseball Hall of Fame. Won three pennants and an MVP. Scouted for the Philadelphia A's and Phillies. He signed Dick Allen, which earns extra points.

3. Vic Willis. This Hall of Famer pitched from 1898 to 1910 and would have won more than 245 games from 1898 to 1910 if the Boston Beaneaters had any offense. Still won 20 games eight times and completed 388 games.

2. Elena Delle Donne. A guard-forward who reached 3,000 points faster than any player in WNBA history. League MVP and scoring leader in 2015. Olympic gold in 2016. Highest career free-throw percentage in pro basketball history (including NBA), at over 93 percent. She once made 20 kills in a college volleyball game.

1. Randy White. We're using tiny type here because the manster (half man, half monster) played defensive tackle for some stinkin' group of Texans. Oh, and he was an NFL Hall of Famer and co-MVP of Super Bowl XII.

Ten Best Philly Pro Players Not Born in This Country

Well, since we just covered the tristate area—and with immigration being such a hot topic—let's take a look at 10 superb athletes to hail from foreign soil. We're excluding Canada not only because it's so close but because it's . . . uh . . . Canada. They drink so much beer up there we're not even sure if it counts as a country.

10. Ben Simmons. As of this writing, he's only two seasons in with the Sixers, but his skill set is so special, this Aussie can't be left off. And if there is another edition of this book someday, we expect him to place much higher than number 10. Now make your free throws!

9. Kimmo Timmonen. This tough-as-nails defenseman from Finland gave everything he had to the Flyers for 519 games.

8. Peter Forsberg. He only played 100 games for the Fly Guys, but when you were once referred to as the greatest player in the world, you must make this list. And how many times have you been reminded that Peter the Great appears on a stamp in his homeland of Sweden? Has anyone ever bothered to check out if this is a big deal? Paul Jolovitz has his picture on a stamp in Sweden, and he's from Alabama.

7. Pelle Lindbergh. The first European goaltender (he was from Sweden) to win the Vezina Trophy after posting 40 victories in 1983–1984. This after being the goalie on the NHL All-Rookie team the previous season. Unfortunately, they would be the only two seasons for Pelle, who tragically died in a car accident on November 10, 1985.

6. Tony Taylor. "Leading off, Tony Taylor!" Boy, how many times did we hear that in our lives? This Cuban native played 14 seasons for the Phils, including a record 1,003 games at second base. Made the defensive play that saved Jim Bunning's perfect game. A real star at Phils Fantasy Camps because—simply put—he's a *nice guy*.

5. Juan Samuel. Second baseman Sammy still holds a Major League record for most at bats by a right-handed batter in a season with 701 for the Phils in 1984—and that's the most by any National Leaguer in a single season. In six seasons, this Dominican made the All-Star team three times and was the first major leaguer to have double figures in doubles, triples, home runs, and stolen bases in his first four seasons. A fun, vibrant clubhouse presence, Juan ended up being traded by the Phils in 1989 in a deal that brought us Lenny Dykstra.

4. Bobby Abreu. Whatever negative thought you might have about our favorite Venezuelan Gold Glover, his offensive numbers are just too overwhelming to ignore. He played nine years with the Phils (18 overall) and hit over .300 with 891 runs and 814 RBIs in our town. This man could flat-out hit, and there are fans out there who argue that he's the Phils' greatest right fielder ever. Just keep him away from any outfield wall.

3. Carlos Ruiz. What a leader this Panamanian was. There are players ranked below him on this list who have better stats, but a World Series ring makes the difference. One of our favorite Phils ever.

2. Joel Embiid. Well, sometimes you just have to go out on a limb. If he got hurt tomorrow, his number two ranking would be too high, but if he doesn't, he could end up being one of the greatest Sixers of all time. Plus, this funky dude from Cameroon is just so much fun.

1. Steve Van Buren. This Eagles great is the only NFL Hall of Famer to be born in Honduras, where his father worked as a fruit inspector. I would wager he's the only *Eagle* to be born in Honduras, a real hotbed for churning out legendary NFL running backs. When Steve retired, he led the entire NFL in career rushing yards.

Hey, we know what you're thinking. How can there be such a list without the Eagles' legendary kicker Horst Mühlman? He's from Germany, and his name is Horst. Then there's Tongan Vai Sikahema and Sweden's Kim Johnsson, but there's only so much room.

Guys Who Were a Pleasure to Coach—and Guys Who Were a Challenge :: Billy Cunningham

Billy Cunningham coached the Sixers for eight years, including the 1982–1983 championship season. His 454 regular-season wins and 66 postseason wins are both franchise records.

A Pleasure

6. Moses Malone. A piece of cake. The first time I met Moses, I told him what we expected in terms of rebounding and throwing outlet passes for fast breaks—something he hadn't had to do in Houston. He immediately accepted it and knew how to do it from day one.

5. Julius Erving. For him to have to listen to me for eight years, well, that couldn't have been an easy thing for a superstar like him. And if he ever had a bad game, you never had to worry about the next one.

4. Harvey Catchings. He pretty much knew his role and accepted it. You really need guys like that willing to come off the bench.

3. Caldwell Jones. He was game for anything. He didn't care if I asked him to cover a guard or a center. He would just nod and go out and do it. Caldwell didn't care if he scored a point, as long as we won.

2. Mo Cheeks. He was like a sponge. You only had to tell Mo something once and he had the ability to apply it from that point on. Such a smart and dedicated player.

1. Bobby Jones. By far the easiest player ever to coach. Bobby would do anything to help the team win. If it meant him playing five minutes or 35 minutes, he didn't care.

A Challenge

6. Andrew Toney. He's my sixth man on this team. I loved Andrew, and he sacrificed some individual talent for the success of the team. The challenge with him was that he didn't always make good decisions. I'll never forget playing the Lakers one year in an overtime game at the Spectrum with about 14 seconds to go. We called timeout and designed a play that would eventually get the ball to Andrew. But, as we broke the huddle, he said, "Just give me the ball and everybody get out of my way." Three Lakers came out at him, and he took a crazy shot. Knocked it down. I walked off shaking my head. That was Andrew—he didn't always make good decisions, but they seemed to work out.

5. Eric Money. He was difficult to coach because he was a point guard with a scoring guard's mentality of "shoot first."

4. Joe Bryant. The issue with Joe, and I mean this in a positive way, was that he thought he should be playing more and have a bigger role on the team. Perhaps he should have, but with all the talent we had, I just couldn't find the minutes for him.

3. George McGinnis. He was a great player. But I think he just lost his love and passion for the game. He went on to greatness in the business world, which shows what he could do when he was motivated.

2. Charles Barkley. I loved coaching him, but he was such a challenge. I think he now understands that I was trying to make him as great as he could be. He showed up the first year at 280 pounds. We had to get him down under 260. He didn't think it was important to run back to half court on defense, but I could see him starting to realize how good he could be and the price he had to pay to get there. I regretted not having the opportunity to push and nurture Charles for more years to help him become his best.

1. Darryl Dawkins. I loved him, but I wished he embraced greatness. Darryl didn't want the responsibility night in and night out. He could have been special. He passed away so young; I really loved him and miss him.

Remember Woody Sauldsberry? We don't either, but he won the NBA Rookie of the Year Award for the Philadelphia Warriors in 1957–1958, averaging 12.8 points per game.

Also in 1957, the Phillies had the top rookie batter (Ed Bouchee) and pitcher (Jack Sanford). The team still finished at .500. Would you have guessed otherwise?

On the other hand, the Flyers have never had a player win the NHL's Calder Trophy for top rookie.

Here are the top 10 seasons ever enjoyed by first-year players in Philadelphia.

10. Ben Simmons, Sixers, 2017–2018. It's one thing to be named NBA Rookie of the Year and another to put up all-around numbers that compare to Oscar Robertson. So shuddup, Donovan Mitchell, and stop carping that Ben should be ineligible because he sat on the bench in street clothes the year before. The last NBA rookie who made passes this smooth and accurate was a guy named Magic. Did you know that the Sixers are the only Philly pro team to even have a rookie of the year since '06? They've had two, the other being Michael-Carter Williams in 2013–2014. If Joel Embiid had played a dozen more games in '16-17, he would have won, too.

9. Del Ennis, Phillies, 1946. Fresh back from World War II, the 21-year-old kid from Olney finished fourth in the National League in batting (.313), fourth in home runs (17 in a dead-ball season), and eighth in MVP voting. So why did local fans boo him so much?

8. Eric Lindros, Flyers, 1992–1993. Lindros scored in his first game as a Flyer and set a franchise rookie record with 41 goals in just 61 games. An omen of the Stanley Cups to come . . . oops. He lost out on the Calder Trophy to Winnipeg's Teamu Selanne, who set an NHL rookie record with 76 goals. Can you still name his orginal line mates on the Crazy Eights? Well, Lindros (No. 88) centered wingers Mark Recchi (8) and Brent Fedyk (18).

7. Allen Iverson, Sixers, 1996–1997. AI averaged 23.5 points and 7.5 rebounds. A nice start to a Hall of Fame career. Unfortunately, he was surrounded by dreck on Coach Johnny Davis's 22–60 squad. Ask people what they remember about Iverson's break-in season and most mention two things: (1) How the coach called a meaningless timeout in a late-season game to help Iverson continue a streak of 40-point games, and (2) how Iverson hilariously wore a white do-rag to the Rookie of the Year Award announcement.

6. Keith Jackson, Eagles, 1988. Buddy Ryan's favorite player and we see why. He caught 81 passes (a franchise rookie record) for six touchdowns as Randall Cunningham's safety valve. Made the Pro Bowl as a starter. We just wish he had held on to that touchdown pass in the Fog Bowl.

5. Richie Ashburn, Phillies, 1948. A five-decade love affair got off to a quick start as Whitey hit .333 (second only to Stan Musial) and led the league with 32 stolen bases. He finished 11th in MVP voting on a team that was 22 games below .500. So how did he not win the Rookie of the Year Award? Alvin Dark of the Boston Braves had less impressive stats, but his team won the pennant.

4. Richie Allen, Phillies, 1964. Entered the Majors with a bang and a 42-ounce bat. Give us a little space, please, to roll out the stats: 125 runs, 352 total bases, 13 triples—all of which led the National League. Hit .318 with 29 homers and 91 RBIs. Played in all 162 games. Also led the league in errors and strikeouts, but we're ignoring that. Allen was a transcendent, stunning talent who hit the longest home runs anyone had ever seen in this town. Alas, he was also the Terrell Owens of his era. Who knew back in the balmy summer of '64 how ugly it would all end?

3. Ron Hextall, Flyers, 1986–1987. Who was this crazy kid from Manitoba? No one had ever played goal like this—wandering into the corners, stick-handling to the faceoff

circles, scrapping with the tough guys. His regular-season numbers were terrific: 37 wins and a 3.00 goals-against average, which were good enough to win him the Vezina Trophy as the NHL's top goalie. But his really brilliant work came in the Stanley Cup Finals, where Hexy kept the Flyers going to Game 7 against the legendary Edmonton Oilers. He won the Conn Smythe Trophy as the most valuable player of the playoffs, and afterward, Wayne Gretzky called him "the greatest goaltender I've ever faced." Heady stuff for a 23-year-old.

2. Grover Cleveland Alexander, Phillies, 1911. We needed to go old school—real old school—at least once here. Like Ashburn, he came to the Phils as a farm kid out of Nebraska and captured the city. As a 24-year-old rookie, Old Pete (no one likely called him that back then) led the league with a 28–13 record. He also finished first in innings (367), complete games (31), and shutouts (7), plus a bunch of stats that no one even knew existed back then, like fewest hits per nine innings. His rookie campaign started a run in which he won 190 games over seven seasons, before the Phils traded him in 1918 for two marginal players and $55,000. He would go on to win 183 more games, mostly with the Cubs. The Phils would go on to stink.

1. Wilt Chamberlain, Sixers, 1959–1960. You expected someone else? The Overbrook High grad came home and transformed the sport. He wasn't just Rookie of the Year; he also won the league's MVP Award as a 23-year-old and relegated Bill Russell to the All-NBA second team.

Wilt had passed up his last year at Kansas to tour with the Harlem Globetrotters. When the NBA finally accepted him, much was expected. His $65,000 rookie salary was the highest in the NBA. He was four inches taller than Russell and broader and more muscular than George Mikan.

Columnists worried aloud whether he would destroy the NBA. He didn't, but he did revolutionize it. Wilt led the league with 37.6 points and 27 rebounds per game. He scored more than 50 points seven times. He played 48 minutes per game. The Sixers improved over the previous season by 17 wins. No one ever made a bigger splash.

Geez, what doesn't Philly's own Questlove do? He's the musical director of The Tonight Show Starring Jimmy Fallon. *He's the cofounder of the Roots, who are not only one of the best recording acts to ever come out of Philly but also rank as one of the best backing bands of all time. They've backed musical acts as diverse as Public Enemy and Bruce Springsteen.*

He's also one of the producers of Hamilton. *And did we mention what an awesome drummer he is?*

Questlove is also a major hoops fan and overall fan of Philadelphia sports. Here are his 10 favorite local players.

10. Reggie White. The Minister of Defense.

9. Brian Dawkins. The Hitter.

8. Joel Embiid. The Process.

7. Jimmy Rollins. J Roll.

6. Charles Barkley. The Round Mound of Rebound.

5. Kobe Bryant. Mamba.

4. Bernard Hopkins. The Executioner.

3. Julius "Dr J." Erving. The Doc.

2. Randall Cunningham. The Human Highlight.

1. Allen Iverson. The Answer.

Your team drafts a guy, nurtures him, develops him into a star. You go out and buy his jersey, figuring it's a safe investment. Next week, he gets traded and you feel like a fool.

So few quality players have spent their entire careers in Philadelphia uniforms that we had a tough time coming up with 10 worthy of this list. Our starting date here is 1970—around when free agency began and players started moving more freely. So you won't find Chuck Bednarik or Paul Arizin or the other old-timers your grandfather still insists "played for the love of the game."

10. Brent Celek. Celek was able to pull off the rarest of achievements—playing 11 seasons for the team that drafted him and ending it at a championship parade. He was a tough, reliable tight end who missed just one game in his career. He adopted Philadelphia, opening several restaurants and sticking around after football ended.

9. Jimmy Watson. The younger of the blue-line brothers from Smithers, British Columbia, spent a full decade poke-checking the puck and steadily clearing the zone. Never glamorous, but he rarely made mistakes. The best homegrown defenseman in franchise history. He also stayed in the area and still coaches youth hockey in Delaware County.

8. Jerry Sizemore. The big, silent Texan was the third overall pick of the 1973 draft (52 slots above another guy on this list) and took a few years to develop into a star. Under Dick Vermeil, he made two Pro Bowls (1979 and '81) and anchored an elite offensive line. Played 12 seasons in green and silver.

7. Randy Logan. The '73 Eagles finished 5–8–1, but give GM Jim Murray credit for a solid draft—Sizemore in the first round, center Guy Morriss in the second, and this 11-year strong safety in the third. At 195 pounds, Logan could hit like a linebacker. A big player in big moments.

6. Andrew Toney. Toney's career ended because of injury and with a nasty divorce from owner Harold Katz, who publicly doubted his pain. The Boston Strangler played just eight seasons, and his prime was really just four. The run may have been short, but it was spectacular. It's been uplifting to see his rapprochement with the 76ers in recent years.

5. Mike Quick. Another magnificent career ended too early. Quick made five Pro Bowls in his first six seasons and seemed headed toward the Hall of Fame when he shredded his knee in a 1988 game at the Vet. He tried a few comebacks but ultimately had to retire at age 31. Quick caught 61 TD passes in his 101 games as an Eagle.

Glen says: I covered that '88 game for the *Inquirer*. Beforehand, I met Quick's mother, who had traveled up from North Carolina. She told me she was reluctant to watch her son play live because the two previous times he had been injured. I told her not to worry. And then . . .

4. Ryan Howard. A fifth-round draft pick in 2001, Howard's path to the Majors was blocked when the Phils signed Jim Thome two years later. We began hearing tales of Howard's prodigious power as he moved up the minor-league system. He won Rookie of the Year in '05 and slugged 58 homers in '06. Howard had an amazing first half to his career. Then the Phils signed him to a $125 million extension that made him untradeable as injuries stole his brilliance.

3. Bill Barber. Scored 30 goals as a 20-year-old rookie—but got robbed when the 1972 Calder Trophy went to the hated Steve Vickers of the Rangers. Barber played 12 great seasons with the Flyers, making six All-Star Games and always being in the right spot to receive the puck for one of his 420 goals. He stuck with the organization in several roles, including coach for two seasons. And he's an NHL Hall of Famer.

2. Bobby Clarke. He was the team's second-round pick in the 1969 draft—the first-rounder was someone named Bob Currier, who never played a single NHL game. Clarke was actually a controversial pick because many thought his diabetes would prevent him from having a lengthy career. Fifteen seasons, two Stanley Cups, and two MVP Awards proved the doubters wrong. Mr. Flyer, less beloved as an executive than as a player, is still around.

1. Mike Schmidt. The odd thing about Schmidt lasting 18 years in red pinstripes is that his relationship with the fans was chilly more often than not. Remember when he ripped us to a Montreal newspaper and then disguised himself in a fright wig when the team came home? We never really loved Schmidt, although by the end we all respected him as the best ever at his position. No player better destroys the canard that Philadelphia fans run their stars out of town.

Philly Stars Who Looked Weird in Another Uniform

The World Champion Phillies scattered, even if we thought they'd play here forever. Chase Utley became the Gray Fox of the Dodgers. Jimmy Rollins wound up with the White Sox. Carlos Ruiz spent a season catching in the rain in Seattle. We weren't comfortable with any of it.

Truth is, it's incredibly rare that even a great athlete plays his entire career with one team—as you saw in the preceding chapter.

But sometimes, it feels downright weird to catch the one-time local hero in another team's laundry. Here are 10 examples that made us rub our eyes in disbelief.

10. Ron Jaworski. Old quarterbacks never die, they just shuttle around the NFL as backups. Jaws gave way to Randall Cunningham in 1988. He moved to Miami as Dan Marino's backup—a nice way to keep your uniform clean. After one season (and just 14 passing attempts), he moved to Kansas City, starting three games as a 38-year-old before returning to Philly to launch a corporate empire.

9. John LeClair. After a decade as a Flyer, LeClair seemed finished in 2004–2005. But the last-place Penguins decided he was worth $3.6 million, so he laced them up at age 36. We hated seeing him skating side by side with Sidney Crosby. LeClair scored just two goals in 21 games his second season in Pittsburgh and was unconditionally released. No sadder words in sports than those.

8. Darren Daulton. He was the captain of Macho Row in 1993, but by 1997 Daulton's career—like the Phillies franchise—was limping along. The Phils sent him (along with Jim Eisenreich) to sunny Florida to play out the string like so many senior citizens. Both looked odd in those aqua-and-black jerseys, but both helped the upstart Marlins win their first World Series. Nice way to go out.

7. Randall Cunningham. Old quarterbacks never die, Part II. Quick: name all the teams Randall played for after leaving Philadelphia. There was Minnesota, of course, where he almost got to the Super Bowl. There was the hated Cowboys in 2000—when he went 0–2 against the Eagles. But we'll bet you didn't remember he finished wearing purple jersey number 1 for the Baltimore Ravens in 2001—a backup to Elvis Grbac.

6. Larry Bowa. The guy's been back and forth in town over decades as player, coach, and manager. And he's probably been an instructor for half the teams in baseball. But where did he end his playing career? No, it wasn't the Cubs, where he was shipped in 1982 as part of the infamous Ryne Sandberg trade. Rather, it was the stinkin' Mets in 1985, when he hit .105 in 14 games and called it quits. Father Time never loses.

5. Simon Gagne. He bounced around a bit after 11 solid seasons in Philadelphia. Won a Stanley Cup with a bunch of Flyers refugees in Los Angeles in 2011. He had a brief return in 2013 and then hung up the skates. One year later, he signed with Boston. He wasn't very good at age 34 (three goals in 23 games), but we like to believe his presence in gold and black haunted the Bruins with a reminder of how he singlehandedly destroyed them in the 2010 playoffs.

4. Reggie White. Of course you remember him leaving when God told him to go to Green Bay and win a Super Bowl. But did you recall that White retired after 1998, spent a year at home, and then signed up for one more season with the Carolina Panthers? He played all 16 games but registered just 5.5 sacks. Just four years later, White passed away in his sleep.

3. Mo Cheeks. Mo spent 11 seasons with the 76ers and learned that Harold Katz had traded him when a TV camera crew met him in his driveway. Not the proper way to send out a legend. Anyway, he had stops with the Spurs, the Knicks, and the Hawks. Then he retired—but came back for 35 games with the 1992–1993 New Jersey Nets when point guard Kenny Anderson got hurt.

2. Donovan McNabb. Old quarterbacks never die, Part III. We all remember McNabb being dealt to Washington on Easter 2010. He started out that season 3–2, including a nationally broadcast win over the Eagles—during which it was leaked that he'd signed a $78 million extension. The number was bogus, and so was his performance. Soon enough he was benched for Rex Grossman. The next summer, McNabb was traded to Minnesota. He started 1–5 for the Vikings and was benched again, this time for Christian Ponder.

1. Harold Carmichael. Cut in 1984 after 13 glorious seasons with the Eagles, Carmichael got picked up . . . by the Cowboys. "I put my head between those stars on the helmet," he recalled later. "I looked in the mirror and said, 'Harold, this is too much.'" Carmichael played in just two games for Dallas before being released. "I packed up as soon as I could and got out of there. I never looked back."

Ten Fastest Philly Athletes

This list holds a special fascination for us since no one has ever thought of your authors of this book as speedy. Plodding? Yes. Slow moving? Check.

Because we lack it, we're fascinated with quickness. It also happens to be the key physical trait that often separates the boys from the men. So here's a look at 10 of the fastest athletes ever to wear a Philadelphia uniform.

For the record, we know Carl Lewis is from Willingboro Township, New Jersey, but we're going to keep this to team sports. That also eliminates Smarty Jones, not only because horse racing is an individual sport, but Smarty also had four legs, and we consider that a little bit of an unfair advantage.

We just wish we could have added Millville's Mike Trout to the list.

10. Sami Kapanen, Flyers. He could watch *60 Minutes* in half an hour.

9. Drew Nolan, Temple basketball. We realize you have to be a Big 5 freak to even remember Drew, but this Owl from the late '60s was so quick he couldn't control his own body and played wildly out of control. He drove legendary Owls coach Harry Litwack out of his mind, but he sure was fun to watch.

8. Craig "Speedy" Claxton. You have to truly earn a nickname like that.

7. Lonnie Smith, Phillies. So lightning-quick he would slip and fall a lot, hence his dynamite nickname, Skates.

6. Michael Vick, Eagles. Rocket ships flew at the speed of him.

5. Bob Dernier, Phillies. The Cubs gave Bob his nickname, the Deer, but the Phils had him first.

> **Big Daddy says:** I was at the Vet on May 15, 1989, when Dernier hit a walk-off, inside-the-park homer in the bottom of the 12th to defeat the Giants. I swear I never saw anyone run the bases that amazingly fast.

4. Richie Ashburn, Phillies. Speaking of inside-the-park home runs, did you know only five players in the history of baseball had more of them than Whitey?

3. Rick MacLeish, Flyers. Oh, to have back those days before hockey helmets, just to see the Hawk's hair flowing down that ice. RIP, Rick.

2. DeSean Jackson, Eagles. We realize this is an old joke, but here it goes: D-Jax was so fast he would hit the bedroom light switch and be under the covers before the light went out.

1. Allen Iverson, Sixers. Philly was blessed to witness one of the quickest human beings with a basketball in his hands ever.

Honorable mention: Michael Bourn, Ken Linseman, Kenny Lofton, Greg Luzinski (just to make sure you're still reading), Mike Quick, Jimmy Rollins, Juan Samuel, Darren Sproles, Jeff Stone, Shane Victorino, Herschel Walker.

Guys Who Came Out of Nowhere

Not all stars are first-round draft picks. Here are 10 (or maybe a few more) Philadelphia heroes who arrived with low expectations but left in high esteem.

10. Dave Poulin. Despite being a finalist for college player of the year awards in 1982, Poulin went unpicked in the NHL draft. He played a season in Sweden, signed with the Flyers, and ended up as the team's captain for six years.

9. Steve Mix. Entered the NBA as a fifth-round pick, which is about one step above towel boy. He was waived by the Detroit Pistons, picked up by the ABA, and waived again five days later. Spent the next year out of the game. Mix came to the Sixers in 1973 as the proverbial last guy on the bench and stayed nine seasons. There's got to be a lesson there somewhere.

8. Andy Reid. Okay, he's not a player. But let's face it: When the Eagles hired the anonymous quarterback coach of the Green Bay Packers to run the show in 1999, who would have thought he would end up the winningest coach in franchise history?

7. Larry Bowa. Unnoticed and undrafted out of Sacramento Community College in 1966. Bowa wasn't seen as much of a prospect coming up. He wasn't taken seriously when he came to the Phils, hitting just .241 his first four seasons. But he made himself into a Major League hitter and a major league pain in the neck—as both shortstop and manager.

By the way, when Bowa was breaking in, Richie Ashburn referred to him as "the single worst hitter I ever saw." Ashburn then spent the rest of Larry's career touting how much he admired Bowa's work ethic to become the player he ended up being.

6. Jason Peters. He played tight end at the University of Arkansas, catching 21 passes his final season. No NFL team was interested in a 320-pound receiver, so Peters went undrafted in 2004 and ended up on the Buffalo Bills practice squad. One position change and nine Pro Bowls later, Peters is a sure bet for enshrinement in Canton.

5. Mo Cheeks. Remember Winford Boynes? Buster Matheney? Terry Sykes? Roger Phegley? All of those guys—plus 31 others—were chosen ahead of Mo Cheeks in the 1978 NBA draft. But only four of the 35 picked over Mo scored more career points, and none had more assists. And just one, some guy named Bird, also ended up in the Naismith Memorial Basketball Hall of Fame.

4. Carlos Ruiz. At 19, he showed up at the Phillies Baseball Academy in the Dominican Republic as a skinny second baseman. He almost quit because he felt like a 10-year-old among the taller, more athletic prospects. The Phils signed him for $8,000. He wound up wearing the red pinstripes for 11 years as the cornerstone backstop during a great era.

3. Seth Joyner. Taken in the eighth round of the 1986 NFL draft, Joyner was actually cut before the season but got called back when another linebacker got hurt. Fortuitous move, eh? Joyner emerged as the most dangerous playmaker on Buddy Ryan's Gang Green defense of the late 1980s. Toss in ninth-rounder Clyde Simmons and undrafted free agent Andre Waters, and you've got some real treasures culled off the scrap heap.

2. Tim Kerr. The 1979 NHL draft went six rounds and 126 players deep. None of those players was this big center from Tecumseh, Ontario, who got labeled by his junior coaches as too lazy to play in the NHL. Somewhere along the way—taking cross-checks in the back, surpassing the 50-goal mark four straight years, performing heroics even while disabled— he shed that image.

1A. Wilbert Montgomery and 1B. Harold Carmichael. What does it say that the Eagles second all-time leading rusher and top all-time leading receiver were, respectively, sixth- and seventh-round picks? Perhaps that the draft is less a science than a crap shoot. Anyway, in this town, where first-round picks too often end up as Marcus Smith or Danny Watkins, we'll take good luck where we can find it.

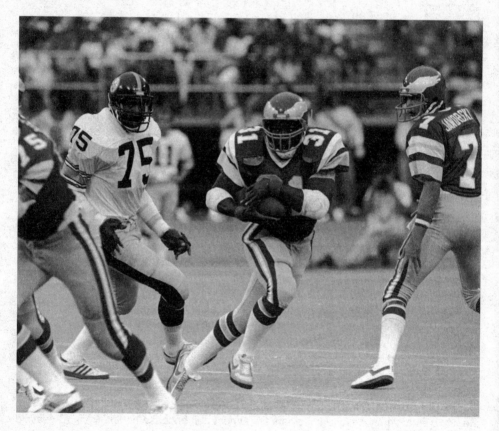

The Best and Worst Sportswriters in Philadelphia ::
Angelo Cataldi

Angelo Cataldi has been the anchor of WIP's popular Morning Show *since 1989. Before switching to radio, Cataldi was an outstanding reporter for the* Philadelphia Inquirer. *In 1987, he was a finalist for the Pulitzer Prize. This is his ranking of the top—and bottom— local sportswriters over the past 30 years.*

The Best

10. Kyle Neubeck. Maybe I have a bias because I contribute twice-monthly columns myself to *Philly Voice*, but Kyle, 29, is the best young sportswriter in Philadelphia right now—and it's not close. His knowledge of the NBA and his dexterity with words present an inside look at the 76ers that belies his age. If you want to know what's really happening with the Sixers, Kyle is the most likely writer in Philadelphia to tell you.

9. Mike Sielski. The best of the current crop of young wordsmiths, Mike is not afraid to take on sacred cows like the Flyers, making his points on Philly.com with a stiletto instead of a sledgehammer. Mike is such a talented writer, he often uses his column for feature stories—something I feel should be kept separate from his duties as an opinion-maker. Otherwise, Mike would be even higher on the list.

8. Jimmy Kempski. The beat reporters who cover the Eagles right now are the best crop ever—Jeff McLane, Les Bowen, and Paul Domowitch of Philly.com, Sheil Kapadia of the Athletic, Tim McManus of ESPN—but what distinguishes Jimmy from the pack is his sense of humor. His stick-figure analysis of the Birds on Philly Voice is just one of his many entertaining devices that remind readers that this, after all, is just sports.

7. Reuben Frank. In this new age of analytics, Reuben has mastered the art of statistics, and he does it in an old-school way, mixing it with potent opinions on the website for NBC Sports Philadelphia. He also ranks among the most entertaining writers, with notes columns that weave in pithy takes with some off-the-wall esoterica.

6. Jack McCaffery. The most courageous columnist since Stan Hochman, Jack is fearless in taking a contrarian position and arguing it vehemently. Even when you don't agree with Jack, you have to admire his ability to provoke. Long a mainstay at the less mainstream *Delco Times*, Jack is every bit as good as the better-known columnists in Philadelphia.

5. Stephen A. Smith. Stephen is known now as a hugely successful curmudgeon on ESPN, but he was the best basketball writer in Philadelphia long before he conquered sports broadcasting. A reporter who frequently broke stories, he did what only the very best beat writers do, offering strong opinions while patrolling the locker room.

4. Jayson Stark. His recent induction to the Baseball Hall of Fame aside, Jayson has been the most entertaining voice of Philadelphia—and national—baseball for decades. A true pioneer in covering sports at ESPN and now the Athletic, Jayson mastered the eccentricities of baseball with astounding stories and implausible statistics. After all these years, he still hasn't lost his fastball.

3. Marcus Hayes. There is only one sports columnist working in Philadelphia who is a must-read every day, and that is Marcus, who is best at developing a provocative—and totally legitimate—opinion and arguing his points with strength and humor. In his previous life, he was a terrific Eagles beat reporter for the *Daily News*.

2. Ray Didinger. Ray actually dropped one spot from the 2006 list, but only because he dialed back dramatically his writing in favor of an equally noteworthy career in broadcasting. Ray's recent 60,000-word addition to the *Eagles Encyclopedia* is a reminder of just how brilliant a wordsmith he has always been. He's also the smartest football writer in Philadelphia history—and is deservedly in the Pro Football Hall of Fame for his extraordinary work.

1. Stan Hochman. Stan's passing a few years ago only enhanced the greatness of his 50-plus years of writing about sports at the *Daily News*. He had all of the essentials for elite status—wit, accuracy, logic, and provocative opinions. A columnist without a strong point of view is just a feature writer. Stan was the best true sport columnist in Philadelphia history. An anthology of his work is planned for 2019. Don't miss it.

The Worst

5. Mark Bowden. The most accomplished journalist of anyone on these lists, Bowden is a best-selling author (*Black Hawk Down*, among others) and a prize-winning reporter who has risked his life on the front lines of major wars and produced vivid accounts of his adventures. Unfortunately, covering the Eagles at the *Inquirer* for two years was his hiatus from journalism. He was a gushing fanboy. You can look it up.

4. Mel Greenberg. The most influential writer covering women's basketball in the past 25 years, Mel has never actually covered the game; he has promoted it. That is not the responsibility of a journalist. For his decades of coverage at the *Inquirer,* Mel received the first media award from the Women's Basketball Coaches Association, among countless other honors. If the coaches love you and you're supposed to be a journalist, there's something wrong.

3. David Murphy. David's writing is like a scone—dense and dry, and ultimately almost impossible to swallow. I cannot recall a single column he has written on Philly.com that I was able to finish. His takes are often murky, overwhelmed by long paragraphs filled with words that require the assistance of Google. I'm not sure who David thinks he's writing for, but it's definitely not the average Philadelphia sports fan.

2. Claire Smith. This may seem like piling on after I named the renowned columnist from both the *New York Times* and the *Inquirer* the number one worst sportswriter on my 2006 list for this book, but the awards keep pouring in for all the wrong reasons. Yes, she was a pioneer, both as a woman and a minority. Unfortunately, trophies don't make her work any less fawning or pedantic. Read it online. I think you'll agree.

1. Frank Fitzpatrick. History is supposed to be boring, and Frank has found a way to make it excruciating. At the *Inquirer* so long, his days actually overlapped with mine 30 years ago—and it's pretty clear Frank is living in the past, with sappy, far-too-long feature stories on topics that have been forgotten for a good reason. His attempts at humorous pieces are even less successful. Sad to say, but it's time for Frank to be history himself.

We set some rules for this chapter. It does not include movies that were shot in Philadelphia but never identify the city (like *Twelve Monkeys* or *The Woodsman*), nor those supposedly set here that were actually made somewhere else (like *The Philadelphia Story*, which was filmed in Culver City, California).

Philadelphia has to be an actual character. That's our law.

10. *Silver Linings Playbook* (2012). The social-misfits-fall-in-love-and-dance vehicle for Bradley Cooper and Jennifer Lawrence is a virtual tour of the city and Delco burbs, from Jeweler's Row to the Lincoln Financial Field parking lots to Bonner and Prendy High Schools. We were a bit annoyed by the portrayal of Eagles fans as face-painting thugs, but, on the other hand, Lawrence looked pretty good in an undersized Birds T-shirt.

> **Glen says**: My wife and I still go to the Llanerch Diner in nearby Upper Darby, sit in the booth where Cooper and Lawrence had their first date, and order Raisin Bran and tea.

9. *The Answer Man* (2009). A nice little gem starring Jeff Daniels as a crotchety author who scores with a self-help book and now just wants to be left alone. Great street shots of the city, and a lot of the action takes place in our favorite local used bookstore, the Book Trader at 2nd and Market. Lauren Graham and Kat Dennings costar.

8. *Invincible* (2006). Another Eagles-oriented movie. It's based on the true story of Vince Papale, who got the nickname from our pal Ray Didinger. We know folks who were annoyed that the film shifted all the real-life Delaware County parts to South Philly. We were more irked that everyone in the film sounds like they were born in Brooklyn. It's not the same damn accent! Great shots of Franklin Field and Pat's Steaks.

7. *Philadelphia* (1993). A courageous (for its time), groundbreaking movie exposing bias against those suffering from AIDS. It opened eyes and changed minds. Terrific acting by Denzel Washington and Tom Hanks, who dropped 50 pounds for his role and won the best actor Oscar. Bruce Springsteen also won an Oscar for the title song, "Streets of Philadelphia." Watch for a nifty Dr. J cameo at the old Spectrum.

6. *Blow Out* (1981). A young John Travolta plays a movie sound technician who accidentally records the murder of a political candidate in this Brian De Palma slasher/thriller. The film failed at the box office because of its depressing ending, but we recommend you give it a watch. There are easily identifiable shots throughout the city—Penn's Landing, Wissahickon Bridge, Macy's in Center City. And, hey, isn't that veteran weather guy Dave Roberts playing a TV newsman?

5. *Creed* (2015). We love the scene where West Coast native Adonis Creed (Michael B. Jordan) is introduced to Philadelphia cuisine and culture by Bianca (Tessa Thompson) over his first-ever cheesesteak at Max's Steaks. She talks about Johnny Brenda's and the Roots and Jill Scott and the Electric Factory (watch for Joe Conklin's name on the marquee). She even explains the meaning of the word "jawn." It's the most Philly-intense scene in the history of the Rocky franchise.

4. *Trading Places* (1983). One of the funniest movies ever made starring *Saturday Night Live* alums—in this case Dan Aykroyd and Eddie Murphy—as well as Jamie Lee Curtis in her glorious, naked prime. The plot is the old *Prince and the Pauper* storyline as Society Hill swell Louis Winthorpe III (Aykroyd) is forced to switch places with homeless street hustler Billy Ray Valentine (Murphy). Largely shot in Center City with scenes at Rittenhouse Square, Delancey Street, the Union League, and the Clothespin sculpture.

3. *The Sixth Sense* (1999). Penn Valley's M. Night Shyamalan has shot at least 10 films in the area. This was the first—and by far the best. Bruce Willis stars as a psychologist trying to help a young boy (Haley Joel Osment) who claims to see ghosts. It's got one of the greatest mind-blowing twist endings in movie history, which we won't reveal except to say that Judy Macnow figured it out less than an hour into the movie.

2. *Witness* (1985). The most memorable scene is the murder at the 30th Street Station, which begins with young Lukas Haas staring in awe up at the Angel of Resurrection statue and ends with him crouched and shivering on a toilet seat, hiding from the murderers in a men's room stall. Most of the movie takes place out in Lancaster County. Outstanding performances by Harrison Ford, Kelly McGillis, and a few barns' worth of Amish folks.

1. *Rocky* (1976). Could there be any other choice? Millions of people have sprinted up the Art Museum steps since this Oscar winner came out. And the great underdog-with-a-huge-heart story is the narrative this city has carried forever. In the famous training scene—as "Gotta Fly Now" plays in the background—Rocky (Sylvester Stallone) runs from the Italian Market, up along Boathouse Row, back down to the Navy Yard, and across town to scale those steps. Saharan marathoners don't cover that much ground in a month.

Honorable mention: *1776, The Big Fan, Birdy, Kitty Foyle, In Her Shoes, Unbreakable, The Young Philadelphians.*

10. Charlie Manuel for Clarence the Angel from *It's a Wonderful Life*. It all started while I was watching that Christmas classic. Clarence made his first appearance, and it hit me like a ton of Gino Giants. Not only did Charlie resemble Clarence, he had that friendly uncle personality to boot. Seriously, he wouldn't even have to act.

9. Jayson Werth for Jesus. I'm not getting blasphemous on you. There have been plenty of movies where an actor portrayed Jesus. Willem Dafoe in Martin Scorsese's *Last Temptation of Christ* comes to mind. Seriously, who looks the part more than Jayson? And some spiritual being helped Werth get that ridiculous contract from the Nationals.

8. Phil Martelli for Peter Boyle in any movie. And to think I grew up four blocks from Phil and knew him when he had hair. Phil (I'm sure he's thrilled to read this) not only resembles Boyle, but he's every bit as funny. Throw in this fact: if Phil hadn't moved out of Southwest Philly, he would have gone to West Catholic High—just like Boyle.

7. Shawn Bradley for Lurch from *The Addams Family*. You rang?

6. Jason Peters for Rick Ross. Not sure if Jason can rap, but he sure looks the part.

5. Howard Eskin for the Burger King. To tell you the truth, I'm surprised the Burger King has not popped up in some Farrelly Brothers comedy or *Game of Thrones*. I would empty Cataldi's bank account to see this on the silver screen. Come to think about it, Howard would make a great Wolfman as well.

4. Carson Wentz for Prince Harry. What I know about the royal family would fit in a shot glass, but you can't wait in the "about 15 items" line at the supermarket or sit in a dentist's office without seeing Harry's mug on the cover of some idiotic magazine. Yes, Carson does look like him, but does this ginger from North Dakota have the acting chops? Who cares? Who knows anything about this Prince Dweeb anyway?

3. Pat Burrell as a cheating fiancé in any romantic comedy. A standard plotline used in romantic comedies for decades. A penniless sweetheart of a guy falls head over heels with a cute chick who is already engaged to some good-looking, philandering dirt bag, yet she's the last to know. Think of Adam Sandler and Drew Barrymore in *The Wedding Singer*. Pat the Bat could play that cheating Casanova in his sleep.

2. Nick Foles as Napoleon Dynamite. Please, Hollywood, we're begging you. Make this rumored sequel and cast Nick. With his luck, the movie would win 10 Oscars.

1. Allen Iverson for Frank Sinatra. Stick with me. Yes, there was Robert Downey Jr. portraying a white actor playing a black soldier in *Tropic Thunder*, but there's never been a biopic with a black guy portraying a white guy. Or vice versa. But I've been comparing Sinatra and Iverson on the air for years. Both come from tough neighborhoods. Both had flamboyant mothers. Both weighed about 160 pounds soaking wet. And, despite their diminutive stature, when Iverson or Sinatra walked into any room with that tough swagger, they immediately became the most intimidating men in it. For the record, no professional actor yet has portrayed Sinatra effectively. I would see this movie on opening day.

Ten Worst Eagles Draft Picks Ever

Boy, we love the NFL draft, don't we? It allows fans to forever say about a player, "Well, he's okay, but for a first-round draft pick, well . . ." Of course, it works the other way when you find a gem like Wilbert Montgomery in the sixth round. But being the whiners we are, it's usually more fun complaining about the busts, isn't it?

10. Freddie Mitchell. Freddie, oh Freddie. A first-rounder in 2001. Freddie was a star at UCLA—on and off the field—having made a couple of appearances on Jay Leno's show. Actually, that's where the problem started. He was just never as good as he thought he was. He was an egotistical guy and a whacked-out quote machine. There were almost as many FredEx fans as there were detractors. Unfortunately for Freddie, Donovan McNabb was in the second camp, and Mitchell was rarely thrown the ball. The numbers "4th and 26," however, are permanently tattooed on Eagles fans' souls.

9. Bernard Williams. The 14th overall pick out of Georgia in 1994, this 6-foot-8 offensive tackle had talent but preferred playing basketball and rolling doobies. There's not a lot of money in that unless you're Cheech and Chong.

8. Jon Harris. Big Daddy was actually with a Virginia alum when the Eagles picked this tall, skinny defensive end with the 25th pick in 1997, and even his friend was stunned. "You gotta be kidding me," he cried, tossing his tuna hoagie at the TV. Ray Rhodes swore by Harris, and he responded with two sacks in two years.

7. Antone Davis. Rich Kotite's first pick for the Birds, which should tell you something right there. A highly regarded offensive tackle out of Tennessee, the Eagles basically traded two first-rounders to get him. To make a long story short, the Packers came out of the whole mess with Brett Favre.

6. Siran Stacy. Okay, so he's not a first-round pick (second round, 1992), but check out these facts about this running back out of Alabama: arrested for allegedly beating up his girlfriend just two weeks after he was acquitted for beating up the same girlfriend. (She didn't show in court.) Lasted one season with the Eagles and never had a single carry. He was also pulled over for driving his agent's car 100 miles an hour down Broad Street. Now there's a parade.

5. Marcus Smith. Chip Kelly targeted six players with the 2014 first-rounder, and all of them went right before the Eagles came on the clock. So the Birds traded down six slots and, in a panic move, selected this Louisville linebacker who had been projected as a third-rounder. After Smith proved a bust, the funniest part was watching Kelly and Howie Roseman try to blame each other for the selection.

4. Leroy Keyes. If the Eagles lost one more lousy game in 1968, they could have ended up with O. J. Simpson instead of this running back out of Purdue. He got switched over to D-back and lasted all of three years with the Birds. Picked third overall to boot.

3. Happy Feller. His name alone earns him a spot here, but there's a lot more. A kicker? They drafted a kicker with the 83rd pick? Happy lasted one season for the Eagles, converting six of 20 field goals in 1970. Not only that, the Birds passed on Joe Theismann to draft him, and they cut Mark Moseley to keep him. Is everybody Happy?

2. Danny Watkins. A hockey-playing, 310-pound volunteer fireman from British Columbia, Watkins made a far better human-interest story than he did a pro guard. He was 26 years old when the Eagles drafted him in the first round out of Baylor and quickly learned he couldn't bully NFL opponents around as he did the younger college kids. He earned $5.9 million for two hideous seasons and then retired. In 2015 Watkins was named Rookie of the Year by the Frisco, Texas, Fire Department. That last sentence is not a joke.

> **Glen says:** The night after Watkins was drafted, I was hosting my WIP show at Chickie's and Pete's while Watkins's biggest champion, Eagles defensive line coach Howard Mudd, was at the bar. I asked Mudd to come on the air. He declined, saying, "Just tell them [Watkins] is going to be fucking terrific," before returning to his order of chicken wings.

1. Kevin Allen. The Eagles passed on Jerry Rice to take offensive tackle Allen with the ninth overall pick in 1985. He passed out from dehydration several times in training camp. He was released a year later after being arrested for rape on a Margate beach and, eventually, sent to prison. At least we got a great quote out of Buddy Ryan, who said Allen was "a good player if you want someone standing around killing grass."

Honorable mention: Michael Haddix, Kevin Kolb, Trevor Laws, Mike Mamula, Jerome McDougle, Leonard Renfro.

Because this is famous twosomes, we doubled the size of the list.

20. Hank Gathers and Bo Kimble. Philly kids from Dobbins Tech playing at faraway Loyola Marymount. Gathers led the nation in scoring as a junior; Kimble did it as a senior. We still get choked up remembering how Kimble honored his fallen friend by shooting his first free throw each game left-handed.

19. Donovan McNabb and Terrell Owens. Ah, what might have been. In just 22 games (including the Super Bowl), they hooked up for 133 receptions, 2,085 yards, and 20 touchdowns. Prorate that over a few years and you could easily forecast a title or two and maybe even McNabb joining T.O. in the Hall of Fame. If one of them hadn't been such a jackass and the other so thin-skinned, this could have been the ultimate Philadelphia pair.

18. Jameer Nelson and Delonte West. The greatest backcourt in St. Joe's history. In 2004, they helped the Hawks become just the second NCAA team in 25 years to finish the regular season undefeated. Both went in the first round of the 2004 draft. West had a middling NBA career, while Nelson defied all the experts and played 14 solid seasons in the pros.

17. Joel Embiid and Ben Simmons. Next time we rewrite this book, we expect this duo to head this list. "Process" architect Sam Hinkie didn't get to stick around to enjoy the fruits of tanking. But Embiid, after dealing with early-career injuries, has become one of the NBA's elite players. Simmons (when he learns to shoot) could join him at the top.

16. Ryan Madson and Brad Lidge. Lidge, the closer, earned the nickname "Lights Out" for his unhittable slider. In 2008, he was 48-for-48 in saves, including the postseason. Madson, who didn't get the glory, became known as "The Bridge to Lidge" for his mastery of the eighth inning. In 2008, manager Charlie Manuel handed them the ball a combined 148 times and never gave it a second thought.

15. Mark Howe and Brad McCrimmon. In 1985–1986, the Flyers' top defensive pairing combined for 32 goals and 114 points. Not bad. What was astounding was their plus/minus marks—plus-83 for McCrimmon and an NHL-best plus-85 for Howe. How did this team lose in the first round of the playoffs to the sub-.500 New York Rangers?

14. Jim Bunning and Chris Short. They combined for 70 starts, 36 wins, and even four saves in the fateful 1964 season. Both made the All-Star team and got MVP votes. Of course, all that we recall is Gene Mauch losing his grip as the Phils began their September swoon and pushing Bunning and Short out to the mound on two days' rest. Their arms were spent, and the season was lost.

13. Aaron McKie and Eddie Jones. The second-greatest backcourt in Temple—and Big 5—history (yeah, we know Jones played some small forward) led the Owls to the Elite

Eight in 1993. Both were drafted in the first round of the 1994 draft and went on to fine NBA careers.

12. Jon Runyan and Tra Thomas. Rock-solid bookend tackles for all those Andy Reid playoff teams. From 2000 to 2008, they combined to play 280 of a possible 288 games, keeping the bad guys away from McNabb. The Eagles have been blessed over the years by strong sets of tackles: Stan Walters and Jerry Sisemore in the 1980s, and Jason Peters and Lane Johnson in the 2010s.

11. Hal Lear and Guy Rodgers. And now, the greatest college backcourt in city history. Not many folks today can say they saw this superb pair when they starred at Temple in the mid-'50s. Lear was a prolific scorer, and Rodgers was the prototype for the passing point guard. They set the standard for the thousands of Philly guards who followed.

10. Merrill Reese and Mike Quick. Just about half of Merrill's 40-plus years calling Eagles games came with this great former wide receiver by his side offering prescient commentary. They're friends away from the booth, and the mutual respect shows in their work. In a way, they're like a musical duo, with Merrill playing lead and Mike providing the percussion.

9. Reggie White and Clyde Simmons. The misconception is that Reggie carried Clyde (you only need first names here). While it doesn't hurt to play with the greatest defensive end of all time, Clyde more than occasionally found himself double-teamed. From 1987 to 1993, the two combined for 162.5 sacks. We're not sure, but that may be a few more than Mike Mamula and Greg Jefferson rang up.

8. Ron Jaworski and Harold Carmichael. What quarterback-receiver tandem holds the Eagles record for touchdown passes? Not Van Brocklin-McDonald. Not Cunningham-Quick. Not McNabb and . . . uh . . . Pinkston? Nope, it was the Polish Rifle and his 6-foot-8 target, who hooked up 47 times from 1977 to 1983.

7. Maurice Cheeks and Julius Erving. They played together for nine glorious seasons on the Sixers. We're not sure exactly how many of Cheeks's 5,003 assists those years ended up in Doc's long fingers, but we've got highlight reels full of evidence.

6. Mike Schmidt and Greg Luzinski. The best 3-4 batting combo in the history of the Phils—and exactly what the club was aiming for when it later paired Jim Thome and Pat Burrell. During their eight years together, they totaled 484 homers—Schmidt's parabolic shots and Bull's upper-deck blasts. Schmidt was always the better player but Luzinski the more popular one. Many fans cried when he was sold to the White Sox in 1981.

5. Eric Lindros and John LeClair. If you count the seasons they played side by side, LeClair averaged 48 goals and 44 assists per 82 games. The rest of LeClair's career, he averaged a scant 25 goals and 28 assists per 82 games. Lindros's production also goes up with LeClair in tow, but not nearly as dramatically. It's fair to say that number 88 had more to do with number 10's success than the other way around. A scoring pair so good that even right winger Keith Jones couldn't screw them up.

4. Carson Wentz and Nick Foles. Two guys sharing one job. It wasn't supposed to be that way, of course. Wentz was on his way to winning the NFL MVP Award in 2017 when he went down with a shredded knee in Week 14. Many fans (and so-called experts) thought the Eagles season was finished. But Foles, the retread backup, so masterfully picked up the cudgel and wound up as the Super Bowl MVP. Much as it made sense, it was tough to see Foles leave in 2019.

3. Allen Iverson and Larry Brown. The all-time odd couple of Philadelphia sports. They gave this town its biggest NBA thrills over the past 30 years. Like an old married couple, they alternately bickered and embraced. Thing was, they were so much alike—undersized point guards raised without fathers, and both always needed to prove something. That's probably why they fought with each other.

2. Chase Utley and Jimmy Rollins. The heart of the nucleus of that team that won the NL East five straight years and ended the city's 25-year championship drought. Both were GM Ed Wade draft picks, so we can thank him for that. Chase and Jimmy played side by side for 12 years, combining to make nine All-Star teams and draw MVP votes 10 times. You can make a decent case that both belong in the Hall of Fame.

1A. Scott Franzke and Larry Andersen. Okay, here's a bonus entry. Phillies fans have not always watched great teams, but the guys calling the games on radio have been brilliant. Scott's easy Texas drawl and understated delivery mesh perfectly with LA's sense of humor and persistent disgust with the umps. This duo pulled off the toughest of tasks—replacing legends. Speaking of which . . .

1. Harry Kalas and Richie Ashburn. You expected something other than Harry and Whitey? The finest broadcasting team we've ever heard. For 22 years, they went together like coffee and donuts. Like beer and barbecue. Bacon and eggs. We'd better stop—we miss them *and* we're getting hungry.

My 10 Favorite Days in Philadelphia :: Jay Wright

How cool is it that the nation's best college basketball coach is a local boy? Because that's what Jay Wright is. Local. He started out at Churchville Elementary, then on to Richboro Junior High, then Council Rock High. After a few assistant coaching jobs, he landed his first head coaching gig at Bucknell before getting the Wildcats—and we all know how that's worked out.

In Philly, we knew Jay before all the titles and the tremendous success. And through it all he has remained the same likable, approachable guy (albeit a very well-dressed one). So it makes sense that when we asked Jay to contribute to this book, he decided to list what he loves most about living in an area that has been his home virtually his entire life. These are his 10 favorite days of the year.

Jay, may you never leave.

10. Opening Day for the Phillies.

9. Tour de Shore, the last Sunday in July. The charity bike ride from the Irish Pub in Philly to the Irish Pub in Atlantic City.

8. July 4th fireworks after a Phillies game.

7. The Friday of Memorial Day weekend. Jersey Shore time!

6. The Mummers Parade, New Year's Day. Take that, Glen.

5. Broad Street Run, the first Sunday in May.

4. The Run the Bridge from Camden to Philly and back, the first Sunday in November. What a view!

3. Monday after Selection Sunday. The Coaches vs. Cancer breakfast on the Palestra floor. It's so nice to see so many folks trying to make a difference.

2. The first Eagles home game of the season. Fall's coming. Merrill and Mike. I love it.

1. Thursday before Christmas. "The Glorious Sounds of Christmas" at the Kimmel. My favorite time of the year.

Best Complimentary Nicknames

The best nickname evolves naturally from fans, writers, and—especially—teammates.

We ignored manufactured nicknames for this chapter—did any Eagles fan ever really call Randall Cunningham "the Ultimate Weapon"? And we bypassed commercial hype—because "the Answer" wasn't anything that fans tagged to Allen Iverson; it was the result of some boardroom brainstorming designed to sell sneakers.

15. The Executioner. Every boxer worth his belt requires a decent ring name. Philadelphia boasted Smokin' Joe, Willie the Worm, and Stanley the Kitten. But the name that could best throw fear into opponents, just by hearing PA announcer Michael Buffer shout it, belonged to Bernard Hopkins.

14. Chooch. The moniker derives from either the Italian *ciuccio*, which means jackass, or the Spanish *chucha*, which means underarm odor. We're not sure which to believe, but it became an endearing term for Phils catcher Carlos Ruiz, who spent a career tipping his cap to a stadium full of fans chanting, "Chooooooch!"

13. The Hammer. If you ever met one of Dave Schultz's fists, you didn't have to ask about the nickname. Just check with Rangers defenseman Dale Rolfe.

12. Lefty. You've got to be damned good to have your nickname stem from a body part—Lou "The Toe" Groza, Elroy "Crazy Legs" Hirsch, Muhammad "The Louisville Lip" Ali. According to baseball-reference.com, there were 181 major leaguers known as Lefty over the sport's history (and none, by the way, as Righty). Just three made the Hall of Fame—Lefty Gomez, Philadelphia Athletics pitcher Lefty Grove, and the guy with 329 wins, Phillies pitcher Steve "Lefty" Carlton.

11. The Process. Sixers fans were deeply divided over GM Sam Hinkie's long-term tanking plan, but Joel Embiid fully embraced it. After Hinkie was forced out, the big center changed his social media profile name to Joel "The Process" Embiid and asked the team's PA announcer to introduce him simply as the Process. Somewhere in seclusion, Hinkie probably smiled.

10. The Polish Rifle. Ron Jaworski, from Lackawanna, New York, earned this for his heritage and his right arm, but it's too bad no one uses this for Jaworski anymore. It's much more descriptive than Jaws.

9. Dr. J. The name preceded Julius Erving to Philadelphia. In fact, it stems from his high school days when teammates marveled at how surgically brilliantly the kids "operated" on a basketball court. The measure of Erving's greatness is that the nickname got its own nickname, just plain Doc. How many guys do you know who can be universally identified by one syllable?

(Note: We got another Doc, with Roy Halladay joining the Phils from 2010 to 2013. We can't imagine another nickname ever being graced by two such great players.)

8. The Minister of Defense. The great Reggie White, an ordained minister from the age of 17, would brutalize a quarterback and then bless the poor sap as he helped him up. Good thing White wasn't Jewish—the Rabbi of Pass Rushers just doesn't have the same ring.

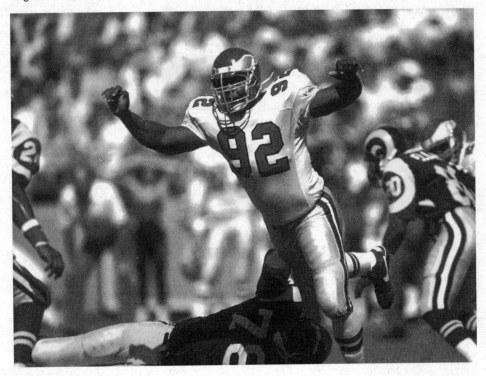

7. The Kangaroo Kid. Like Julius Erving, Billy Cunningham earned his tribute on the New York City playgrounds—in this case, Erasmus Hall High in Brooklyn (which also happens to be the alma mater of Barbra Streisand and Moe of the Three Stooges).The nickname, of course, is a nod to Billy C's great leaping ability.

Trivia question: Can you name the other Naismith Memorial Basketball Hall of Famer who shares this nickname?

Answer: Yeah, we didn't remember Jim Pollard either, although he coached at La Salle from 1955 to 1958.

6. The Man. It's rare we know the exact moment a nickname was born, but Chase Utley's occurred on August 9, 2006. Against the Braves, Utley hit a bases-clearing double and then hustled to score from second on a Ryan Howard comebacker to the pitcher. As Utley crossed home, Harry Kalas exploded, "He's safe at home plate! Chase Utley, you are the man!" The tag aptly stuck for the rest of Utley's career.

5. The Big Dipper. Wilt Chamberlain hated being called Wilt the Stilt. Felt it made him sound freakish. Didn't like Goliath either, for obvious reasons. But he liked the Big Dipper. Friends shortened it to Dipper. Real close friends knew him as Dippy.

4. Concrete Charlie. The thing that no one knows is that the moniker—so perfect for rock-hard Chuck Bednarik—didn't come from anything having to do with football. It came from Bednarik's off-season job of selling concrete up around Bethlehem. At his prime, Bednarik earned just $28,000 a season with the Eagles.

3. Chocolate Thunder. These days, there would be protests over the political incorrectness of such a reference. But Darryl Dawkins was a funny guy who gave himself a funny nickname. Indeed, Dawkins was such a character he gave titles to his dunks, including the Go-Rilla, the Yo-Mama, and—after shattering a backboard over Kings forward Bill Robinzine in 1979—the Chocolate Thunder-flying, Robinzine-crying, Teeth Shaking, Glass-breaking, Rump-roasting, Bun-toasting, Wham-bam, Glass-breaker-I-am Jam.

2. The Voice of God. We're not sure how many people are still alive who remember John Facenda as a newsman at WIP-AM and, later, as Philadelphia's first prominent anchorman at WCAU-TV. But everyone heard his stentorian voice intoning about "the frozen tundra of Lambeau Field" for NFL Films. Facenda's pipes were so good that he could make a fumble-filled clunker sound like an epic gladiatorial battle.

1. The Boston Strangler. We'll just leave the words to Larry Bird: "Do I remember Andrew Toney? The Boston Strangler? Yeah, I remember him. I wish we would've had him. He was a killer. We called him the Boston Strangler because every time he got a hold of the ball we knew he was going to score. He was the absolute best I've ever seen at shooting the ball at crucial times. We had nobody who could come close to stopping him. Nobody."

Best Nicknames That Were Meant as Anything but a Compliment

15. The Rat. Kenny Linseman looked like a rat, leaned forward on his skates like a rat, and played chippy, nasty hockey like a rat. Today, he says he regrets that nickname. But as a young player, he embraced it, once posing for a magazine cover with a rubber rat on his shoulder.

14. Bottom Line. As in Bottom Line Braman. Credit the late, great Stan Hochman for succinctly labeling the Eagles cheapskate owner, Norman Braman. Also known as That Guy in France.

13. Dr. Strange Glove. Dick Stuart was your big, beefy classic power hitter who slugged 28 homers for the Phils in 1965. Unfortunately, if you flipped him a baseball from across the kitchen table he would drop it, which is why he wore six different uniforms in his 10 big-league seasons.

12. Big Dog. Funny thing is, Big Dog was put on Glenn Robinson back in his college days and was first meant as a compliment, as in, "Leader of the Pack." By the time Robinson got to Philly, it was meant as an insult, as in, "What a mutt."

11. Sammy Sleeves. Eagles QB Sam Bradford said he preferred billowy jersey sleeves because "I just don't like to feel restricted. I just don't like them touching my arms. I'm kind of weird about it." Weird, too, were his darting eyes, blank stares, and gawky appearance.

10. Losing Pitcher. With a career record of 45 wins and 89 losses, Phils hurler Hugh Mulcahy got his tag because the words "Losing Pitcher" always ran next to his name in the box score. On a separate note, Mulcahy is the answer to this trivia question: Who was the first major leaguer to join the armed services after Pearl Harbor? He probably thought he'd be safer on the front lines than the pitcher's mound.

9. Mr. Universe. Flyers goalie Ilya Bryzgalov didn't get this moniker because of his abs and pecs. He earned it for otherworldly comments about the universe made during the HBO show 24/7, which previewed the 2012 Winter Classic. Bryz was a "humangous" free agent bust who couldn't blend with teammates or handle the pressures of playing goal in Philadelphia.

8. Highway 59. Opponents mocked Eagles defensive end Mike Mamula—playing off his jersey number and his inability to stop the run. "If you want to go a long distance, just go through Highway 59."

7. Titleist Head. Teammates hung this on a young Mike Schmidt, comparing his facial pockmarks to a dimpled golf ball. And you thought Phillies *fans* were rough on Schmitty?

6. El Pulpo. Antonio Alfonseca only pitched one season for the Phils (2007) but will long be remembered for his Spanish nickname, which translates to the Octopus and stems from his having six fingers on each hand and six toes on each foot. As a teenager, Alfonseca declined to have surgery for the polydactyly, saying it helped him throw a better sinker.

5. Honey Buns. It seems like a term of endearment, but the center on the Eagles 2004 Super Bowl team, Hank Fraley, merited the name because of his doughy belly as much as for his sweet demeanor.

4. Dirty. Just as every guy named Rhodes becomes Dusty, every guy named Waters becomes Muddy or Dirty. In the case of late Eagles safety Andre Waters, the designation fit. It was *Monday Night Football* announcer Dan Dierdorf who started it.

3. Head. Former Phil Dave Hollins carried this one for years because of A) his extra-large cranium (supposedly, he wore a 7-7/8 cap), and B) he was a major head case. No one, of course, had the guts to call him this to his face.

2. The Fog. A perfect name for Flyers coach Fred Shero, who seemed in a perpetual daze. Ever hear about the time he went for a walk between periods of a game in Atlanta and locked himself out of the arena?

1. Toast. Marvelous. Just right. What do you call a cornerback who repeatedly gets burned? In Izel Jenkins's case, Toast was the ideal handle. There is debate whether Jenkins or Giants defensive back Elvis Patterson was the first to be named after singed bread. No matter. We'll take ours with green jelly.

Guys Whose Names Sound Dirty (but Aren't)

15. Wendell Smallwood, Eagles running back, 2016–2018

14. Anatoli Semenov, Flyers center, 1994–1996

13. Heinie Sand, Phils shortstop, 1923–1928

12. Dick Pierce, Phils outfielder, 1883

11. Seth Morehead, Phils pitcher, 1957–1959

10. Wagon Tongue Keister, Phils outfielder, 1903

9. Harry Kane, Phils pitcher, 1905–1906

8. Dick Harter, Penn basketball coach, 1966–1971

7. Charlie Fuchs, Phils pitcher, 1943

6. Moise Fokou, Eagles linebacker, 2009–2011

5. Karl Dykhuis, Flyers defenseman, 1994–2000

4. Harry Cheek, Phils catcher, 1910

3. John Booty, Eagles defensive back, 1991–1992

2. Antonio Bastardo, Phils reliever, 2009–2014

1. Brian Baldinger, Eagles guard, 1992–1993

The Super Bowl champion Eagles of 2017 featured star players Chris Long, Fletcher Cox, Jason Peters, and Lane Johnson. They delighted in making fun of their own last names, frequently posting pictures on social media standing side by side, with captions reading like, "I can't go anywhere without my Long Cox."

Nine Old-Time Baseball Players We'd Want to Party With

9. John Boozer, Phils pitcher, 1962–1969

8. Billy Brewer, Phils pitcher, 1997–1999

7. Rich Dubee, Phils pitching coach, 2005–2013

6. Johnny Lush, Phils pitcher, 1904–1907

5. Lil Stoner, Phils pitcher, 1931

4. Johnny Walker, A's catcher, 1919–1921

3. Bud Weiser, Phils outfielder, 1915–1916

2. Bobby Wine, Phils shortstop, 1960–1968

1. Charles Yingling, Phils outfielder, 1894

Spelling Bee

Yeah, we don't understand why ESPN considers this a sport either, but if they're going to cash in on spelling bees, we don't want to be left out.

Here are 20 of the all-time most challenging names in local sports history, listed in alphabetical order by last name. If you're reading this, of course, you can't take the quiz. But run these names by a friend. If he can correctly spell 10 of them—first *and* last names—he'll probably beat you in Scrabble. If he can spell 15, he ought to be working on a newspaper copy desk. And if he can spell all 20, tell him we said thanks for buying the book (he's cheating).

A. Porfirio Altamirano, Phillies pitcher

B. Nnamdi Asomugha, Eagles cornerback

C. Ilya Bryzgalov, Flyers goalie

D. Viacheslav Butsayev, Flyers forward

E. Shayne Gostisbehere, Flyers defenseman

F. Kurt Gouveia, Eagles linebacker

G. Joe Lefebvre, Phillies outfielder

H. Timothé Luwawu-Cabarrot, Sixers forward

I. Billy Melchionni, Villanova and Sixers guard

J. Bill Mlkvy, Temple forward

K. Marty Mornhinweg, Eagles offensive coordinator

L. Dikembe Mutombo Mpolondo Mukamba Jean-Jacques Wamutombo,
Sixers center

M. Antero Niittymäki, Flyers goalie

N. Branko Radivojevič, Flyers forward

O. Mike Rogodzinski, Phillies outfielder

P. Hank Siemiontkowski, Villanova forward*

Q. Junior Tautalatasi, Eagles running back

R. Daniel Te'o-Nesheim, Eagles defensive end

S. Halapoulivaati Vaitai, Eagles tackle

T. John Vanbiesbrouck, Flyers goalie**

---

* Not counting Mutombo's splendid seven-part moniker, Hank Siemiontkowski's name is the longest of any athlete who ever played on a local sports team. Big Daddy once played a summer league game where only five players showed up for each team and he was forced to cover Hank Siemiontkowski the entire game. According to the box score, Big Daddy was narrowly outscored, 44–2.

** Big Daddy knows so little about hockey (he once referred to the "blue line" as the "blue route") that the first time he heard Vanbiesbrouck being talked about on WIP, he thought his name was Van Biesbrouck—as in, first name Van, last name Biesbrouck.

The Great Book of Philadelphia Sports Lists

The Great Philadelphia Nickname Quiz

Here are 50 nicknames hung on local sports figures. If you can associate 40 with the correct player, coach, or executive, you've earned your master's degree in Philadelphia sports. If you get fewer than 20, you're required to buy another copy of this book and study it.

1. Ash Can
2. Axe Man
3. Bedrock
4. Big Balls
5. Big Bird
6. Big Piece
7. Big Ragu
8. Big Red
9. Boxcar
10. Bubba Chuck
11. Bull
12. Bundy
13. Car Bomb
14. Crash
15. Dutch
16. Five-for-One
17. Flockey Hockey
18. Flyin' Hawaiian
19. Fred X
20. Fridge
21. Ghost
22. Ginger Jesus
23. Green Goblin
24. Hollywood
25. Hound

26. Jellybean
27. Jimmy Buckets
28. Johnny Vermont
29. Keith the Thief
30. Lights Out
31. Little Dictator
32. Mad Dog
33. Moose
34. Nails
35. Nicky Six
36. Pat the Bat
37. Pope
38. Razor
39. Rico
40. Sarge
41. Sauce Castillo
42. Secretary of Defense
43. Shady
44. Shake and Bake
45. Sheriff
46. Trash Man
47. White Lightning
48. Whitey
49. Wild Thing
50. World

Answers:

1. **Barry Ashbee,** Flyers
2. **Jeremiah Trotter,** Eagles
3. **Steve Bedrosian,** Phillies
4. **Chip Kelly,** Eagles coach
5. **Don Saleski,** Flyers
6. **Ryan Howard,** Phillies
7. **Donte DiVincenzo,** Villanova basketball
8. **Andy Reid,** Eagles coach
9. **Ed Hospodar,** Flyers
10. **Allen Iverson,** Sixers
11. **Greg Luzinski,** Phillies
12. **Chris Therien,** Flyers
13. **Dan Carcillo,** Flyers
14. **Richie Allen,** Phillies
15. **Darren Daulton,** Phillies
16. **Von Hayes,** Phillies
17. **Ron Flockhart,** Flyers
18. **Shane Victorino,** Phillies
19. **Freddie Mitchell,** Eagles
20. **Todd Fedoruk,** Flyers
21. **Shayne Gostisbehere,** Flyers
22. **Carson Wentz,** Eagles
23. **Jalen Mills,** Eagles
24. **Cole Hamels,** Phillies
25. **Bob Kelly,** Flyers
26. **Joe Bryant,** Sixers
27. **Jimmy Butler,** Sixers
28. **John LeClair,** Flyers
29. **Keith Allen,** Flyers GM
30. **Brad Lidge,** Phillies
31. **Dick Vermeil,** Eagles coach
32. **Fred Carter,** Sixers, or Ryan Madson, Phillies
33. **André Dupont,** Flyers
34. **Lenny Dykstra,** Phillies (also, the Dude)
35. **Nick Foles,** Eagles
36. **Pat Burrell,** Phillies
37. **Paul Owens,** Phillies GM
38. **Ray Emery,** Flyers
39. **Eric Desjardins,** Flyers
40. **Gary Matthews,** Phillies
41. **Nik Stauskas,** Sixers
42. **Garry Maddox,** Phillies
43. **LeSean McCoy,** Eagles
44. **Bake McBride,** Phillies
45. **Rodney Buford,** Sixers
46. **Gregg Garrity,** Eagles
47. **Richie Ashburn,** Phillies
48. **Bob Dernier,** Phillies
49. **Mitch Williams,** Phillies (also went by Mitchie Poo)
50. **Lloyd B. Free,** Sixers

Any list like this starts with tennis great Lisa Raymond, but the Wayne native took herself out in order to write this chapter. She is an 11-time grand slam doubles winner who was ranked for 137 weeks as the number one women's doubles player in the world. She won the bronze medal in mixed doubles for the United States in the 2012 Olympics.

Raymond won the United States Federation Cup both as a player (2000) and a coach (2017). She currently coaches that team, along with captain Kathy Rinaldi-Stunkel, and is the owner of the Star FitClub group fitness gym in Somers Point, New Jersey.

10. Mary Ellen Clark, diver. This Radnor High School alum was an Olympic bronze medalist in 1992 and 1996. Clark was voted one of the top 10 women athletes in the country by the United States Olympic Committee in 1996.

9. Mary Decker, runner. Unfortunately this Jersey native is known more for the unfortunate incident at the 1984 Los Angeles Olympics (the favorite to win the gold in the 3,000 meters, she collided with Zola Budd and was unable to finish the race) than for her standout career. The 1983 world champion would be back four years later to compete in the 1988 Olympics. In 2003 she was inducted into the Track and Field Hall of Fame.

8. Tara Lipinski, figure skating. Born in Philly, until just recently Lipinski held the record for the youngest US figure skating champion at 14 years old. That record was broken by 13-year-old Alysa Liu in 2018. The 1998 Olympic Games gold medalist in Nagano, Lipinski would later go on to be a top analyst alongside Johnny Weir for NBC.

7. Elena Delle Donne, basketball. From Wilmington, this University of Delaware grad is currently one of the biggest names in women's basketball. A 2016 Olympics gold medalist and 2015 WNBA MVP for the Washington Mystics, she was also named a Special Olympics global ambassador in 2014 for her tireless work in the community.

6. Kathy Jordan, tennis. The King of Prussia native was someone I looked up to while growing up. A seven-time grand slam doubles champion, Jordan was one of the world's top singles and doubles players. She is an Australian Open singles finalist with wins over the great Chrissy Evert. She grew up in a tennis family: her sister, Barbara, is a fellow grand slam winner, and her father, Bob, is a well-respected coach in the Philadelphia area. I was fortunate enough to practice with Kathy when I was young, which was a thrill for me.

5. Carli Lloyd, soccer. The New Jersey native is a two-time Olympic gold medalist, a 2015 world champion, and two-time FIFA player of the year. Those are just a few of her accomplishments. She has been on the US National Team since 2005 and is the first woman to score three goals in one FIFA World Cup game.

4. Betsy King, golf. From Reading, Betsy King was among the world's best golfers in the 1980s–1990s and is an LPGA legend. The winner of six majors and 34 tour events, King was the LPGA money leader and Player of the Year in 1984, 1989, and 1993. King led the Americans to victory as captain of the 2007 Solheim Cup team.

3. C. Vivian Stringer, basketball. You can't speak about women's basketball legends without mentioning this great player and current Rutgers coach. In 1993, she was named Naismith Coach of the Year, *Sports Illustrated* Coach of the Year, and *USA Today* Coach of the Year. She is the first woman to lead three different teams to the NCAA Final Four. In 2001 Stringer won her 1,000th game at Rutgers. One of the coolest facts about her is she is the third woman—and the first African American woman—to have a building named after her at the Nike headquarters.

2. Immaculata College Women's Basketball Team. Also known as the Mighty Macs, this women's team won the first three national championships (1972–1974) of the Association for Intercollegiate Athletics for Women. They played in the first-ever televised women's college basketball game in 1975 and had a movie made about them titled, of course, *The Mighty Macs*. In addition, Coach Cathy Rush was inducted into the Women's Basketball Hall of Fame in 2000 and the Naismith Memorial Basketball Hall of Fame in 2008.

1. Dawn Staley, basketball. It would be impossible to put together a list of great local female athletes without Dawn Staley right up at the top. The Philly native is a three-time Olympic gold medalist and played in both the ABL and the WNBA. She is currently the head coach of the University of South Carolina, where she led her team to the NCAA title in 2017. On a personal note, Dawn and I were both winners in 1992 for the Honda Award (best collegian athlete in our sport). It was cool to be part of that with my fellow Philadelphian.

The 10 Best Things about the Palestra

10. It's *still* great. I wish everyone would stop waxing nostalgic about it. There are still many, many great sold-out games a year there. Just go.

9. Those weird windows on the ceiling. Name another arena where light pours though the roof during a day game. It makes for really odd lighting, which further adds to its uniqueness.

8. You can take a trolley to it. I have always said that the main reason college football wasn't big in this town was because you couldn't take a trolley to a big-time game. I don't believe the 36 has a stop in Happy Valley. But the greatest teams in the country (Duke, Kansas) have come to the Palestra since it opened in 1927, and you can still get there on SEPTA.

7. Everyone shares the same concourse. Whether you're sitting in the front row or at the tippy-top with your back against a radiator, everyone ends up lumped together in the same tiny hallway at halftime—unlike the Wells Fargo Center (or whatever they call it these days), which separates its fans by ticket price like the *Titanic*.

6. The location. Plopped right down in the middle of a beautiful college campus. Not a meat warehouse in sight.

5. It's loud. Ask any opposing coach to name the loudest venue in the country and to a man he'll tell you it is the Palestra. There's no carpeting anywhere. Not one seat has a cushion. No tiled ceiling. There's nothing to absorb any sound.

4. The soft pretzels outside. "Cheaper outside than inside." Not to mention that the guy you buy them from inside isn't wearing crummy-looking gloves with the fingers cut out of them.

3. Divided by two. When it's a Big 5 battle, you get one team's fans on one side of the building and the other team's fans on the other. This just doesn't happen anywhere else.

2. Every seat is great. Granted, very few of them have backs, and you're in trouble if you're sitting next to anyone even 20 pounds overweight. But every seat is right on top of the players. If Hickory High coach Norman Dale (Gene Hackman) asked a player to tell him what brand of gum an opponent was chewing, well, not only could his player smell the Dentyne, but most of the fans in the stands could as well. And it seats almost 9,000, which makes this even more amazing. This is no small arena.

1. No luxury boxes.

John Chaney is a Philadelphia legend who began his career coaching Simon Gratz High in 1966. He had 10 successful years at Cheyney State (how often does the coach's name match that of the school?) and led the Temple Owls for 25 seasons before retiring in 2006. He won 741 career games, took Temple to 17 NCAA Tournaments, and reached the Elite Eight five times.

John didn't want to rate this list, so the names are in alphabetical order.

Chuck Daly, Penn. He took Penn, an Ivy League school, to the Final Four (in 1979), which was a tremendous accomplishment. You just can't overlook what Chuck Daly did before he became such a successful NBA coach.

Fran Dunphy, Penn and Temple. He had a few tough seasons toward the end, before stepping down in 2019. But remember: he did a lot at Penn with very little. He was perhaps second in the Ivies to Petey Carril (of Princeton). Fran won nine Ivy League titles; Petey won 13. Fran would have surpassed that record if he didn't move to Temple.

Tom Gola, La Salle. Tommy is the one who came along at a time when La Salle was going through problems (because of a scandal), and someone like him was really needed. He inherited a team that had many good players and took them to great heights. Tommy was an All-American player. He's in the Hall of Fame. And he happened to be one of our great coaches and someone I respect highly.

Ken Loeffler, La Salle. I did not know him, but I knew of him. He took that La Salle team (in 1954) to the NCAA championship. The next year they went back to the Final Four, against the Bill Russell team from the University of San Francisco. He is certainly somebody we should respect as being one of the greats.

Harry Litwak, Temple. Harry was one of the creators and another Hall of Famer. Before I got involved in this, coming out of high school, he was always someone I looked at as being special. He produced a number of great players—Guy Rodgers and Hal Lear, among many others. He also was one of the first to produce the 3-2 zone, one of the zones that we used as well.

Herb Magee, Philadelphia University. Herbie finally got into the Naismith Memorial Hall of Fame. He won a national championship at the Division II level. He certainly was one of the best-kept secrets in this city. He should have been coaching at the Division I level, but he coached a Division II team and went largely unrecognized. He is certainly one of the great minds and one of the great shooting coaches in basketball. I really revere him highly.

Rollie Massimino, Villanova. He won a national championship here against one of the hot-button teams of all time, Georgetown. What else do you need to say?

Speedy Morris, La Salle. Speedy is just Philadelphia. He certainly made a great transition from being one of the great high school coaches in the city, to coaching women's basketball, to running a successful men's team at La Salle. He is one of our overlooked great coaches. I admire him and love him dearly.

Jack Ramsay, St. Joseph's. He was always innovative and creative. He is another Hall of Famer from St. Joe's and the one who created, and wrote books on, the full-court pressure defenses he employed. One of our most innovative and creative coaches, he won titles here in the Big 5 and also in the NBA.

Jay Wright, Villanova. Well, what he's contributed in recent years is tremendous. Winning one national championship is so hard. Winning two? Close to impossible. I love that I turn on my TV to an NBA game and see those kids who played for him. All that, plus he's a great diplomat for the entire Philadelphia basketball community.

We have been blessed with amazing coaches who grew up in the area, including Jay Wright, John Chaney, and Phil Martelli. But each of those men would tell you Speedy Morris is right there as well. He won titles at Roman Catholic and St. Joe's Prep, and he also took La Salle University to four NCAA Tournament appearances.

To watch Speedy coach in the legendary Roman Catholic bandbox of a gym was a special treat. Speedy would begin a game in jacket and tie. After the first call to go against him, the tie would loosen. Eventually it would come off completely, followed by his suit jacket—which would be hurled to the floor. The last step would be his shirt tails hanging out. He's the winningest coach in the history of the Catholic League and a Philadelphia treasure. Here are the coaches who gave him a run for his money.

10. Buddy Gardler, Cardinal O'Hara. He could really coach, and I always tell people he is the best coach never to win the Catholic League Title. Buddy is the second-winningest coach in the 100 years of the Catholic League with 560 wins. He passed away recently, and he is missed by his family and many friends.

9. Sean Tait, Father Judge. Some coaches are good at doing more with less, and that is Sean Tait. Every time my prep team plays Judge, the game comes down to the final minute. Sean is a disciple of Princeton coach Pete Carril, and sometimes I think that it is Coach Carril behind the bench. If you fall asleep, you will be back-doored to death.

8. Dan Dougherty, Episcopal Academy. My second season at Penn Charter, we won the Inter-Ac championship, and we were one game away from going undefeated. It was senior night, and we had a standing-room-only crowd looking forward to celebrating an undefeated season. Dangerous Dan had other ideas, and his famed secondary break won out.

7. Jim Fenerty, Germantown Academy. Jim's favorite play is called Patriot, and he runs it a lot. It's a man-to-man play with a lot of movement, and we "defend" it with a zone defense. It is usually a close game, and Jim is a formidable opponent. Fenerty is the second-winningest coach in Philadelphia history with 632 victories in 37 years.

6. Bill Fox, Father Judge. We won back-to-back titles in '73 and '74, but rookie coach Bill Fox had other ideas about us winning our third. Fox coached Judge for 29 years, winning 545 games. Fittingly, Father Judge's court is now named in his honor.

5. Mark "Max" Levin, Overbrook High School. Another terrific coach with extraordinary talent. We lost back-to-back city title games to Overbrook, and in the last one played in 1980, Overbrook was 30–0 and ranked number one in the country. We were 31–2, number five in the state, but not ranked nationally. The game was televised, and it was standing room only at the Palestra. Down one with eight seconds remaining, our Randy Monroe was fouled. He calmly made the first shot but missed the second, sending the game into overtime. Overbrook controlled the OT for a 65–56 victory.

4. Joey Goldenberg, West Philadelphia High School. His Speedboys were one of the best teams in Philadelphia in the '70s and '80s. We defeated West Philly in a defensive battle, 38–35, for the 1974 city title. It was the last time a Catholic League team defeated a public school team for the title. West Philly got even four years later, when they defeated our Roman Catholic Cahillites 57–54.

3. Jim Purcell, Cardinal O'Hara. Jim Purcell was a thorn in my side during my first five years as a high school coach. We lost three times to O'Hara, including a playoff loss on a triple-overtime buzzer beater. The following year, 1969, we won the Catholic League title for the first time in 27 years. Jim retired in 1972.

2. Carl Arrigale, Neumann-Goretti High School. In our first few years at the Prep, we did well against the Saints, winning six of eight games. After that, Neumann-Gorretti beat us 13 straight times, including Catholic League championship games. We finally broke the streak in 2018, upsetting Neumann in the first round of the playoffs. It was their first loss at home to a Catholic League team in 10 years. I consider Carl Arrigale the most successful coach in the history of the Catholic League. I had the pleasure to coach Carl at Penn Charter in 1984. He was the most valuable player and led us to the Inter-Ac championship.

1. Morgan Wootten, DeMatha High School. I have coached against DeMatha four times and lost all four. Wootten is probably the finest high school coach in America, and he is in the Naismith Memorial Basketball Hall of Fame with over 1,200 victories. The Hall honors Morgan every year with an award in his name. I was honored to receive the award in 2016 in Chicago.

Honorable mention: Roman Catholic's Dennis Seddon, Chris McNesby, and Matt Griffin. I have to mention my alma mater and three coaches that cause me some pain when I coach against them.

To be honest, we could push this list past 100, so we limited eligibility to guys who got in trouble while actually playing in Philadelphia—leaving out the likes of Irvin Fryar (convicted, along with his mother, of mortgage fraud after he retired) and Craig MacTavish (who served a year in jail for vehicular homicide before he got here). The criterion also leaves out Edwin "Alabama" Pitts, who came to the Eagles in 1935, right out of a five-year armed-robbery stretch in Sing Sing Prison. These are not necessarily the most serious infractions, just the most interesting.

10. Jahlil Okafor. Hey, we've all exceeded the speed limit on the way to Jersey. But Okafor morphed into Kyle Busch one late night in 2015, reaching 108 mph on the Ben Franklin Bridge and then telling police, "Oh, man. My car just goes really fast without kinda knowing." The *Speed Racer* episode came shortly after he was suspended for two games for getting in a fight outside a Boston bar. The third overall pick of the 2015 draft, Big Jah lasted less than three seasons in Philadelphia, his stats declining every year.

9. Nigel Bradham. According to police, the Eagles linebacker broke the nose of a cabana boy at the Hilton Bentley Miami in 2016, after an argument over how long it took to bring an umbrella that Bradham and his friends had ordered. His group hightailed it from the scene, but police found them through a cell phone and receipt left behind in the sand.

8. Ed Bouchee. In February 1958, Bouchee, a 25-year-old Phillies first baseman, pleaded guilty to a series of sex offenses—specifically, indecent exposure involving young girls. He received a sentence of three years' probation and was ordered into a rehab program. Here's the amazing part: in May, the Phils brought him back for the rest of the season. And the season after that. And by most accounts, there was no uproar from the fans. Somehow, we don't think that putting a pedophile in the starting lineup would go over so well these days.

7. Lenny Dykstra. We could write a book on the transgressions that landed this creep in prison, but we'll focus on one from 1991. Headed home from a teammate's bachelor party, Dykstra wrapped his brand-new Mercedes around a tree in Radnor and broke a few bones. Teammate Darren Daulton, riding shotgun, fractured the orbital socket around his left eye and missed several months of play. Legendary stories emerged around the late-night romp, but we can only print what we know to be true—or at least what won't get us sued. Anyway, Dykstra was charged with drunken driving, but his record was expunged after he entered a program for first-time offenders. His later crimes did not earn such leniency.

6. Josh Huff. Chip Kelly's pet project was arrested on the Walt Whitman Bridge in 2016 carrying a 9 mm Smith & Wesson handgun, six hollow point bullets, and a bag of weed. He was also cited with driving under the influence. Huff was headed home from practice when the arrest occurred. In addition to all those transgressions being against the law (obviously), they violated an NFL policy against bringing weapons to the workplace. Huff insisted he had not taken the guns, ammo, and drugs to the NovaCare Center but merely stopped somewhere to pick them up on the way home. The Eagles didn't buy his story and cut him two days later.

5. Allen Iverson. AI was arrested in July 2002 after police said he barged into a West Philly apartment—toting a gun—and threatened two men (one of whom was wearing hot pants) while looking for his wife, with whom he had fought earlier that night. A judge later dismissed all the charges. All we are left with is the memory of the week-long media stakeout around Iverson's Gladwyne home, including hovering helicopters. The British royal family never drew so much paparazzi.

4. Mychal Kendricks. Finally, a nice white-collar crime to write about. Kendricks, a linebacker who spent six seasons with the Eagles, pleaded guilty in 2018 to securities fraud and conspiracy. Turns out the Cal grad benefited (to the tune of about $1.2 million) from illegal inside tips given to him by an investment bank analyst. Kendricks was paying the guy off in Eagles tickets and invitations to nightclub promotions.

3. LeSean McCoy. They didn't call him Shady for nothing. McCoy had a series of incidents over the years, including accusations of throwing a woman out of a "party bus" and having an ex-girlfriend shaken down over some jewelry he gave her. But the one that resonated was a literal run-in with the law, when Shady got into a bar fight and allegedly beat up two off-duty Philly cops.

2. Ugueth Urbina. For sheer weirdness, this one earns top-two billing. The Phils setup man was arrested in his native Venezuela soon after the 2005 season. Several workers on his farm claimed that Urbina accused them of stealing a gun. He then, they claimed, attacked them with a machete and followed that up by dousing them with gasoline and setting them on fire—three times. Urbina was convicted of attempted murder and served more than seven years in prison.

1. Kevin Allen. The Eagles reached up to draft this stiff of a tackle in 1985—passing up Jerry Rice, by the way. He played one terrible season and then was convicted of raping a woman on the beach in Margate, New Jersey, in October 1986. Allen served 33 months in prison after a jury chose to believe that he "mistakenly believed that the woman consented to have sex." In a column written from prison, Allen said he hoped to return to the NFL—a plan, fortunately, the Eagles did not agree with.

Philly Athletes Who Acted—The Best and the Worst

Every actor thinks he's an athlete, and every athlete thinks he's an actor. Most often, they're wrong. But dozens of Philadelphia athletes have tried being in the movies. While most have been closer to Lawrence Taylor than Laurence Olivier, a handful shined on the big screen. Or at least they didn't embarrass themselves.

Here are lists of the best and worst acting jobs ever by Philadelphia sports. We did not include any in which the athlete played himself, for better (Charles Barkley in *Space Jams*) or worse (Ian Laperrière and Scott Hartnell in *This Is 40*). And we extended it out to include some folks who didn't actually play the games but made their living around it.

Oh, and we really enjoyed Nick Foles as Napoleon Dynamite. Wait, what?

Ten Best

10. Joe Klecko. We include Klecko because of his years at Temple, not his fame as a member of the Jets' New York Sack Exchange. And we include Klecko because the Chester native was terrific in Dick Richards and Jerry Jameson's 1986 *Heat* starring Burt Reynolds (not to be confused with Michael Mann's slicker 1995 *Heat* that featured Val Kilmer, Al Pacino, and Robert De Niro). This one is a punch-'em-up vehicle set in Vegas. Klecko plays a mob bodyguard who, in stunning slow motion, tosses a guy through a window. And he doesn't even spoil it with a Mark Gastineau sack dance.

9. Roman Gabriel. This may be a cheat, since the acting role came four years before Gabriel arrived in Philadelphia in 1973 as the Eagles' so-called savior of a quarterback. Still, we had to include Gabriel's performance in *The Undefeated,* simply because he got to portray John Wayne's adopted Cherokee son, Blue Boy. How many actors get to break into the business playing side by side with a legend like the Duke?

It didn't do much for Gabriel's thespian career, however. He only ever acted in one other movie.

8. Tim Rossovich. You could have predicted an acting career for Rossovich when he first showed up as an Eagle in 1968 with sideburns and a bushy mustache and drew attention by eating glass and setting himself on fire. Heck, his college roommate at USC was Tom Selleck, after all. By the late '70s, he was out of football and into Hollywood as an actor and stuntman. He appeared in more than 15 movies, and his finest work came in the Michael Keaton–Henry Winkler comedy *Night Shift*, playing a menacing pal to the coroners-turned-pimps.

7. Jack O'Halloran. Back in the 1960s, Irish Jack was a 6-foot-6 heavyweight contender out of Runnemede, New Jersey, who battled future heavyweight champs George Foreman and Ken Norton. You're more likely to recall him as Kryptonite villain "Non" in *Superman* and *Superman II*. A scarier, more intimidating mute never lived. O'Halloran made other notable movies (he was great as lug Moose Malloy in *Farewell, My Lovely*), but his *Superman* role brought him a guaranteed lifetime income attending superhero conventions. There was even an action figure with his likeness.

6. Bob Uecker. Somehow he converted six seasons—including two for the Phillies—as a dreadful backup catcher (career batting average: .200) into a five-decade career in comedy. Uecker had success in standup, television (*Mr. Belvedere*), and dozens of commercials. But his finest work came as cynical flask-sipping announcer Harry Doyle in the feature movie *Major League*. Think about this: How many times over the years have you heard a wild pitch greeted with the shout, "Juuusssst a bit outside"? That's Uecker's tagline from the movie and his contribution to the lexicon.

5. Julius Erving. Doc plays a hoops superstar surrounded by teammates resembling the Village People in *The Fish That Saved Pittsburgh*. He wears the tightest basketball shorts in history, dribbles in time to disco music, and nearly trips over his platform shoes in one scene. He finds himself upstaged by Flip Wilson and Jonathan Winters and has to deliver lines like "I've learned to lean and walk on air, and listen to the rhythm inside my body." Still, it works. And it works because you can tell that Doc is playing it for fun. As seriously and earnestly as he played the game, Erving is in this campy film for the laughs. Watching it, you feel like you're in on the joke.

Erving recently said that *Fish* was his second-favorite movie of all time, trailing only *The Great Escape.* Us? We'd call it a draw.

4. Stan Hochman and Al Meltzer. Okay, maybe the two Philadelphia media legends are actually playing themselves in *Rocky V,* but since they're both identified as "conference reporter," we're going with it. Stan steals the scene with his putdown of tomato can Tommy Gunn: "He's a second-rate fighter with so much glass in his jaw, he ought to be a chandelier." Stan told us later that he improvised the line, thinking it was much better than what was in the script. He also told us that he received an annual royalty from the film, which he described as "almost enough to take Gloria [his wife] out for breakfast."

3. Wilt Chamberlain. Personal prejudice here, but we thought the Dipper stole the show in *Conan the Destroyer* as Bombaata, the 7-foot bodyguard to the queen with the unstoppable finger roll. After all, who other than Wilt could upstage a cast that included Arnold Schwarzenegger, André the Giant, and Grace Jones? Watch carefully the scene where Wilt single-handedly crashes down a stone wall. As he picks up the rocks to throw them, you can clearly tell they're made of foam rubber.

2. Tex Cobb. The former heavyweight contender acted in great movies (*Diggstown*) and terrible movies (*Ernest Goes to Jail*). But his classic performance came in the Coen Brothers' comedy *Raising Arizona*, in which he played Leonard Smalls, the Lone Biker of the Apocalypse. Watch as Tex shoots that tiny little lizard off the rock. Marvel as he figures out the whereabouts of the cons just by sniffing their hair grease. This, of course, was Cobb's second-greatest contribution to the arts. His greatest was getting pasted by Larry Holmes in a fight so one-sided that it spurred Howard Cosell to swear off boxing forever. For that, we thank you, Tex.

1. Tim Brown. You may better remember the great Eagles halfback from the classic football scene in *M*A*S*H* (not exactly an acting reach), but his work in another Robert Altman film, *Nashville*, was far superior. Brown plays Tommy Brown (hmmmm, how'd they come up with that name?), a country singer modeled after Charley Pride. Not only can he act, but he's called upon to warble a tune, "Bluebird," and proves he can sing as well.

Ten Worst

10. Todd Zeile. The former Phils infielder plays Mullet in *Dirty Deeds*, a 2004 teen sex romp that bills itself as a poor man's *American Pie*. A very poor man's. On the other hand, Zeile passed along something in his DNA. His daughter, Hannah Zeile, aptly plays young Kate Pearson in the hit NBC drama *This Is Us*.

9. Bo Belinsky. He pitched two seasons for the Phils in the mid-'60s. That's the least of Belinsky's accomplishments. Bobo was a New Jersey pool-hall rat who pitched a no-hitter as a rookie with the Angels, hung with Frank Sinatra, and performed truly horribly in the 1967 malt-shop flick *C'mon, Let's Live a Little*. His greatest feat was being engaged to Hollywood sex bomb Mamie Van Doren for about a year. For further research, look her up on Google images. That alone will justify whatever you paid for this book.

8. John Kruk. What was Kruk's famous line? "I'm no athlete, lady, I'm a baseball player." Well, he was no actor, either. Ever see Kruk as Lanz in the Wesley Snipes–Robert De Niro flick *The Fan*? Let's put it this way: compared to that, his work in *The Best Damn Sports Show, Period* was Shakespearian.

7. Reggie White. We will always love Reggie for his Hall of Fame play as an Eagle and his commitment to make the world better. His semiautobiographical flick, *Reggie's Prayer,* is well intentioned but about as tolerable to most guys as a *Judge Judy* marathon. Reggie stars as Reggie Knox, a retired player who coaches and counsels troubled high schoolers. Costars include ex-Eagle Keith Jackson as his assistant coach and Brett Favre and Mike Holmgren as janitors. Really.

6. Dick Allen. He portrays a scout in *Summer Catch*, a disappointing movie about Cape Cod League baseball. Presumably, he's searching for the next Dick Allen.

5. Bernard Hopkins. We won't go too hard on his work in *State Property 2*. Let's just say we wouldn't blame him if he sent director Damon Dash on a one-way trip to Palookaville.

4. Joe Frazier. His friend Sherman Hemsley (a.k.a. George Jefferson from *The Jeffersons*) roped Frazier into playing Terrible Tucker in *Ghost Fever*, a terrible film that combines boxing, the supernatural, and torture. Trust us, the worst torture is that foisted on the viewers. Remember the beating that Smokin' Joe took from George Foreman? This was worse.

3. Pete Rose. Director Mark Tinker had a sense of humor when he cast Rose as Ty Cobb in the 1991 made-for-TV film *Babe Ruth*. The movie itself is outstanding—better than both the William Bendix and John Goodman versions. But Pete? We would bet you 7-to-5 that he was horrible.

2. Muhammad Ali. We'll always consider the Greatest a Philly guy for his years in Cherry Hill and Fairmount Park. And we'll always marvel at his showmanship and skills. But Ali should have never agreed to take a shot at acting in *Freedom Road*. In the 1979 film, Ali stars (if that's the word) as Gideon Jackson, an ex-slave in 1870s Virginia who gets elected to the US Senate. He stares at the camera at inopportune times, mumbles through his monologues, and looks ready to punch out costar Kris Kristofferson half the time. Actually, that may have helped the movie.

1. Jeff Lurie. We're not even considering *V. I. Warshawski, Detective in High Heels*—a stinkbomb Lurie produced before redeeming himself with the Oscar-winning documentary *Inside Job*. We're merely focusing on the Eagles owner's brief on-camera gig in the 1998 made-for-TV monstrosity called *The Garbage Picking Field Goal Kicking Philadelphia Phenomenon*. Lurie plays the taproom pal of Tony Danza's lead character, Barney. Aside from appearing about as comfortable in a corner bar as Snoop Dogg in a nunnery, Lurie utters this immortal line, "Hey, did you hear about the Eagles' new owner? I hear he's a great guy!"

Hey, could you be more self-serving? I hear you're an egomaniac!

Mo Cheeks came to the Sixers in 1978 and directed the team's offense for 11 seasons as one of the smoothest, greatest point guards in NBA history. In 2018 he was inducted into the Naismith Memorial Basketball Hall of Fame.

5. Micheal Ray Richardson (1978–1986: New York Knicks, Golden State Warriors, New Jersey Nets). It's a shame that more fans don't remember him—although Sixers fans sure do from when he and the Nets eliminated the Sixers in the first round of the 1984 playoffs. At 6-foot-5 he was one of the first tall point guards, and that really gave me a lot of problems.

4. Norm Nixon (1977–1989: Los Angeles Lakers, Los Angeles Clippers). Quick and smart—and a real scorer. With all the other great guys he teamed with on the Lakers, he's become a forgotten great player.

3. John Stockton (1984–2003: Utah Jazz). He was incredibly competitive. Mean and nasty. He'd bump you, hit you, whatever.

2. Isiah Thomas (1981–1994: Detroit Pistons). I swear he could play today. The first point guard who didn't always have the "pass-first" mentality—yet he was a great passer. He could really break you down off the dribble. Tough and mean. He gave me fits to guard him.

That's my list.
  Wait a minute, here. Isn't Mo forgetting somebody? Wasn't there a number 32 on the Lakers who broke the Sixers fans' hearts on many occasions? How could he not even bring up you-know-who?

1. Magic Johnson (1979–1991, 1995: Los Angeles Lakers). Oh, him? He doesn't count. I mean, he was so great and unique that he's a list unto himself. Plus, he was so tall I only guarded him if my whole team was in foul trouble. The best floor leader ever.

Bob Kelly played 11 seasons for the Flyers, scoring the Stanley Cup–winning goal in 1975. He is better remembered by fans, however, as the aggressive, hard-hitting left winger who amassed 1,285 penalty minutes. He was too modest to put himself on this list, although he certainly belongs.

10. Ian Laperrière, 2009–2010. Lappy came to the Flyers at age 36, at the end of his career. Still, he was one of the toughest guys in the NHL even then. He would do whatever it took to help his team—even if that meant blocking a puck with his face. He probably had 250 NHL fights, and he won most of them.

9. Riley Cote, 2006–2010. Riley was 6-foot-2 and played in an era when heavyweights like Derek Boogaard and Eric Cairns were going 6-foot-7. But he never was afraid of a challenge; he'd just wade in and throw at the big guys. He typified what a Flyer was all about in my mind.

8. Paul Holmgren, 1975–1984. He went after me when I played for Washington in 1981. Boy, was he a hard hitter. Homer always went after the toughest guys—Nick Fotiu, the Carlson brothers, anyone with a reputation. He was very in shape, very ripped.

7. Craig Berube, 1986–1991, 1998–2000. He had 1,139 penalty minutes as a Flyer and more than 2,000 during his time in the league. Very inspirational. Chief used to drink down in my basement. He'd take out his teeth and put them on the bar, and you'd see his knuckles, all scraped up. He really enjoyed fighting.

6. Dave Brown, 1982–1989, 1991–1995. He was a big, tall, standup guy who would just stand back and throw fists. Sometimes, he would take two or three punches for every one he threw, but his were harder. I remember the 1987 brawl against Montreal in the Finals. Dave came out of the locker room in just pants and skates—nothing else. He went after their toughest guy, Chris Nilan, who wanted no part of Brownie.

5. Rick Tocchet, 1984–1992, 1999–2002. His 1,817 penalty minutes are a franchise record. He was a fully developed player who could score and play defense, and boy, could he fight as well. Pound for pound, he's one of the toughest ever. The girls liked him too, eh? When my daughter was 12 years old, his was the jersey she wanted.

4. Mel Bridgman, 1975–1982. I watched him break in with us. He went after the toughest players we played against, like Curt Fraser of Vancouver, who was a 200-pounder when there weren't a lot of those around. Mel pumped weights when other guys weren't yet into that. A pit bull. Not the best-looking guy around, but as tough as they come.

3. Donald Brashear, 2001–2006. He was the most legitimate heavyweight the Flyers had in many years. He was a fearless player who would go into every dangerous corner.

When the rules changed to de-emphasize fighting, he was able to hone his skills. He didn't embarrass you as a player.

2. Dave Schultz, 1971–1976. My teammate, the Hammer. He was instrumental in changing the way the rest of the league looked at us, the Broad Street Bullies. Dave fought all the heavyweights back then, like Noel Picard and Joël Bouchard. A great fighter; he threw like a jackhammer.

1. Behn Wilson, 1978–1983. Not only was he the toughest fighter ever, he was also unpredictable. He would spear you just as easily as look at you. He was even nasty with his own teammates. One day he went after Ken Linseman during a practice. They really went at it before the other guys—led by Paul Holmgren—stepped in.

Honorable mention: Glen Cochrane, 1978–1984; Todd Fedoruk, 2000–2007; Dave Hoyda, 1977–1979; Jack McIlhargey, 1974–1977, 1979–1981; Al Secord, 1988–1989.

Anthony SanFilippo is West Philadelphia born and raised and has covered the Flyers and NHL since 2000 for ComcastSportsNet.com (now NBCSNPhilly.com), the Delaware County Daily Times, the Associated Press, and currently CrossingBroad.com. He hosts a Flyers-centric podcast called Snow the Goalie *and learned everything he knows about broadcasting from his days producing Glen and Big Daddy's WIP shows in the 1990s.*

Believe it or not, there was a time for the Flyers when searching for good goaltending was not the equivalent of handing a toddler a *Where's Waldo* book.

Bernie Parent is, of course, a legend. He backstopped the franchise's only two Stanley Cup championships. And while no other goalie was even able to do half that, for a short period after Parent, the Flyers did have reliable goaltending.

Pete Peeters, Pelle Lindbergh, and Ron Hextall all took the team to the Stanley Cup Final. Lindbergh and Hextall each won the Vezina Trophy as the NHL's best goalie, and Peeters was the primary goalie during the Flyers' 35-game unbeaten streak, the longest such streak in North American professional sports.

But since Hextall was traded as part of the mega-package for Eric Lindros, the search for stability in net is now three decades long.

Maybe young phenom Carter Hart will finally break that drought for a championship-caliber goalie. But there has been a diverse collection of vagabonds, hopefuls, heartbreakers, and outright dreck standing in the crease in the Orange and Black since that trade.

There have been 59 goalies to play at least one game for the Flyers. In honor of that continued search for the Holy Grail, here are the 10 worst:

10. Ilya Bryzgalov. Talent-wise, he wasn't this bad. Off the ice, he was a dumpster fire. He splintered the locker room. He ticked off his coaches and general manager. When they had seen enough, the Flyers bought out his absurd contract—and are still paying him not to play. He was a delight to the writers, because you never knew what he would say next, but his antics set the franchise back for the better part of a decade.

9. Antero Niittymäki. Niitty was a great guy off the ice and a space cadet on it. He played in an era when defense was king and still had a GAA of 3.01. His crowning moment came when he let in a goal from the opposing blue line because he was watching the video scoreboard hanging over center ice and not the play in front of him. Asked after the game what he saw happen on the goal, head coach Ken Hitchcock responded, "A lot more than Niitty."

8. Ken Wregget. He has the highest GAA of any Flyers goalie who played in at least 100 games (3.55). He also is one of only three goalies to have a losing record for his Flyers career with at least 40 starts. He was the primary goalie on the 1989–1990 Flyers team that snapped a streak of 17 consecutive years making the playoffs. The only good thing about Wregget is he was part of the trade that brought Mark Recchi to Philadelphia.

7. Dominic Roussel. In five years with the Flyers, he had a save percentage of .895 and a GAA of 3.18. He and the guy listed next battled it out to replace Wregget as the starting goalie. Both tried, both failed.

6. Tommy Söderström. He was acrobatic in net, but he had to be because he was only 5-foot-9. There was so much net to shoot at. He posted five shutouts as a rookie but came back in his second season with a GAA of 4.01. That's all GM Bob Clarke needed to see. He traded Söderström to get a second tour of duty from Hextall.

5. Mark Laforest. He has one of the all-time great nicknames (Trees). Unfortunately, he didn't have the game to match. Laforest lasted only 38 games with the Flyers. He won 10 of them. His Flyers GAA was a lusty 3.91 as Hextall's backup from 1987 to 1989. He did, however, earn one big win—stopping all 16 shots he faced in the Alumni game before the Winter Classic at Citizens Bank Park in 2011, relieving Bernie Parent. So, there's that.

4. Petr Mrázek. How bad was Mrázek after he was acquired at the 2017–2018 trade deadline? So bad that when the Flyers made the playoffs, they opted to use two injured goalies ahead of him. He played only 17 games but had a 3.22 GAA and only six wins. One would think that as a former goalie, then-GM Ron Hextall would have recognized Mrázek's shortcomings before trading for him. What a waste of a third-round pick.

3. Bobby Taylor. This is almost sacrilegious because Taylor was such a beloved teammate and color analyst for the Flyers for a long time. But Chief was a terrible goalie. He backed up Parent, and if Bernie had ever got ten hurt during those years, the Flyers would still be without a Cup. Taylor has the worst GAA of any Flyers goalie with more than five appearances (4.05) except for one guy—who is number one on this list. Thank goodness for Bernie, eh?

2. Michael Leighton. Anyone else still have nightmares about that Patrick Kane goal in Game 6 of the 2010 Stanley Cup Final? If the Flyers had anyone else but Leighton in goal, they might have won that Cup. Anyone. He returned the following year in the playoffs after not playing all season, had a terrible game in Buffalo, then went AWOL for 24 hours. He was a train wreck. The Flyers soon parted ways with him. It was a little too late, however.

1. Stéphane Beauregard. Who's that, you say? Beauregard (which makes me think of the janitor on *The Muppet Show*) was part of the Roussel-Soderstrom error . . . uh . . . *era* of goaltending for the Flyers. He played 16 games in 1992–1993. He won three. He had a 4.41 GAA. His save percentage was a pitiful .854. He allowed four goals or more in half the games he played, including nine in one game against the New York Islanders. He's very forgettable, you say? Yeah, I wish I could forget his play. But I can't.

A Philadelphia Frankenstein

What if you had the ability to create the perfect sports figure from the best attributes of everyone who's worked in this town? Here's what we came up with:

Left arm—Steve Carlton. Four Cy Young Awards and 329 Major League wins. Hey, when your nickname is "Lefty," you're an easy choice for this one.

Left fist—Joe Frazier. Just ask Ali.

Right arm—Sonny Jurgensen. The Eagles have had dozens of quarterbacks since Christian Adolph Jurgensen III. None could fling the ball as far as him.

Right fist—Dave Schultz. In an era when hockey players really fought, no one wanted to battle the Hammer.

Knuckles—Chuck Bednarik. He claimed to have broken his fingers dozens of times. We don't doubt it. His hands looked like a jumble of tangled tree roots.

Fingers—Dikembe Mutombo. We all imitated the finger waggle. The guy's digits resembled yardsticks.

Hands—Jimmy Rollins. Averaged just eight errors a season and earned four Gold Gloves during the Phils' great run.

Wrists—Chase Utley. In his prime he could flick those wrists and drive the ball out of the park. Especially at Shea Stadium.

Forearms—Greg Luzinski. Looked like Popeye.

Elbows—Gary Dornhoefer. He would back into the crease and swing his arms around, usually catching the opposition goalie in the neck. Dorny amassed 1,494 career penalty minutes, all of them, we assume, for elbowing.

Biceps—George McGinnis. Looked a lot stronger than he played, to be honest.

Shoulders—Wilt Chamberlain. He stood under the net and pushed away Bill Russell with those broad shoulders.

Hair—Oscar Gamble. Best Afro ever. Google it.

Sideburns—Richie Allen. Completely badass.

Forehead—Placido Polanco. It was a widescreen TV.

Eyes—Brian Westbrook. The little guy could find a hole the size of the eye of a needle among all those 300-pound linemen.

Ears—Donovan McNabb. He could always hear criticism, even when it was whispered.

Nose—Rod Brind'Amour. Won a poll among readers of the *Hockey News* in 2008 for largest beak in the NHL. Once, when his nose was broken (for the fourth time) by Ed Jovanovski, his response was, "I was kind of hoping that would straighten it out."

Jaw—Mike Keenan. He would stand behind the bench, jutting it out, looking like a guy imitating Mussolini.

Mouth—Curt Schilling. Sometimes incisive, too often inane. It still hasn't stopped running.

Beard—Jayson Werth. Unfortunately, there's not enough competition in this department. Werth really let it go that one year he tried out for ZZ Top. If Bryce Harper grows his out, he could steal this spot.

Mustache—Andy Reid. That big red twitching paintbrush.

Brains—Billy Cunningham. We never met a smarter coach. Although, if you asked Chip Kelly, he'd tell you that he deserves this spot.

Back—Herschel Walker. If you needed to know the difference between a latissimus dorsi and an erector spinae, you just had to look at Herschel from behind. He exercised 18 hours a day to resemble an illustration from *Gray's Anatomy.*

Abs—Terrell Owens. All those crunches in the driveway weren't for nothing.

Chest—Reggie White. An absolute barrel.

Belly—Ken Hitchcock. A smart coach whom players cited as an example that not all fat men are jolly.

Rear end—Jaromír Jágr. All that skating power derived from those glutes. We wish he'd stayed here longer.

Thighs—Roy Halladay. It was his great push off the mound that made him perfect.

Calves—Charles Barkley. For a guy that size to lead the league in rebounds, something had to give him that leaping ability.

Left foot—David Akers. Who else?

Right foot—Jake Elliott. Or maybe Carli Lloyd.

Toes—LeSean McCoy. His Twitter handle, appropriately, is @CutOnDime25. He changed direction better than anyone since Barry Sanders. We were sorry to see it end ugly.

Forelocks—Smarty Jones. We're not really sure what a forelock is, to be honest.

Heart—Brian Dawkins. Give him the nod for soul, as well.

Balls—Allen Iverson. Would drive into the land of 7-footers to put up a feathery layup, take a huge hit, and then do it again.

Pituitary gland—Shawn Bradley. If he only had a heart.

Spleen—Larry Bowa. Tamer now, but, man, he could spit venom.

Asshole—Norman Braman. Enough said.

Ten Local Athletes Who Don't Need a Mask on Halloween

Mind you, the two of us realize we don't look like Idris Elba or Ryan Gosling. But, as we used to say in the neighborhood, here are some folks who "fell out of the ugly tree and hit every branch on the way down."

10. Lane Johnson. If you were getting ready to get in a bar fight and you saw bouncer Lane Johnson headed your way, that fight would break up in a South Philly second.

9. Lenny Dykstra. Pigpen from *Peanuts*. The scratching, the spitting. Lenny could have had the starring role in *Caveman*. Even centerfield at the Vet was disgusting by the time Lenny was through with it, thanks to all the tobacco stains.

8. Rick Tocchet. Nose broken a dozen times. Eight thousand stitches to his face. Just a day at the office for hockey players. Could easily go out for Halloween as Frankenstein—as is.

7. Jakub Voráček. If they ever brought back the TV series *The Life and Times of Grizzly Adams*, Jakub wouldn't even have to audition.

6. Tex Cobb. Several claims to fame. As a boxer, Tex's fight against Larry Holmes was so ugly and one-sided that it prompted Howard Cosell to retire as a boxing commentator. As an actor, Tex appeared in more than 30 movies, including some good ones like *Raising Arizona* and *Uncommon Valor*. Somehow he never got cast in a romantic lead. We wonder why. Had a face that resembled a sack of nails. Extremely funny and likeable guy.

5. Odubel Herrera. Blond dreadlocks. Blond goatee. Really?

4. Tyrone Hill. Skeletor from *He-Man and the Masters of the Universe*. If you ever want to know how truly bad former NBA star Charles Oakley is, he once punched out this former Sixer—the scariest-looking cat ever to wear shorts. Over a poker bet no less. Tyrone also once got a photo op with Faith Hill when she performed in Philly because of the last-name connection. Wonder if someone has a copy of that adorable portrait.

3. Chuck Bednarik. Even these days, in his seventies, Concrete Charlie could cuss out every man in a packed barroom and *no one* would accept the challenge. His *hands* are scary looking.

2. Manute Bol. We never believed the story that this 7-foot-6 former Sixer once killed an African lion with a spear. No way would the lion have gotten that close. RIP, Manute; we loved you.

1. Gritty. Yes, he's hilarious. But if you were walking down a street late at night and Gritty was walking toward you, you'd drop dead of a heart attack.

Big Daddy's Favorite Chrome Domers

In honor of my follicly challenged writing partner (must get cold up there, eh, Glen?), I thought I'd salute our skullcap-wearing friends. First up, there must be something about coaching that makes these poor souls pull their hair out. These are in no particular order, except for number one. (And don't peek ahead!)

The Coaches

10. Terry Francona, Phillies. See what managing in this town can do? By the time he got to the Red Sox and Cleveland, he had no more hair left to lose.

9. Harry Perretta, Villanova. Fans think it was coaching women that drove the long-time Villanova coach nuts. But Harry's hair started falling out years before that, from all the times I schooled him on the basketball courts of the Observatory on West Chester Pike.

> **Glen says:** Hey, BDG, I heard it was the other way around!

8. Craig Ramsay, Flyers. Just looking at Craig used to put the Flyers to sleep on the bench.

7. Ian Laperrière, Flyers. Lappy's been an assistant under *three* different head coaches. I guess his head's so blinding, no one can make out exactly who he is.

6. Rollie Massimino, Villanova. When he would flip out on the sidelines, his well-placed comb-over would swing from one side to the other. RIP, Rollie; you coached the most perfect game hoops fan ever saw when you upset Georgetown for the NCAA title in 1985.

5. Jack Ramsay, St. Joe's, Sixers. Come on, be honest. Give him some gold hoop earrings and tell me Jack couldn't have made a living playing Mr. Clean at conventions. RIP, Doctor.

4. Gabe Kapler, Phillies. If Gabe truly uses coconut oil as much as he says he does, then that explains the hair loss. If he doesn't watch himself, blindness will be next. Some fans think he already is.

3. John Lucas, Sixers. Tell me John didn't look like he popped out of Aladdin's lamp.

2. Phil Martelli. Is there one bald joke left in the world that Phil hasn't used? At least all he has to do before he goes out is straighten his tie. Whoops . . . I think Phil just used that line at a banquet.

1. Rich Kotite, Eagles. The first time I saw Richie the K at a press conference, I thought he was there to fix a pipe leaking from the Vet ceiling. Then he stepped up to the podium and started talking.

The Players

10. Raúl Ibañez, Phillies. In his three seasons with the Fightins, he averaged over 23 HRs and 85 RBIs, and each one seemed clutch. We miss the "Rauuuuuuuuul" cheer.

9. Clay Dalrymple, Phillies. I'll never forget the first time I saw Clay take off his cap to wipe his brow at Connie Mack Stadium. What a shock! Bald. Not strong, virile, Michael Jordan bald, but bald like your Uncle Harry. This couldn't be. Not a Phillie. Not a Major League baseball player. Say it ain't so, Clay.

8. Ed Van Impe, Flyers. Back in the Flyers' Stanley Cup days when NHL players wore no helmets, there was no hiding it if you had a full head of skin.

7. World B. Free, Sixers. Not even a name change from Lloyd to his current moniker could stop the erosion on top of his head.

6. Terrell Owens, Eagles. Just wanted to see how many different lists T.O. can make in one book. "Are you truly bald or is that just a fashion statement?" "NEXT QUESTION!"

5. Lane Johnson, Eagles. We never miss an opportunity to throw an offensive lineman some love. No one else does. And this big Texan just might be headed to the Hall of Fame.

4. Charles Barkley, Sixers. I remember when the Round Mound of Rebound had hair, but like everything else about Chuck, he just wanted to "be like Mike" in every way.

3. Bernie Parent, Flyers. Television hair ads. Radio. Billboards. Newspaper ads. You have to hand it to Bernie. Not embarrassed in any way by his baldness. Nor should he be.

2. Eddie George, Abington High. If you're going to be bald, this is the way to go. The most intimidating, baddest-looking mother on the planet. A dead ringer for actor Woody Strode, for those of you old enough to remember.

1. Matt Geiger, Sixers. He comes in at number one, not because he was ever any great shakes as a player, but just think, we would have been denied years of watching the greatness of Allen Iverson had this handsome fellow not invoked his own no-trade clause to stop a swap involving him and AI.

Glen's List of Guys with Great Hair and Guys with Bad Hair

Great Hair

10. Cole Hamels. Male-model handsome with flowing locks. Chris Gimenez, a Rangers catcher when Hamels pitched out there, said he'd sometimes walk to the mound just to discuss it. "I'll talk about how the wind's kind of fluttering his hair. I would be like, 'Dude, your hair looks solid right now.'"

9. Rick Tocchet. The Flyers winger boasted a blow-dried pompadour in the 1980s that drove the young girls wild. Alas, that's long gone. Lots of men go bald, but in his case, it was a shame.

8. Jalen Mills. We actually debated whether the "Green Goblin" belongs on the "great hair" or "bad hair" list. By his own admission, the Eagles cornerback said he resembles a lime Skittle. But the patch of green is fun and funny, and it's a tribute to the franchise he plays for. We just always have this urge to grab a nine-iron, place a golf ball up there, and swing away.

7. Rick MacLeish. In the days before all NHL players became faceless, helmeted entities, there was no more exciting sight than to see the Flyers winger speeding up ice, his long mane flying behind him.

6. Jay Wright. If the title-winning Nova coach wasn't such a nice guy, we'd resent him for his George Clooney looks, impeccable tailoring, and charming style. The hair is salon perfect with just a few flecks of gray. Unlike some of his colleagues, Jay can dress down a ref without his shirttail flopping or his hair flying around.

5. T. J. McConnell. For a guy who runs around so much, the Sixers point guard never has a single strand out of place. Looks like a 1965 ad for Vitalis. Former teammate Dario Šarić said McConnell uses a half jar of hair gel a day. "You need to touch T. J.'s hair," Šarić said. "It's unbelievable. It's like plastic."

4. Darren Daulton. He accomplished the perpetually tanned surfer-dude-with-muscles look. Dutch loved whipping off his catcher's mask and helmet on foul pops, the better to show off his sweet lid. Daulton sold more tickets to females than any player in Phillies history.

3. Allen Iverson. For a while, Al had someone traveling with him on road trips to do his hair a different style for every game. The results ranged from tragic (that flat tire-tread pattern) to magnificent (the Crossover, a series of crisscrossed cornrows resembling a basketball net). Probably did more to influence hairstyles among America's youth than anyone since the Beatles.

2. (Tie) Oscar Gamble, Garry Maddox, Bake McBride. And every other Phillie who sported an Afro back in the 1970s. My own personal favorite was Gamble, whose baseball cap rested about 20 inches above his eyebrows. I still keep around a 1975 baseball card of Gamble, in which his mass of hair, squeezed under a batting helmet, spills out like earmuffs on steroids.

Of course, the patron saint of Afros is . . .

1. Julius Erving. In the ABA days, they actually once presented the "Biggest Afro Award," which Doc lost by a hair (sorry) to Darnell Hillman. The 'do was part of the fashion, the grace, the magnificence of Doc. The greatest hairstyle of all time, and no one wore it better than Julius.

Honorable mention: Chuck Daly, Ben Hawkins, Kyle Korver, Jeremy Roenick, Tim Rossivich, Isaac Seumalo.

Bad Hair

10. Donovan McNabb. Well, sometimes. Forgive us for suggesting that McNabb was an Iverson wannabe—at least follicly—but, between the cornrows, the faux Afro, and the squashed-down do-rag look . . . well, we just wish he could have come up with his own act. A square guy trying to look cool never fools anyone.

9. Vance Worley. "The Vanimal" came to the Majors sporting a Mohawk, which eventually evolved into that shaved-on-the-sides, styled-to-a-point-on-top look that made his head resemble a lit matchstick.

8. Riley Cooper. He sported the redneck greased-back ponytail look which, let's face it, certainly fit the man.

7. Armen Gilliam. Known to all as "Gumby"—a nickname bestowed by Charles Barkley—during his disastrous three-year stint with the Sixers. Gilliam was 6-foot-9 on one side of his head, 6-foot-6 on the other.

6. Odubel Herrera. He showed up in 2018 sporting shaggy mini-dreadlocks with bleached tips and a yellow beard, all of which made him look like he was in a Cowardly Lion costume.

5. Macho Row. Call it what you like—the Tennessee top hat, the Kentucky waterfall, the Canadian passport—we'll stick with the traditional name and tell you that the 1993 Phils clubhouse boasted more mullets than all the Great Lakes combined. The most impressive, of course, belonged to Mitch Williams. We loved when he doffed his hat to reveal it after each save.

4. Scott Hartnell. The winger had a fright-night head of hair that resembled *The Simpsons* character Sideshow Bob. To his credit, he had a sense of humor about it. In a 2012 commercial for a local auto dealership, the director is heard off camera asking, "Can we get another wig on him?" Speaking of which, the Flyers once held a game where they gave out free Hartnell wigs to the first 5,000 fans.

3. Pete Rose. Sported the ultimate bowl cut during his Phillies seasons, a tribute to his intellectual hero, Moe. Later shifted to a poorly dyed red crewcut, which resembled a sack of rusty nails.

2. Andrew Bynum. The 7-foot slug turned heads, though never with his play in this town. The oddest of many odd styles was the half-cornrows, half-electric shock look.

1. Freddy Mitchell. Remember the "Frohawk"? This bust of a first-round pick couldn't draw enough attention to himself as a talented player, so he tried stunts like wearing furs, moping, and transforming his head into something out of *Spaceballs*. He unveiled this monstrosity for the 2004 NFC Championship, boasting afterward, "Now everybody is trying to get the Frohawk." We're still waiting for the second person, Chief.

Honorable mention: *Michal Handzuš, Nerlens Noel, Don Saleski, Dario Šarić, Keith Van Horn, Jake Voráček's caveman look, Gritty.*

Phil Martelli grew up a hoops junkie in Southwest Philadelphia. He was the head men's basketball coach at St. Joseph's from 1995 to 2019. In 2003–2004, he led the Hawks to the NCAA Elite Eight. In 2019, he was hired as an assistant coach at the University of Michigan.

We asked Phil to give us a list of the greatest games or players in Big 5 history.

Coach Martelli says: The Big 5 continues to be a treasured institution in Philadelphia and a crown jewel envied by all involved in college basketball throughout the nation. Others express their admiration by constantly remarking, "How can five schools so geographically close, competing so fiercely, still be so connected?"

The simple answer: we are Philly!

The deeper answer: all of us involved now are just the latest. We are not the greatest, and we honor our history to illustrate this togetherness and comradery.

For this project I requested that each school provide their one game that cannot be forgotten and their greatest team. Thanks to each school's basketball historian (or debate starter) who supplied the answers. I appreciate Jack Scheuer and Don DiJulia for providing their insight for the 20 greatest college players to represent a Philadelphia Big 5 school.

La Salle University

Greatest game in school history: La Salle 74, Villanova 67. February 8, 1969, at the Palestra. Two top-10 teams in one of the most anticipated Big 5 games in history.

Best-ever team: A tie between the 1953–1954 national champions and the 1968–1969 team (23–1, number two in final AP poll). If you need to pick just one, flip a coin.

University of Pennsylvania

Greatest game in school history: Penn 72, North Carolina 71. March 11, 1979. UNC was the top seed in the East Regional, but the Quakers—seeded ninth out of 10 teams in the region—knocked off the Tar Heels at Reynolds Coliseum in Raleigh, North Carolina. It marked the first time UNC lost an NCAA Tournament game in its home state, and it would be 39 years before it would happen again.

Best-ever team: The 1970–1971 team went undefeated through the regular season and won two NCAA Tournament games before falling to Villanova in the East Regional final. They spent the entire season ranked in the AP Top 10, ending with a number three national ranking. Five players were NBA draft picks: Dave Wohl, Corky Calhoun, Bobby Morse, Alan Cotler, and Phil Hankinson.

Temple University

Greatest game in school history: Top-ranked Temple 98, number 10 Villanova 86. February 10, 1988, at McGonigle Hall.

Best-ever team: The 1987–1988 Temple team finished 32–2 and was ranked number one for the final six weeks of the regular season.

Villanova University

Greatest game in school history: NCAA championship game. Nova 66, Georgetown 64. April 1, 1985, in Lexington, Kentucky.

Best-ever team: The 2017–2018 national champions—36–4, most wins in program history, and won six NCAA Tournament games by an average of 17 points.

St. Joseph's University

Greatest game in school history: SJU 49, number one DePaul, 49. March 14, 1981. Second round of the NCAA Tournament. SJU's John Smith scores at the buzzer on a pass from Lonnie McFarlan.

Greatest team: The 2003–2004 team was a number one seed in the NCAA Tournament and went undefeated during the regular season. Finished 30–2 after losing to Oklahoma State in the Elite Eight. Led by National Player of the Year Jameer Nelson and All-American Delonte West.

Coach Martelli's All-Time Top 20 College Players in Philadelphia History

20. Rick Brunson, Temple

19. Bob McNeill, St. Joe's

18. Jerome Allen, Penn

17. Ernie Beck, Penn

16. Bill Mlkvy, Temple

15. Hal Lear, Temple

14. Mark Macon, Temple

13. Mike Bantom, St. Joe's

12. Larry Cannon, La Salle

11. Kerry Kittles, Nova

10. Corky Calhoun, Penn

9. Cliff Anderson, St. Joe's

8. Michael Brooks, La Salle

7. Howard Porter, Nova

6. Ken Durrett, La Salle

5. Paul Arizin, Nova

4. Tom Gola, La Salle

3. Jameer Nelson, St. Joe's

2. Guy Rodgers, Temple

1. Lionel Simmons, La Salle

My Most Memorable Eagles Calls :: Merrill Reese

The dean of NFL broadcasters, Merrill Reese, has been the Eagles radio play-by-play announcer for more than four decades.

10. December 2, 1990, at Buffalo. Randall Cunningham's amazing scramble-and-pass.

The call: *"Cunningham is back. He's being trapped. He ducks under three men. He's looking . . . he's rolling . . . he's heaving it deep down field for Barnett—who leaps and has it! At the 40, at the 35, 30. Barnett's gonna scooooore! Touchdown! Unbelievable! A 95-yard touchdown to Fred Barnett!"*

Merrill remembers: "It ended up as the second-longest touchdown in franchise history. Unfortunately, the Eagles lost the game. Afterward, Randall was asked if he ever amazed himself, and he answered, 'Yeah, sometimes I even amaze myself.' Of course, that got him in trouble, but all he did was answer honestly."

9. October 19, 2003, at the New York Giants. Brian Westbrook's punt return saves the season.

The call: *"Westbrook—dangerous every time he has his hands on the football. The snap to Feagles. He gets it away. It's a wobbler, bounces across the 20. Westbrook takes it. Looks for running room, up to the 25, the 30, to the 35, 40, 45, midfield, 45, 30, 25, 20—Brian Westbrook! He's going, he's going! Touchdown, Brian Westbrook! Eighty-four yards, no penalty flags! I don't believe it! Brian Westbrook has just exploded, and with 1:16 remaining, this place is in a state of shock!"*

Merrill remembers: "Brian Westbrook's terrific return beat the Giants at the Meadowlands. This came late in the game when the Eagles needed a big play. It came on the heels of a tough loss in Dallas and launched the Eagles to a nine-game winning streak."

8. October 3, 1993, at New York Jets. Eric Allen's incredible interception return.

The call: *"Thornton, the tight end, goes into motion. Esiason, play action, he's back, he's firing—and it's intercepted by Allen! Spinning at the 10, out to the 15, the 20, cutting to his left at the 25, 30, Allen to the 40, Allen to the 45, 50, 45, 40, Eric Allen down the far sidelines, steps over a man, he's going to gooooo! Eric Allen with a miraculous return of an interception, and the Eagles take the lead! Eric Allen with an absolutely miraculous return, getting help from a block by Ben Smith. Ninety-four yards, and the Eagles lead!"*

Merrill remembers: "This was as great and exciting a play as I've ever seen. It was a tough game, in which the Eagles lost Randall Cunningham and Fred Barnett to season-ending injuries. They were down, 30–28, with time running out when Allen made this remarkable play. It ended with him seeing Cunningham next to the end zone on crutches and then handing him the ball."

7. September 24, 2017, vs. the Giants. Jake Elliott's 61-yard field goal wins the game at the final whistle.

The call: *"Here we go. Hold your breath. The ball is spotted. The kick is away and the kick is . . . it's goooooooddd! And the Eagles win! They win! Sixty-one yards! The longest kick in Eagles history! We forgive him for missing the 30-yarder last week. Oh my goodness, 61 yards! What a game, do you love it? What a game! As the Eagles defeat the New York Giants, 27–24!"*

Merrill remembers: "The Eagles led this game early, but the Giants took over and tied it. I remember Alshon Jeffery got out of bounds with one second left to set up the field goal. I was thinking there wasn't much pressure on Elliott because no one figured he could make it. If it was a 40-yarder, there would have been expectation, but who expected him to make one from 61 yards? And outdoors? Well, he took a shot, and he sure made it."

6. December 10, 1995, vs. the Cowboys. Groundhog Day, or Fourth and One—twice.

The call:
Merrill: *"The Eagles stopped them once; can they do it again? It will be fourth and one, and Switzer's going for it again."*
Stan Walters: *"I think Switzer should be punting here."*
Merrill: *"I wish he were punting here."*
Stan: *"He's got a lot of confidence in his offensive line."*
Merrill: *"Can they do it again? They could pass, too, to Novacek, who's in motion. Here they go. Fourth down. They go to Smith and the Eagles stop him again! They stop him again! And this time they can't take it away! The same play—it's Groundhog Day!"*

Merrill remembers: "In a 17–17 tie, the Cowboys had fourth-and-inches at their own 29. Their coach, Barry Switzer, decided to go for it, and Emmitt Smith was stopped for a loss by the Eagles' defense. But the official's whistle had blown to signal the two-minute warning, so the play didn't count. Dallas got another chance. Switzer decided to go for it again and called the same exact play. I had just seen the Bill Murray movie, *Groundhog Day*, where he wakes up in the same day again and again, and that's what came out of my mouth."

5. November 10, 1985, vs. Atlanta. In overtime, Ron Jaworski and Mike Quick hook up for the longest pass in Eagles history.

The call: *"Second down and 10 for the Eagles. Jaworski retreats, he's looking . . . he fires the football over the middle. Complete to Quick. He's going to go—25, 30, 35, 40, midfield, 45, 40, 35, 30, 25, 20—Mike Quick, touchdown! The Eagles win! The Eagles win! Forget the extra point! Jaworski to Quick, 99 yards and the game is over!"*

Merrill remembers: "I was worried that the Falcons might win the game on a safety. The Eagles had been in five overtime games before this and lost four of them. So I wasn't that confident before the pass."

4. January 11, 1981, NFC Championship Game vs. Dallas. Wilbert Montgomery scampers 42 yards for the opening touchdown.

The call: *"Second down and 10 for the Eagles. The Cowboys have six defensive backs in the game. Jaworski hands off to Montgomery. Up the right side—25, 20, 15, 10, touchdown! Montgomery exploded up the right side and the Eagles have scored first. Wilbert rambled 42 yards. The block—Sisemore and Peoples. And the Eagles have struck!"*

Merrill remembers: "I knew, and I think everyone in the Delaware Valley knew right at that moment that the Eagles were going to the Super Bowl."

3. December 19, 2010, at the New York Giants. DeSean Jackson's punt return caps a miracle comeback.

The call:
Merrill: *"Fourteen seconds to go, 31–31. Matt Dodge to punt; gets a high snap. Gets it away. It's a knuckler. Jackson takes it at the 35, drops it, picks it up. Looks for running room. He's at the 40. He's at the 45, midfield, the 40! He's gonna go! DeSean Jackson! I don't care if he jumps . . . dives . . . he's running around, and he's in the end zone, and there's no time! And the Eagles win! The Eagles win!"*
Mike Quick: *"This is Miracle in the Meadowlands, Number 2!"*
Merrill: *"He ran around until all the zeroes were on the clock. The Giants fans can't believe it, and the Eagles have just pulled off the most remarkable win I have ever seen."*

Merrill remembers: "That game was so one-sided at halftime, I told listeners that I thought the Eagles had missed the team bus and were still back at their hotel. But Michael Vick directed them to a terrific comeback. Right before this final play, Mike Quick said to me, 'There's no way they'll punt it to DeSean.' But they did. When he started downfield, it was like the Red Sea parted. He got to the one and started dancing. I thought, 'Just get into the end zone first.'"

2. November 19, 1978, at the New York Giants. Herm Edwards performs the original Miracle at the Meadowlands.

The call: *"Under 30 seconds left in the game. And Pisarcik fumbles the football! It's picked up by Herman Edwards. He's at the 15, 10, 5, touchdown Eagles! I don't believe it! I do not believe it! I do not believe what has just occurred here, ladies and gentlemen. As Pisarcik came forward, he fumbled the football, Charlie Johnson hit him, and Herman Edwards picked it up and ran it in for a touchdown!"*

Merrill remembers: "I didn't realize until the next day what I had seen. And I never thought it would be one of those plays that every fan would see—on ESPN, HBO, highlight shows— thousands of times. It's one of the strangest plays in NFL history."

1. February 3, 2018. Final play of Super Bowl LII. Tom Brady lofts a Hail Mary.

The call: *"What a game. We will never forget this—hopefully with joy in our hearts. Eagles by eight. Brady lines them up. He's back again. He steps up. He's hit . . . he stumbles . . . he is throwing it deep for the end zone. And it is . . . batted around and . . . incomplete! And the game is over! The game is over! The Philadelphia Eagles are Super Bowl champions! Eagles fans everywhere, this is for you! Let the celebration begin!"*

Merrill remembers: "I was nervous, only because we were seated in the opposite end zone 110 yards away. I didn't want to blow the definitive call of the Super Bowl. I was using binoculars, doing everything I could to see. I was thinking more about doing my job than the situation and what was at stake. When Brady let it go I wasn't that worried about him converting. He didn't have the arm strength of Aaron Rodgers. The height wasn't there on that throw. It proved to be a very close play, but we were all delighted at how it turned out, weren't we?"

Ah, the pressure of being Joe Conklin. When a new player, coach, owner, or anyone at all famous captures Philly's imaginations, Joe not only has to get the voice and vocal quirks down, he has to be hilarious doing it. No wonder he's certifiably insane.

We asked him to name the favorite new voices he's had to perfect since the last time this book came out in 2006. Here's his list—sports, politics, and, uh, law enforcement:

10. Bernie Sanders. Crazy Bernie! Nobody wants to hear about socialism, but who would have thought Trump would be scarier than Bernie?

9. Gabe Kapler. Standard deep, confident pipes, along with a laser focus on his shifts. Look how ripped I am, dude.

8. Detective Brown. A defecation caper in the stairwell of a Lower Merion library produced this fake character. I put a standard Northeast Philly accent onto a Main Line civil servant. We call him back when I need him in a pinch.

7. Tom McCarthy. Hahahahahahahahahahaha.

6. Brett Brown. A combination of the Gorton's fisherman and Sol Rosenberg from *The Jerky Boys*. And he loves to pontificate, which is always helpful.

5. Barack Obama. For a guy who was an electric orator, he was a pretty boring president. I still bring him back for March Madness picks.

4. Gary "Sarge" Matthews. I miss Sarge almost as much as I miss Harry Kalas. He might be the most inadvertently entertaining Philly broadcaster we've ever had. Sarge tickles every time.

3. Ilya Bryzgalov. Ilya's voice started with me copping Borat, and it only shifted slightly. Years after retirement, he's still getting paid and he's still in my act. High five!

2. Joel Embiid. Jo-Jo has a unique voice that starts like a breathy version of my bicycle horn impression. He's a media darling, social media sensation, and great copy. I wish he wouldn't shoot so many three-pointers.

1. Donald Trump. He's the gift that keeps on giving. The challenge is making the parody more outrageous than the original. It's tough to out-trump Trump.

Ten Funniest People from Philadelphia

We've disqualified hilarious people like Dom Irrera, Joe Conklin, Jay Black, Craig Shoemaker, and Cozy Morley (RIP) because they happen to be friends of Big Daddy.

10. Rob McElhenney. We know what you're thinking. Rob's not even the funniest dude of the *It's Always Sunny in Philadelphia* cast. How could you be with Charlie Day and Danny DeVito hanging around? But he created the show for crying out loud, and we're talking 153 episodes here for this St. Joe's Prep grad.

9. Larry Fine. Okay, what exactly did he do? He was a member of the Three Stooges, and that's enough for us. Questioning his contribution is sort of like asking if Ringo Starr was really a great drummer. Who knows how the Stooges or the Beatles would have turned out with a different roster? Did you know that the left side of Larry's face was so calloused from Moe slapping him that it was permanently numb? He never felt a thing. Out of respect, go check out his mural at 3rd and South.

8. Bruce Graham. Talk about prolific—this Ridley High alum has written 14 movies and 15 plays that have been produced around the world. We guarantee that as you are reading this, one of his shows is being acted out somewhere. Really, he should be way better known by the Philly public, who primarily know him from the hilarious *The Philly Fan*. He also was a tremendous influence on Ray Didinger's *Tommy and Me*. Even when Graham (no relation to Big Daddy) writes something you would consider deadly serious, such as *The Outgoing Tide,* which is about Alzheimer's, there's still many gut-busting laughs. *Tide,* by the way, starred the late John Mahoney from *Frasier.* Do yourself a favor. Go out and see one of his shows; you won't regret it.

7. The Phillie Phanatic. We know what you're thinking—isn't Big Daddy friends with him? Well, he's a very difficult guy to get to know. He doesn't talk much. Seriously, anyone who thinks his act has grown stale . . . well, let's just say that *you've* grown old. Watch the kids when he's doing his thing. They're laughing as hard as kids ever laughed since he burst on the scene back in the '70s. There was a Sixers game back on a Sunday afternoon in '83 when they were making their championship run. During a key timeout in the fourth quarter, the Phanatic came over from the Vet, charged down the Spectrum aisle onto midcourt, and drove the crowd wild. It's one of our favorite memories from that sensational year. Beyond all that, *you* try working in that heat.

6. Jack Klugman. Yes, Walter Matthau's portrayal of Oscar Madison is tough to beat. Jack, however, expertly portrayed Oscar for five years and never missed one joke. A fine dramatic actor also. If you don't believe us, check out *12 Angry Men.*

5. Sherman Hemsley. Big Daddy's daughter Keely was born the same year *The Jeffersons* ended its 10-year run, but ask her who her all-time favorite TV character is. Without missing a beat, she'll tell you, "George Jefferson." Who doesn't know someone like George?

Sherman kept refining him year after year. Did you know that Sherman played the same George Jefferson character in five different TV shows? Can you name them?

4. Will Smith. Admit it—you almost forgot how funny he is, didn't you? He's so talented in so many areas that you don't immediately recall all of his funny stuff. Six seasons of *The Fresh Prince of Bel-Air*, great comedy in the *Men in Black* series, countless videos, *Independence Day*, and on and on and on. When his career is done, he might be the biggest star ever to come out of this town. There's not a field he hasn't conquered. And he's still Philly "street" funny.

3. Peter Boyle. *Young Frankenstein, The Dream Team, Joe, Steelyard Blues*. Boyle had a stroke in 1990 and couldn't even talk for six months—then went on to star for nine sensational seasons on *Everybody Loves Raymond*. What a career. Big Daddy once presented this fellow West Catholic grad with an award at a Communion breakfast. A very nice man who came close to entering the priesthood in his early years. You may know that this La Salle University grad is the son of early Philadelphia TV star Uncle Pete Boyle. But we'll bet you didn't know that the best man at Peter's wedding was . . . John Lennon. RIP, Pete; we really miss you.

2. W. C. Fields. We know the movies seem dated. But consider this: today, more than 60 years after his death, people who don't have a clue who he was still affect many of his voice mannerisms. Did you know he turned down the title role in *The Wizard of Oz*? Once the biggest comedy star in the world, Fields was a wise guy who never refused a drink. Boy, that doesn't sound too Philadelphia, now does it? In the early '70s, you couldn't go into any Wildwood summer rental without seeing that famous poster of him playing cards.

1. Tina Fey. You know how you have to obtain certain numbers before you even get considered for an athletic Hall of Fame? Well, check out these stats for our favorite Upper Darby High alum. Start with 174 episodes of *Saturday Night Live*. Add 138 episodes of *30 Rock*. There's your 300 wins and 500 homers right there. She's starred in movies, including *Mean Girls,* a once-in-a-generation comedy that's also now a Broadway musical. She created and produced *The Unbreakable Kimmy Schmidt*. Did we mention that if all she did was host award shows with Amy Poehler, she *still* would have made this list?

Johnny Callison's Memories of 1964

Johnny Callison passed away in 2006 at age 67. We believe the interview he did with Big Daddy for this chapter may have been his last.

For those too young to recall 1964, we'll recap the ecstasy and eventual agony. The Phillies started the season strong and had a 6½-game lead with 12 left to play. The city was out of its collective mind, and World Series tickets were already printed. But Cincinnati's Chico Ruiz stole home on September 21 to beat the Phils, 1–0, starting a 10-game losing streak. In the end, the Phils lost the pennant to the Cards in what many still consider the biggest collapse in the history of sports.

Callison played right field and was the driving force behind the Phils' success that year. After his baseball career ended in 1973, the Oklahoma native stayed in this area, working as a popular bartender and residing in Glenside. He joked that he was one of the last baseball stars who had to work in the off-season.

Who better to talk to about that gut-wrenching season than a man who was the first sports idol to many in this town? Here were Callison's top—and bottom—memories of '64.

10. Richie Allen. "I took one look at this guy and I knew he was going to be something special. Despite his image, Richie was a great, great guy. They booed him right away, which I could never figure out."

9. Jim Bunning's perfect game. "Everyone says you're supposed to stay away from a pitcher when he's pitching a perfect game, but Jim wouldn't stay away from us. He was stalking up and down the dugout saying stuff like, 'You guys better start diving for balls, I'm pitching a no-hitter!' I went two for four in that game with a home run, but nobody remembers that—nor should they. It was a great experience to be part of. A special, special day for Jim. Did I want to make the final out? Well, let's just say that would have been all right, but it was just as fine that I didn't."

8. Johnny's walk-off three-run home run in the All-Star Game. "This was a moment I'll never forget. A major thrill. I hit a fastball off Dick Radatz. My mother-in-law and sister-in-law were in New York for the game with my wife, who was expecting our daughter, Sherrie. When I hit the homer, my wife thought she was gonna deliver right there."

7. The city's mood through the summer. "I was living in Glenside and everywhere you went—the dry cleaners, the gas station—everyone knew who I was. The town just went crazy. It was a lot of fun. Everyone was rooting for us. They were so starved for a winner."

6. Chico Ruiz steals home. "I wasn't thinking steal at all. I had never seen anyone steal home in a game I was playing. When he started running, I thought, 'What is this guy, crazy? Who steals home with Frank Robinson at the plate?' Ruiz did that on his own. He had to, it was so insane. (Was there any way of knowing that was the beginning of an oncoming disaster?) Oh, no. It was just one loss. Remember, I played for a Phils team that had lost 23 straight in 1961."

5. Johnny hits three homers against the Braves in a late-season loss. "No one even remembers that. In fact, I hardly remember it at all myself because we lost. I remember it not being any big thrill at all."

4. Elimination Day, October 3, 1964. "Well, I remember feeling shitty and just plain exhausted if you want to know the truth. We knew that the city had not had a winner for a long time and that we let everyone down. We did our part by winning the final game, but, unfortunately, the Mets didn't do theirs and lost to the Cards."

3. Did manager Gene Mauch get tight in shortening his rotation? "I don't think so. I think he went with that rotation (Bunning and Short) to try to win it quickly so he could give us all a rest before the World Series. We had been playing every day. In fact, it was the first time all year he was nice to us. Usually he was cussing at us all for something. I still think we would have won the thing had not Frank Thomas gotten hurt." (Thomas was acquired in late July and contributed mightily but broke his thumb on September 8.)

2. Losing the MVP award. "Well, everyone says I would have got it had we won, but we didn't." (Ken Boyer of the pennant-winning Cardinals won it.)

1. How he remembered 1964 years later. "It was the closest team I ever played for. Everyone was pulling for each other all year. It was a team with no jealousy."

The Best Philly Players Who Never Won a Championship

"It don't mean a thing if you ain't got that ring!" That's not exactly how the song goes, but welcome to the world of a pro athlete. You can have an amazing career, but if you never win a title? It's like the Tin Man in *The Wizard of Oz* lacking a heart.

Okay, maybe that's a stretch. But it *is* like there's something incomplete about a player's career. It's missing something. We imagine there's been an athlete who has lofted the Lombardi Trophy or hugged the Stanley Cup and whispered to it, "You complete me."

Geez, let's stop with these lame movie references.

Anyway, often it's just luck that keeps a player from attaining a title. A bad break. An injury. It's Gary Anderson of the Vikings missing his only field goal of the year. (More on that soon.)

Here are the 10 greatest Philly athletes who never won the big one.

10. Donovan McNabb. We don't know if there has ever been a winner in this town (any sport) with fewer fans. He helmed the Birds for 167 regular-season and 16 playoff battles, yet never captured our hearts. Oh, he has plenty of supporters who think he deserves to be in the Hall of Fame—a campaign led by, well, McNabb himself. And he has just as many detractors. You cannot deny his 98 regular-season and nine playoff wins. And then there's the issue of, "Did he or did he not upchuck?"

9. Randall Cunningham. The "Ultimate Weapon." Although he never got close to the Super Bowl in his 11 seasons with the Eagles, he was just one shanked Gary Anderson FG away from quarterbacking the Vikings against John Elway in Super Bowl XXXIII. What a matchup that would have been. Instead we got stuck watching the Broncos rout Chris Chandler and the Atlanta Falcons in Elway's final game. Randall, you deserved one.

> **Big Daddy says:** I deserved to see Randall in that Super Bowl—since it's the only one I ever attended.

8. Brian Westbrook. We know Randall already had the nickname, but Westbrook certainly was the Eagles' "ultimate weapon" during the Andy Reid era. He played 107 games with the Birds (many fans forget he ended his career with the Niners), plus 11 playoff games. Gained 104 yards and scored a TD in Super Bowl XXXIX but didn't get that victory cigar. God, we loved watching him play.

The following seven players are all in their respective Halls of Fame. But alas, no rings.

7. Mark Howe. He played 1,355 professional games, including 594 with the Flyers. That doesn't include three trips to the Stanley Cup finals. Had there not been a little-known player by the name of Wayne Gretzky in his way, who knows how it would have played out? Howe, by the way, sustained one of the most gruesome injuries ever, getting impaled through the tailbone by the pointed piece of metal that used to sit in the back of the goal. After all that, he's still not considered as tough as his father, Gordie.

6. Robin Roberts. Pitched 19 years in the majors. At age 23, his 1950 Whiz Kids got swept by the Yanks in his only World Series appearance. He started 472 games for the Phils and—get ready for this—completed 272 of them.

> **Big Daddy says:** At one of the first sports banquets I ever emceed, Robin Roberts (whom I had never met) approached me at the end and said, "Hey, kid, did you get your check yet?" I shyly replied, "Yes," and Roberts muttered to me, "Well, cash it tomorrow. I don't trust these guys." Words of wisdom. Thanks, Robin.

5. Eric Lindros. Oh, the expectations. Those expectations. It's like being voted "Most Likely to Succeed" in your high school yearbook.

4. Charles Barkley. You could make a case that he's the greatest NBA power forward of all time, which perhaps should rank him even higher on this list. But his 610 games as a Sixer are a little light, and the one NBA Final he did go to was not with the Sixers but with the Suns in 1993.

3. Richie Ashburn. Whitey played 2,189 games in the bigs—including 1,794 with the Fightins. The closest he got to the titles was in 1950 with those Whiz Kids. Ashburn's chances were hurt because he played when there were no playoffs. It was simply the winners of the National League and American League squaring off in the World Series. There was no wild card chance or opportunity that someone else might knock out a favorite, creating an easier path for you.

2. Brian Dawkins. It so pains us to put the number two next to the name Brian Dawkins. Seriously, how can you do that? We know this ranking is going to irk a lot of you, but that's the fun of a list, eh? What a winner he was. Five NFC Championship games. Five! Adding that single Super Bowl appearance—and loss—to the résumé just makes it that much more heartbreaking.

1. Allen Iverson. We're not saying he's the most talented player on this list, although Allen certainly put up amazing numbers and MVP stats. Beyond that, although he had flaws as a player, you cannot deny the toughness he displayed every time he went down that lane and was hammered to the court. The 2001 Finals against the Lakers were as close as he ever got—and the Sixers certainly didn't fall short because of AI. Consider yourself lucky that we lived in a town that got to witness the greatest-ever player of his height.

Honorable mention: Richie Allen, Harold Carmichael, Claude Giroux, Ron Hextall, Ron Jaworski, Tim Kerr, John Kruk, Wilbert Montgomery, Brian Propp, Jim Thome.

Bonus List: *Oh, why stop now? Just for the heck of it, we compiled a group of the 10 best players of the last 50 years to never win a championship: Ernie Banks, Charles Barkley (the only athlete on both lists), Elgin Baylor, Barry Bonds, Dick Butkus, Ken Griffey Jr., Karl Malone, Dan Marino, Barry Sanders, John Stockton.*

Best Endings

10. Double Doink, January 6, 2019. The defending champion Eagles managed to win five of their last six games in 2018 to squeak into the playoffs as the lowest-ranked wild card team. Their reward was to take on 12–4 Chicago and its NFL-best defense in Soldier Field.

The Eagles trailed 15–10 with five minutes to go, but Nick Foles (stop us if you've heard this one before) performed his magic to drive them for a touchdown. A missed two-pointer meant the Birds had a 16–15 lead.

The Bears got the ball back with 48 seconds left. The Eagles defense—so good all afternoon—slipped up, and Chicago managed to drive to the 25. There were just 15 seconds left when Bears coach Matt Nagy used his final timeout to call upon Cody Parkey (a former Eagle) for the game-winning field goal.

Parkey gracefully put one through the uprights—but wait, Eagles coach Doug Pederson had called his timeout just before the kick, so it didn't count. Pederson was aiming to ice Parkey, who calmly lined up to do it again, and . . .

The field goal attempt skimmed the gloved finger of Eagles defensive tackle Treyvon Hester. It started to hook, ricocheted off the left upright, made a physics-defying bounce off the goalpost, and fell harmlessly to the ground. Doink, doink, jubilation.

By a fingertip, literally, the Eagles won the game and moved on to play New Orleans.

9. Chooch saves the no-hitter, October 6, 2010. Roy Halladay pitched only the second postseason no-hitter in baseball history, beating Cincinnati 4–0 before 46,411 ecstatic fans at Citizens Bank Park. Most of it looked easy, as Doc threw 25 first-pitch strikes past the 28 batters he faced.

But the last pitch provided the drama. Reds second baseman Brandon Phillips swung wildly at a gyrating curveball and knuckled a dribbler 10 feet in front of home plate. Phils catcher Carlos Ruiz pounced toward the ball, just as Phillips tossed his bat in the same vicinity.

Ruiz sifted through the mess—rolling bat, spinning baseball, baserunner headed up the line. He dug out the ball, dropped to one knee, and snaked his throw around Phillips into Ryan Howard's yawning glove.

As teammates celebrated, Ruiz sighed in relief. "If I don't make that play," he said, "oh, my God, I'm gonna feel bad."

8. Concrete Charlie sits on the title, December 26, 1960. The Eagles led Green Bay, 17–13, with less than a minute to go in the pre–Super Bowl NFL title game at Franklin Field. QB Bart Starr led his team downfield, completing four straight passes to put the Packers at the Eagles' 22 as the second hand of the old-fashioned clock swept toward its upright position.

Starr hit fullback Jim Taylor on a swing pass, and Taylor turned to bull his way toward the end zone. But middle linebacker Chuck Bednarik met Taylor head on at the Eagles' 10, wrestled him down, and then sat atop Taylor until time ran out.

"You can get up now, Jim," Bednarik finally said. "This fucking game is over."

The game proved to be the only postseason loss of Packers coach Vince Lombardi's career. Bednarik and his teammates each received $3,500 as their championship reward.

7. Keith Primeau ends the marathon, May 4, 2000. The guy who never seemed to connect in the playoffs ended the third-longest game in NHL history by rifling the perfect shot under the crossbar past Penguins goalie Ron Tugnutt. It came in the fifth overtime to give the exhausted Flyers a 2–1 victory. Players said that by the end—2:35 a.m., to be exact—they felt like they were skating in oatmeal.

The seven-hour contest took it all out of the Penguins. The Flyers won the next two games—and the series.

6. Bobby Clarke makes an overtime statement, May 9, 1974. The Big Bad Bruins—two-time winners of the Stanley Cup—seemed invincible in the '74–75 Finals, especially after winning Game 1. The Flyers trailed in Game 2 at the Boston Garden but tied it with 52 seconds to go on a wrister from Moose Dupont, of all people.

Twelve minutes into OT, Clarke took a pass from Bill "Cowboy" Flett and backhanded one at goalie Gilles Gilbert. The Bruins goalie made the save but was on his back as the puck bounced out. Clarke gathered it and lifted one high into the net for the victory.

It was the Flyers' first win in Boston in nearly seven years, and it made a statement. "I don't see how everybody can have doubts about us now," Clarke said. "We know we can beat them there."

Which, of course, they did on their way to the Flyers' first Stanley Cup.

5. Miracle at the Meadowlands I, November 19, 1978. One of the great twist-of-fate endings ever in the NFL. With the Giants leading the Eagles, 17–12, and the clock ticking down, all New York QB Joe Pisarcik had to do was kneel over the ball. He didn't, of course.

Herman Edwards's 28-yard return of the fumbled handoff with 20 seconds remaining didn't just become one of the most replayed moments ever in football or the ultimate reminder for offensive coaches not to eschew the victory formation at the end of games. It also served as a turning point for the Eagles. They won three of their last five games in 1978 to make the playoffs for the first time in 18 years.

4. Rollins's defense captures the division title, September 27, 2008. The Phils led the Mets by 1½ games as they headed into Game 161 against the Washington Nationals. Lidge—40-for-40 in save opportunities—took the mound in the ninth with a 5–3 lead and a chance to clinch the NL East.

Except that Brad "Lights Out" Lidge was anything but his nickname on this afternoon. He quickly allowed four baserunners and a run. Nats cleanup hitter Ryan Zimmerman came up with just one out and a chance to win the game.

Zimmerman connected on a Lidge slider, rocketing a groundball headed for centerfield. But Phils shortstop Jimmy Rollins went to his knees and stabbed the sharp gounder. He flipped it to Chase Utley at second and rejoiced—along with all of us—as Utley's relay throw completed the game-ending—and division-winning—double play.

Little more than a month later, the Phils won their first World Series in 28 years.

> **Big Daddy says:** I watched this game with my long-suffering sports nut stepfather-in-law, Phil Hurst. A tremendous guy, Phil was so proud of the first issue of this book that he bought 20 copies to give away as gifts, without ever telling me. He has since passed away, but I'll always think of him when this play comes up.

3. Miracle at Meadowlands III: DeSean's punt return, December 19, 2010.
The Eagles trailed the Giants 31–10, before QB Mike Vick led them on three fourth-quarter touchdown drives. With 14 seconds left in a tie game, Giants punter Matt Dodge kicked an ill-advised line drive.

DeSean Jackson bobbled it at his own 35, retreated to the 28, and then, amazingly, ran right up the middle past seven or eight Giants who overpursued. Jackson got two great blocks along the way and ended up dancing along the goal line before crossing in as time ran out.

Both teams entered that game at 9–4, and the Eagles' victory cleared their path to the division title. It was the first time in NFL history a game was won with a walkoff punt return.

2. Buzzer beater wins national title for Nova, April 4, 2016.
First, North Carolina's Marcus Paige hit a twisting three-pointer with 4.7 seconds to go to tie the NCAA title game at 74–74. A great, acrobatic shot.

Villanova's Ryan Arcidiacono took the inbounds pass, ferociously dribbled up court, and scooped the ball to trailer Kris Jenkins behind the three-point line. Jenkins lofted his shot exactly six-tenths of a second before the red lights illuminated around the game clock.

His shot swished through. Game over, as a TV camera caught former Nova coach Rollie Massimino hugging everyone in the stands. The Wildcats claimed their second championship in one of the greatest NCAA Finals ever.

1. Hail No, Super Bowl LII, February 4, 2019.
Brandon Graham's strip sack of Tom Brady led to a Jake Elliott field goal, giving the Eagles a 41–33 lead with 1:05 left. The Patriots got the ball back with no timeouts and 91 yards to go.

But, as NBC color analyst Cris Collinsworth repeatedly barked, Tom Terrific had performed magic before, so no Eagles fan was breathing easy. New England got to midfield, and with nine seconds left, Brady launched one toward 6-foot-6 tight end Rob Gronkowski in the end zone. Nine seconds seemed like nine years, as six Eagles defenders surrounded Gronk and the jump ball batted around a few times . . . before harmlessly hitting the ground.

It took a few moments for announcers, and even the players, to realize the game was over. The Eagles won their first Super Bowl in one of the most nail-biting finishes ever.

6. John Lucas III sinks St. Joe's, March 27, 2004. Ten seconds. Three incredible mood swings. With a trip to the Final Four at stake, Pat Carroll hit a late three-pointer to put the Hawks up by one. We were all booking flights to San Antonio. But in the blink of an eye, John Lucas III (yes, the son of the one-time Sixers coach), who was 2-for-11 from the three-point line before that, drilled a long one.

Then, College Player of the Year Jameer Nelson got a good look, but his fadeaway jumper ticked off the rim. Phil Martelli's Hawks—undefeated in the regular season—went home empty. Absolutely crushing.

5. Kawhi Leonard's four-bounce fadeaway, May 12, 2019. We've suffered through buzzer beaters before, but none as heartbreaking as Leonard's Game 7 stunner that pushed Toronto past the Sixers in the 2019 playoffs. The prayer launched from the corner bounced not once, not twice, but four times before gently dropping through the net to break the 90–90 tie. Would the Sixers have won in OT? We'll never know.

4. Tommy Hutton fumbles away a Monday-night win, September 15, 1997. The Cowboys led the Eagles, 21–20, with seconds to play. Things looked hopeless until Ty Detmer hit a wide-open Freddie Solomon, who sprinted to the Dallas 4-yard line. The Eagles called timeout with four seconds to go, setting up a potential game-winning field goal by former Cowboy Chris Boniol.

The snap from Morris Unutoa was right into the hands of holder Tommy Hutton, who bobbled it, dropped it, then bobbled it again. Boniol froze in his approach. No kick. Hutton stumbled toward the end zone with the ball and proceeded to fumble again. Cowboys win.

Look at all the names in the three previous paragraphs and tell me that wasn't the worst era of Eagles football.

> **Glen says:** I watched this game—alone—in my den. I was so excited at the prospect of a late Eagles win that I rose from my chair and began dancing. As Hutton botched the snap, I kicked out in anger and actually broke my right pinkie toe against a coffee table. Two decades later, it still aches in cold weather—a lifetime reminder of my hatred for Tommy Hutton and Chris Boniol.

3. Black Friday, October 7, 1977. Game 3 of a best-of-five NLCS against the Dodgers. The series was tied at a game apiece. The Phils had a 5–3 lead in the ninth with two outs, nobody on, and reliever Gene Garber on the mound.

In every game situation that season, manager Danny Ozark replaced defensive liability Greg Luzinski with Jerry Martin. Not this night. Up came 41-year-old Vic Davalillo, who incredibly beat out a bunt. Then, 39-year-old Manny Mota lifted a flyball to left that Luzinski butchered, allowing Davalillo to score and—when Ted Sizemore messed up a relay—Mota got to third (most fans have forgotten Sizemore's key error over the years).

Davey Lopes then hit a smash that caromed off Mike Schmidt right to shortstop Larry Bowa, who quickly threw to first. Replays show that the throw beat Lopes, but umpire Bruce

Froemming blew the call, allowing the run to score. A throwing error by Garber and single by Bill Russell brought in Lopes. Final score, 6–5.

The Dodgers finished the series the next night, beating Steve Carlton, 4–1, in a steady rain.

> **Big Daddy says:** I was at this game and will always remember the 20-minute walk to the car with my brother, followed by a 40-minute drive to his apartment. Neither of us spoke a word.

2. Patrick Kane's invisible goal sinks the Flyers, June 9, 2010. If a goal gets scored and nobody sees it, does it really count?

Unfortunately, it does, as the Flyers and their fans learned in this Cup Finals Game 6 overtime, won by Chicago's young superstar. Kane got the puck in the corner, 4:06 into OT, and wristed a high one toward the shoulder of Flyers goalie Michael Leighton. It certainly didn't look dangerous at the time.

Here's the play, described by our favorite hockey broadcaster, Doc Emrick: "There's Kane in the corner, trying to shake (Kimmo) Timonen. Threw one in front and they sc—oh my, it rattled around and it's kicked on back and . . . oh, they score! We saw no light, we saw no signal, but they are celebrating at the other end of the ice."

As the Blackhawks dropped their gloves and sticks and began partying on the Wachovia Center ice, Flyers players and fans joined Emrick in watching the replay to figure out what had happened. Turns out Leighton never moved on a stoppable shot. We've held a grudge against him ever since.

1. Joe Carter walks it off, October 23, 1993. Where else did you think we'd finish?

All these years later, it still hurts to talk about it. So let's get this over with.

The Phils had rallied from a 5–1 deficit with a five-run seventh inning in Game 6 of the World Series. Now, they took a 6–5 lead into the bottom of the ninth. Manager Jim Fregosi called on his closer, Mitch Williams. As was his style, the Wild Thing put on two baserunners—future Hall of Famers Rickey Henderson and Paul Molitor.

With one out, up came Carter. The count went to 2–2, with Carter chasing a couple of sliders. Williams tried to throw a fastball up and in, but, well, control was not his thing, so the pitch dropped down over the middle of the strike zone.

And Carter, of course, drove it out of the park for the 8–6 Blue Jays win. World Series over. Hey, we don't want to discuss it anymore.

Harvey Holiday spun everyone's favorite numbers on 98.1 WOGL for more than 30 years. He retired at the end of 2018.

10. "Love Train" by the O'Jays. "People all over the world, join hands!"

9. "Me and Mrs. Jones" by Billy Paul. Almost makes infidelity sound noble.

8. "I'll Always Love My Mama" by the Intruders. How can a song go wrong when its composers are Gamble & Huff *and* McFadden & Whitehead?

7. "I'll Be Around" by the Spinners. Another Sigma Sound masterpiece.

6. "Betcha by Golly Wow" by the Stylistics. "You're the one that I've been waiting for."

5. "Only the Strong Survive" by Jerry Butler. The Iceman comes to Philadelphia and makes a perfect record.

4. "Disco Inferno" by the Trammps. A groove to make you move.

3. "Expressway to Your Heart" by the Soul Survivors. The first top-10 hit written by Kenny Gamble and Leon Huff. Charlie and Richard Ingui sing it like they've been stuck on the Schuylkill for hours.

2. "La La Means I Love You" by the Delfonics. The most gorgeous example of Philadelphia's falsetto harmony.

1. "If You Don't Know Me by Now" by Harold Melvin and the Blue Notes. "We've all got our own funny moods. I've got mine, woman you've got yours too."

Big Daddy's Favorite Songs That Mention Philly

Don't you hate rules? Who doesn't? Unfortunately, this list is going to stick to one very important rule. The song *must* mention Philadelphia somewhere along the way. It doesn't matter if it's in the title or if "Philly!" is shouted out just one time. Them's the rules.

Why? Because I remember the first time I heard my hometown mentioned in a song like it was yesterday and how amazed and proud I was.

So let's get right to it. I am going to go in opposite order this time because, well, number one explains it all.

1. "Dancing in the Streets," Martha & the Vandellas. *Philadelphia* magazine once called to get my memories of summer camp, and I just laughed because no one from Southwest Philly went away to camp. Camp came to us in the form of a couple of city recreation workers who set up camp every day at Patterson schoolyard at 9:00 a.m. and split by 4:00 p.m.

They organized games like dodgeball and volleyball. There would be arts and crafts, and every Friday Mr. Sheridan brought this little record player with a built-in speaker that played 45s. A 45 was a . . . uh . . . well . . . forget it.

It quickly became my favorite moment of the week. The girls would start dancing, and even at 10 years old, well, I found it was terrific.

But one afternoon he put on this song, and at about 1:26 into the song, Martha gives a shout-out to "Philadelphia, PA!" I couldn't believe my ears. That's my town! I can't tell you why it meant the world to me, but it just did. It was the first time I ever heard "Philadelphia" in a song, and I still get a kick out of hearing it today.

2. "Motownphilly," Boyz II Men. And they're from Philly! For a vocal group that's world famous for their soft-touch ballads, this tune is exciting and always uplifting. This was their very first single and was written by all four members of the band. "And all the Philly steaks you can eat!"

3. "I-76," G. Love & Special Sauce. What a fun track, particularly if you're a Sixers fan. G is a Germantown Friends School grad who you might have sat next to when his name was Garrett Dutton. He's a unique, eccentric talent who combines acoustic blues and folk with rap. And he makes it all work. You have to love a ditty that mentions "Cottman," "Parkline Drive," "Fishtown," and "South Philly." Not to mention half of the 1983 Sixers.

4. "Fall in Philadelphia," Hall & Oates. Off their very first LP, *Whole Oats*. Some people thought that was the name of the band for a while. I was stocking shelves in a West Philly Acme when I heard DJ Michael Tearson play this for the first time. Harry, a coworker, yelled from another aisle, "Hey! Did they just say Philadelphia?" Who knew then that these Temple students would go on to become the biggest-selling musical duo of all time. "I'm gonna spend another fall in Philadelphia," just in time for the Birds.

5. "Summertime," DJ Jazzy Jeff & the Fresh Prince. Quick, name another entertainer who has conquered music, TV, and movies like Overbrook's Will Smith? If you're keeping score at home, four of the first five songs were performed by Philly folks. "A place called the plateau is where everybody goes." Yes, a shout-out to Belmont Plateau. Also one of the best summer songs ever.

6. "Philadelphia Freedom," Elton John. I was never a big fan of this song until I started noticing just how loud Jersey Shore bar patrons would scream out the words whenever a band or solo acoustic guys would perform it. I saw how the combination of lyrics, melody, and alcohol (and God knows what else) stirred the masses, and I couldn't help but find myself singing along as well. All for a long-forgotten professional tennis team. "'Cause I live and breathe this Philadelphia freedom."

7. "Lay Your Body Down (Goodbye Philadelphia)," Peter Cincotti. Every music list should have a song on it that you may not be familiar with, as long as it's deserving of a slot. And this song certainly is. It's fun to share music. Sent to me by a listener, and I haven't stopped enjoying it since. Please YouTube it, or find it however you obtain music these days. "Remember Philadelphia when the world was young and warm."

8. "Philadelphia Morning," Bill Conti (*Rocky* soundtrack). I have often said the soundtrack to *Rocky* is one of the top five soundtracks of all time. And to think the score wasn't even Oscar-nominated. Unfortunately, "Gonna Fly Now" never mentions Philly, so we can't use it here. This song is Track 2, Side 1, and if you are not familiar with this cut, YouTube it. It's slow, beautiful, sad, and tense all wrapped up in one, and you'll absolutely love it. By the way, the song "Gonna Fly Now" did get an Oscar nod but lost to Barbra Streisand's lame "Evergreen."

9. "Streets of Philadelphia," Bruce Springsteen. This Oscar winner finishes this low only because it's such a downer that I am rarely in the mood to actually play it. And I get this. The script to the movie *Philadelphia*, which Springsteen had to work with, was not exactly *Dumb and Dumber*. A line doesn't get more Philly street gritty than "Ain't no angel gonna greet me." During his acceptance speech, Bruce muttered, "Geez, this is the first song I ever wrote for a motion picture, so I guess it's all downhill from here."

10. "Punk Rock Girl," the Dead Milkmen. The video was in solid rotation back in the day when MTV aired such things. Also from Philly, the Milkmen saluted the unique clothing store Zipperhead as well as the Philly Pizza Company. Any song that rhymes "punk rock girl" with "Minnie Pearl" is all right in my book.

Honorable mention: It killed me to leave off Bobby Rydell's "Wildwood Days" simply because it never mentions Philly, because as we all know, Wildwood is a Philly neighborhood like Port Richmond is. But rules are rules. Chuck Berry gives a nod to "American Bandstand, Philadelphia, PA" on "Sweet Little Sixteen." James Brown includes "Philadelphia" in "Night Train," a song that salutes nine different cities (unlike "I've Been Everywhere," which mentions 91 North American cities but not Philadelphia). The Orlons' "South Street" is a fun song as well. I didn't quite know what to do with "Here Come the Sixers," a theme song from the mid-'70s that I still play on my show. It felt like it should be on another list, but, boy, do I love that song. I actually own a vinyl copy. A vinyl record is . . . uh . . . well . . . forget it.

12. Tom Dempsey. He was born with no right hand and no toes on his right foot. So what better job than to pursue than NFL placekicker? Dempsey played four seasons (1971–1974) with the Eagles after gaining fame for kicking a then-NFL-record 63-yard field goal with New Orleans. I can still see him in my mind's eye, using that modified, flattened steel-toed shoe and smashing the ball with that old straight-on style.

11. Tim Kerr. He kept coming back from shoulder and knee surgeries that would have driven a lesser man into retirement. But those setbacks were trivial compared with the death of his wife 10 days after she gave birth to their third daughter in 1990. He came back from that, too, to raise his children, play another two seasons, and start a foundation, Tim Kerr Charities.

10. John Cappelletti. As a Penn State senior in 1973, he rushed for 1,522 yards on Saturdays and worried the rest of the week about his young brother, Joey, who was dying of leukemia. When they awarded John the Heisman Trophy, he broke from his prepared speech to say, "They say I've shown courage on the football field, but for me it's only on the field. Joey lives with pain all the time. His courage is round the clock. I want him to have this trophy. It's more his than mine, because he's been such an inspiration to me." There wasn't a dry eye at the New York Athletic Club.

9. Chris Coste. Like every American kid, he grew up dreaming of becoming a major leaguer. For 11 years, Coste toiled away in the minors as a slow-footed catcher (think Crash Davis without the power or Kevin Costner's good looks). He amassed more than 4,000 plate appearances from the Canadian outback to Venezuela before finally, at age 33, getting the call up to the Phils. Coste even ended up with a World Series ring. A walking, crouching lesson in persistence.

8. Bobby Clarke. You may have forgotten that when Clarke was drafted in 1969 as a 168-pound teenager, many so-called experts believed that his diabetes would curtail an NHL career. Clarke proved them wrong and became a Hall of Famer and three-time MVP. His medical condition drove him to play with an ethos—losing is worse than dying—that stuck with the franchise for decades.

7. Vince Papale. Every beer-league ballplayer has visions of trying out for—and making—the big club. Papale actually did it with Dick Vermeil's Eagles in 1976, winning a roster spot at rookie coach Vermeil's open-call workout with a bunch of other regular Joes. He played four remarkable years with the Eagles and did some exceptional things off the field, too. Somebody ought to make a movie about this guy. Huh, what's that?

6. Adam Taliaferro. In his fifth game as a Penn State freshman in 2000, the Voorhees Township native sustained a paralyzing spinal injury while making a tackle. Although he was given just a 3 percent chance to ever walk again, he pushed through a year of rehab and celebrated by jogging onto the field at the start of Penn State's 2001 opener. Taliaferro started a foundation to help others with spinal cord injuries. He went on to law school and today serves as the deputy majority leader in the New Jersey General Assembly.

5. Mo'ne Davis. I don't know what you were up to at age 13 (my own answer is not publishable), but this young woman was throwing a 73-mile-per-hour fastball. She was the first African American girl to play in the Little League World Series and the first girl to earn a pitching win and shutout. Made the cover of *Sports Illustrated* and got a phone call from First Lady Michelle Obama. An inspiration for every young girl wanting to pursue sports. "I never thought at age 13 I'd be a role model," she told ESPN. "I always wanted to be a role model, but being a baseball role model is really cool."

4. Jim Eisenreich. He was so troubled battling Tourette's syndrome early in his career that he briefly retired. By the time he came to Philadelphia at age 33, medication and his determination to succeed had made Eisenreich into a valuable player. Before nearly every Phillies game in the mid-'90s, you'd find Eisenreich giving a pep talk to a visiting youngster, explaining how obstacles could be overcome.

3. Chris Long. He was so appalled by the violent white-nationalist protests in his hometown of Charlottesville, Virginia, that Long donated his entire $1 million base salary in 2017 to charities providing scholarships and promoting educational equality. I could have just as easily slotted Malcolm Jenkins, Carson Wentz, or several other members of the Super Bowl LII Eagles into this slot. I've covered sports in Philadelphia for more than three decades. Never have I seen a group of players more dedicated to one another, their fans, and the city in which they play.

2. Brian Dawkins. All those years Eagles fans were cheering his greatness on the field, few knew Weapon X's struggles with depression. It came out in his moving Hall of Fame induction speech in 2018, when Dawkins told an audience in Canton, Ohio, and on national TV that his wife had to talk him out of suicide during his playing career. "There's hope," he said. "There is something on the other side of this. Don't stay where you are. Keep moving. Keep pushing through." He established the Brian Dawkins Increase Foundation, so named because it aims to help people increase their quality of life—mentally, physically, and spiritually.

1. Jon Dorenbos. Too much of a storybook to be true—except that it is. When Dorenbos was 12, he entered foster care after his father murdered his mother. He taught himself magic to ease his woes and provide a way to meet other kids. He went undrafted after playing as a long snapper at UTEP but sent a tape of himself to each NFL team and eventually got signed by the Buffalo Bills. Dorenbos played 14 seasons, including 11 with the Eagles—and, far as anyone recalls, never made a bad snap. When he was traded to the Saints in 2017, a physical revealed an aortic aneurism, which required immediate surgery and ended his career. "I wouldn't wish this on anyone," he said during recovery, "but it certainly has given me an appreciation for every day of life." An outgoing player, always terrific with fans, Dorenbos has gone on to become a Las Vegas headliner for his sleight-of-hand magic.

7. Michael Vick. Look, if there was a fire and I could only save my dog Beau or various relatives and in-laws, Beau would win every time. Sorry, Uncle Fred, but that's how much I love Beau and the other two beagles I formerly owned, Dutch and Morgan. So, I realize even seeing Vick's name on that list might drive you out of your mind. I have said on the air that if you find what Vick did to be unforgivable, I could never blame you. But hear me out. After Vick got out of prison in 2009, he never got in any trouble again. And don't forget, Vick was in other various types of hot water *before* dog fighting. So what reason would any of us have to believe that at 29 he would walk the straight and narrow? I'm not going to give him an award, but he's proof that occasionally, rarely, a leopard can change its spots. He did the crime, he served his time, and he made the most of it. We can get *something* out of that, right?

6. Gary Papa. When a freakish series of events landed me in sports talk, the first game I went to was a *Monday Night Football* game, in which the Eagles beat the Houston Oilers, 21–6, on October 24, 1994. I quickly found out where the free food was and walked into the Eagles' food court. I admit I was a bit nervous wondering if I even had the right to be there. So what happens? Gary Papa, who was the number one sports broadcaster in town, yelled out to me "Big Daddy!" I knew he had come to a couple shows of mine over the years, but I wasn't expecting this grand welcome. It really made a difference and sent a message to the rest of the press. Years later, in the summer of 2008, Gary was dying of cancer. He was sporting a bald head, and he and John Clark were at one of my shows in Sea Isle City. Gary was having a ball, and he was so much fun to hang around with. When I got sick with the Big C myself only a year and a half later, I often thought of how Gary decided to spend his last days with dignity and humor—and I used it for motivation. So here's to you Gary; I hope you watched the Birds win the Super Bowl wherever you are.

5. Charlie Manuel. I admired Charlie for conquering his "country bumpkin" image to become a true folk hero in this town. That was no small task. Compared to what Charlie had to overcome in real life, however, putting up with the likes of Howard Eskin is mere child's play. First of all, Charlie was born in a car in West Virginia, and you have to love that right there. He was one of 11 children and the oldest son. His father committed suicide when Charlie was 19, leaving behind a note telling Charlie that he now had to take care of the family—and Charlie was already married with a child. Because of these responsibilities, Manuel had to turn down a basketball scholarship to *the University of Pennsylvania* and play minor league baseball because his family needed the dough. So don't think for a second that someone making fun of him because of the way he talked bothered Charlie one iota. Love you, Charlie.

4. Jay Wright. Boy, the Nova haters are going to rip me for this one, but Wright has now won two championships with an incredibly clean program, and you'd be hard-pressed to name me a college basketball coach you'd rather coach a big game than Jay. You name the coach—Coach K, Tom Izzo . . . I'm going with Jay Wright. And he's a local Council Rock nice guy to boot.

3. and 2. Ron and Pete. Local youth leagues are the backbone of American sports. You can't name a pro athlete who can't credit some coach he had before he even got to high school for making a difference. And these coaches do it for free because they love it. Unfortunately, we've all also seen the opposite—like the Tom Cruise flick where a nightmare of a high school coach really screws up a kid's potential college career. I had one of those nitwits. Maybe you did also. So I count my blessings that both my daughters were coached by these two great men. They taught the game, there was discipline, but first and foremost, they made sure all the kids had fun—which is most important. And you know what? They won. They proved you could do it all the right way and still win. Way to go, guys; you have really helped make the community better.

1. Angelo Cataldi. Despite his self-deprecating image as a goofball and his rep as a lunatic to work with, Angelo is one of the hardest-working cats I ever met. He's in at the studio, every stinkin' day, a full two hours before he goes on the air. And we're talking 3:30 a.m. He's completely prepared and virtually everything I learned about talk radio I learned from him.

For example, when I first started, my show was dominated with topics such as, "Who are the best Phillies first basemen ever?" Or, "What's your favorite football movie?" Too often I let those topics control the show instead of allowing the current news of the day dominate the conversation. Angelo taught me that those fun lists were good as a side topic, as long as you were more concentrated on what was the most important story of the day.

None of his advice ever attempted to change what my true personality was and how important it is that I stay consistent with that. And I know Al Morganti is credited with dreaming up "Wing Bowl," but it was Ang who made it what it became—18,000 screaming maniacs, floats, wingettes, eaters, entourages, all assembled at 6:00 a.m. It became, and will remain, the greatest radio stunt ever concocted.

So since I already mentioned Al, let me make sure that I mention Rhea Hughes, who, in my opinion, is the greatest female radio broadcaster in this town's history. Not that I mean to single her out as a woman, because she would be terrific at her job as a man, but I do think that is worth bringing up. Name me another woman who has had Rhea's longevity.

The Eagles' fifth-round pick in 1998, Michigan State alum Ike Reese was a special teams standout here for seven seasons, making the Pro Bowl in 2004. He played 112 consecutive games in Eagles green, starting just five at linebacker, but always being a factor in all aspects of special teams. These days, Reese is cohost, along with Jon Marks, of the 94-WIP Afternoon Show.

These are Ike's 10 special teams standouts:

10. Chris Maragos. I love a core special teams guy, and that's him—being part of every phase of it. That Chip Kelly unit, when Dave Fipp started, was the best in the league for three years, and Chris was the best player on that squad.

9. Kamu Grugier-Hill. He's got great speed. When a key tackle is made, number 54 is always there. He's blocked kicks, recovered fumbles, everything. He reminds me of myself, but he's a better athlete because he can kick off. Remember that game when he came in and got touchbacks on his kickoffs?

8. Sean Landeta. The GOAT. He could boom it, directionally punt, or pin you down inside the 10 with coffin-corner kicks. I didn't always listen to kickers, but I learned so much playing with Sean. He played on great teams and had so much knowledge.

7. Vince Papale. He didn't have the longest career, but anyone who goes to a tryout at age 30 and makes an NFL roster is worth my respect. His story is the stuff dreams are made of. It's like a Hollywood movie—which, in fact, it was.

6. Jake Elliott. He made great kicks during the greatest season in franchise history. The 61-yarder against the Giants stopped an early-season slide. And nothing was bigger than the 48-yarder in the Super Bowl. That kick doesn't get talked about because of the Philly Special and Brandon Graham's strip sack, but that rookie gave us an eight-point lead with a long, clutch kick. If he missed that, Tom Brady had a chance to come back from just five points.

5. Brian Mitchell. My man, B Mitch. He's a Hall of Famer in my opinion. He was a big reason why we made the playoffs for the first time in 2000. We didn't have the strongest offense, but we had a solid defense, and his returns so improved our field position. Plus, he instilled in the young teammates that *we* could be difference makers. His toughness and mentality helped make (special teams coach) John Harbaugh the coach he became.

4. DeSean Jackson. Action Jackson. How many times does he show up in the highlight reels? He was in so many big plays, none bigger than the one at the Meadowlands. The first guy to make the Pro Bowl on both offense and special teams. Still the most electrifying returner I've ever seen.

3. Brian Westbrook. Some guys enter the league and regard playing on special teams as a slight, but never B West. He had to divide time between special teams and offense and always gave it his all. He always came up with the big play at the right time. And, hey, don't forget I was part of blocking for him on Miracle at the Meadowlands, Number 2.

2. David Akers. The all-time leading scorer in franchise history (1,323 points) probably deserves to be number one, but there's no way I can have a kicker at the top. David made five Pro Bowls as an Eagle and was very clutch and accurate. Kickers don't get a lot of respect, but to a man, we all knew he was a tough guy. He prided himself on being a football player, not just a kicker.

1. Ike Reese. Any of these other guys could be here, but I put myself at the top because I was drafted as a special teams player and did it with pride. I was captain of the unit playing alongside a lot of these guys. Harbaugh entrusted me with being out there as a leader, and during those seven seasons, we finished top five in the league in five different seasons. I'm happy to be the standard bearer for a team that I loved.

The Worst Bosses in Philadelphia Sports History

You think you work for a cheapskate or a numbskull? Consider these front-office losers.

10. Bryan Colangelo. It's not that he made only terrible moves during his term as Sixers president of operations—although trading up with the Celtics to draft Markelle Fultz was an all-time stinker. More so, it's the bizarre story that cost this two-time NBA Executive of the Year his job. Colangelo's wife, Barbara Bottini, got busted running three Twitter burner accounts on which she roasted current and former 76ers players. And you thought your wife was a blabbermouth.

9. Jack Ramsay and Don DeJardin. It's tough to tell where the bad work of Ramsay ends and DeJardin's begins, but, together, these two general managers turned the Sixers from a 68–13 NBA Champion to a 9–73 disaster in just six seasons. The hideous Wilt trade. Giving away Chet Walker and Wali Jones. Making first-round draft choices from 1967 through 1972 of—are you ready?—Craig Raymond, Shaler Halimon, Bud Ogden, Al Henry, Dana Lewis, and Fred Boyd.

8. Paul Holmgren. He spent eight seasons putting the Flyers in salary cap hell. Example: he signed old and injured Chris Pronger to a seven-year deal, of which Pronger was able to play just one healthy season. He traded emerging players for overpriced slop. In the grand Flyers tradition, when Homer was eventually relieved of his job in 2014, he was promoted upward to team president.

7. Jerry Wolman. Owned the Eagles from the 1964 through 1968 seasons, during which they went 28–41–1. Awarded a 15-year contract to Joe Kuharich, whose name you will see again very soon. Went bankrupt during his tenure as owner (who loses money in the NFL?) and was forced to sell. That's a triumvirate of terrible. A nice guy, by all accounts. But you know the saying . . .

6. Chip Kelly. The opposite of a nice guy. As Eagles coach, Kelly went 26–21 (and 2–14 with the Niners afterwards). As a general manager, he alienated ownership, players, assistants, PR people, and the nice folks working the cafeteria line down at the practice facility. Kelly wouldn't talk to anyone outside his small cadre of favored assistants, and Eagles employees were instructed not to say hello to him if he walked by. We haven't even gotten to his personnel decisions. DeMarco Murray. Need we say more?

5. John Quinn. Quinn was the Phillies vice president and general manager from 1959 to 1972. That's an astounding 14 seasons with no postseason appearances. Quinn ran an organization that was infamous for being paternalistic toward black players and cheap toward everyone. Once, he was caught paying a young Bahamian outfielder, Tony Curry, several thousand dollars under the minimum because Curry didn't know any better.

4. Jack Pastore. Here is a list of all first-round pitchers picked during Pastore's two stints as Phils scouting director in the 1980s: Tony Ghelfi, Kevin Romine, Brad Brink, Derek Lee (no, not the good one), Blas Minor, and Pat Combs. Over five drafts, he picked dozens of pitchers. Not a single one enjoyed a Major League career in which he retired with at least 40 victories and a winning record. Seriously, you could throw a dart and come up with better results.

3. Joe Kuharich. Take Rich Kotite as a coach and Harry Gamble as a general manager, combine the weakest elements of the two, and you've got Kuharich, who ran the Eagles under Wolman from 1964 to 1968. We'll deal with his coaching in another chapter, but as general manager he traded stars like Sonny Jurgensen, Tommy McDonald, Irv Cross, and Maxie Baughan for virtually nothing. A franchise that entered the 1960s as the NFL champs left it as one of the weakest. Plus, he had the kind of paranoid demeanor often compared with Captain Queeg.

2. Gerald Nugent. He owned the Phils from 1933 to 1942, a decade when they finished last six times and next-to-last the other four. After Chuck Klein won the Triple Crown in 1933, Nugent traded him rather than give Klein a raise. Nugent was finally forced out by baseball's other owners, leaving the franchise to be run by the commissioner's office for a season. Eventually it was sold to a lumber tycoon named William D. Cox. Nine months later, Cox was banned for life by Commissioner Kenesaw Mountain Landis for gambling on Phillies games. We can't imagine he was betting on the Phils to win.

1. Norman Braman. You were expecting anyone else? No owner ever alienated the fan base like Bottom Line Braman. He seemed like an evil character from a Dickens novel (or Disney: think Scrooge McDuck), constantly squeezing the joy from our football team and the nickels from our pockets. He was a native Philadelphian who ran the club as an absentee landlord, monitoring player holdouts from his villa in France. He ran the most profitable franchise in the NFL yet kept players' and coaches' salaries among the bottom five. Hell, he even charged his players for sanitary socks (a story Glen was proud to break in the *Philadelphia Inquirer*). And when free agency arrived in 1992, and Braman could no longer keep players under his penny-pinching prices, well, that was the end of any success the Eagles had under his tenure.

Dishonorable mention: Russ Farwell, Brad Greenberg, Ed Stefanski.

Joe Sixpack is Don Russell, a longtime Philadelphia newspaperman and beer drinker. He is the author of three books about beer, founder of Philly Beer Week, and cohost with Glen Macnow of What's Brewing TV. *This is in chronological order.*

10. Robert Hare's Porter.

"I drink no Cyder, but feast upon Phyladelphia Beer, and Porter. A Gentleman, one Mr. Hare, has lately set up in this City a Manufactory of Porter, as good as any that comes from London."

—John Adams, letter to wife, Abigail, 1774

And it wasn't just Adams who enjoyed the stuff. George Washington, a frequent customer, made Hare's dark ale a cornerstone of his nationwide "buy American" policy after the Revolution. Today, dozens of breweries—including Yards, located a few blocks from Hare's colonial brewery—make a version of the historic beer.

9. John Wagner's Lager.
John Wagner arrived in the city from Bavaria aboard a clipper ship, a container of murky liquid stashed in his luggage. The year was 1840, and that liquid was yeast—specifically fresh newfangled lager yeast he'd spirited from his homeland. He set up a small home brewery near Poplar Street in Northern Liberties and made what is generally regarded as the first cold-fermented lager beer in America. The German immigrant's brewery didn't really pan out, but no matter. Lager fermentation would soon replace ale as America's dominant type of beer, and a historic marker now shows the site of Wagner's brewery.

8. Bergner & Engel Tannhauser Export.
Within 10 years of Wagner's first brew, Philadelphia emerged as a leading brewery city specializing in German lager. By 1870, Bergner & Engel was the second-largest brewery in America, and it was just one of about 90 breweries in the city. Its Tannhauser Export lager was famous around the world, establishing Philly as a brewing capital before Milwaukee and St. Louis would come to dominate the industry.

7. Schmidt's.
Prohibition utterly destroyed Philadelphia brewing. Where the city once had about 100 breweries, by the 1950s, there were only four remaining. The largest—and oldest—was Schmidt's. Opened in 1860, it brewed from a massive plant on Girard Avenue in Northern Liberties. While the rest of the country switched to Budweiser, Pabst, and Schlitz, Philadelphia could proudly enjoy "One Beautiful Beer" while watching Phillies games. Until 1987. After a century and a quarter, Schmidt's succumbed to competition from the much larger national brands, and for the first time in its history, Philadelphia was left with no breweries.

Big Daddy says: What, no Ortlieb's?

---

6. Yuengling Lager. Philly has always had a soft spot for the underdog, which may explain why a small, family-run brewery from coal country has always been so popular around town. Its sweet corn flavor is unmistakable, especially compared to so many bland macrobrews. It's so iconic around town, all you need to say is "Lager," and every bartender will know you're talking about Yuengling, America's oldest brewery.

5. Dock Street Bohemian. Just after Schmidt's closed, the city began to bounce back with new brewpubs and breweries. Dock Street opened at Logan Square in the late '80s and began making all-grain recipes without filler ingredients, like corn and rice. With its Bohemian Pilsner—the city's first world-class twentieth-century microbrew—Dock Street showed Philadelphia exactly what we were missing when we drank cheap BudMillerCoors.

4. Yards ESA. The spurt of new, local breweries continued through the 1990s, as beer drinkers started to get the idea that something special was happening. Specifically, this beer: Yards Extra Special Ale, the first fresh, cask-conditioned ale made in Philadelphia since the Prohibition. Malty and beautifully hopped, the beer gained exceptional flavor through additional fermentation after kegging. There was nothing else like this British-style ale in the region. It was Philadelphia's first signature microbrew (not to mention Joe Six-pack's wedding beer).

3. Victory HopDevil. In today's world of uber-hopped IPAs, it's hard to remember that just 25 years ago, hoppy American ales were a rarity. Hops were to be balanced with ample malts, not shoved into your face; even India pale ales weren't so full of the bitter buds. It was Downingtown's Victory Brewing that crushed that barrier, producing a superbly bitter ale as one of its year-round flagship brands—the first of its kind on the East Coast when it was introduced in 1996.

2. Nodding Head Ich Bin Ein Berliner Weisse. When the now-closed Center City brewpub introduced this tart wheat beer about 2001, few knew what to make of it. Berliner Weisse, fermented with lactic acid bacteria and often flavored with fruit syrup, was a nearly extinct style from northern Germany, and very little of it was exported to America. But Philly fell in love with Nodding Head's version and drank it so much that the tiny brewpub could claim without argument that it made more of the style than any brewery outside of Europe. As out-of-town brewers got a taste, the beer's fame spread. Today, Berliner Weisse is made by no fewer than 3,000 American breweries.

1. Tröegs Mad Elf. When Tröegs Mad Elf was introduced in 2002, very little of the holiday honey-and-cherry strong ale was brewed, and not many got a taste. By the next year, however, word had spread, and stores were shocked to find long lines at their doors. Mad Elf was the region's first cult beer—a brand whose assertive flavor and short supply spawned mad devotion. Today, it's mainly those cult beers that get all the attention from beer freaks.

P. J. Whelihan's has been serving the Philadelphia area since opening its first pub in 1993. They now have 23 restaurants, with two more getting ready to open as of this writing. Why? It's not rocket science. Every brand of beer you can imagine, terrific food (they provided Wing Bowl with its wings, after all), TVs broadcasting sports wherever you look, and great attached outdoor bars. And get this novel thought: it's all reasonably priced. The servers aren't hard on the eyes either.

Jim Fris is the CEO, but we know Jim as a down-to-earth nice guy who we'd see unloading wings off a truck on Wing Bowl morning. So we thought we would ask Jim to name his favorite area sports bars. Who better to ask than a man who has to stay atop his competition?

Jim didn't want to rank one above another, so these are in alphabetical order.

Barnaby's, Havertown, PA. Delco's sports headquarters.

Chickie's and Pete's, South Philly location. Crab fries and ballgames. You can't beat that one-two combination.

City Tap, Logan Square, Philadelphia. A giant video screen, good food, lots of taps with a great beer selection.

Fado, 1500 Locust Street, Center City. An Irish pub where soccer takes priority.

Field House, 1150 Filbert, Center City. They've got 40 beers on tap and 50 TV screens. It's a Penn State fan headquarters.

Maggie's Waterfront Café, Delaware Ave, Northeast Philly. The Northeast's sports hangout, right on the river.

McGillin's, 1310 Drury Lane, Center City. Come for the history, stay for the game.

Misconduct Tavern, 1511 Locust Street, Center City. They offer upscale pub fare and a killer beer list.

SugarHouse, 1001 N. Delaware Avenue. All bets are *on*. You can't beat sports and gambling.

Xfinity Live!, Stadium complex. For before, during, and after the games. Great victory celebration beers.

The Best Cheeseburger in the Delaware Valley—A Debate

"Hamburgers—the cornerstone of any nutritious breakfast."
—Jules Winnfield, *Pulp Fiction*

Glen says: In 2016, I went in search of the greatest burger in town. Over the course of six weeks, I ate 51 cheeseburgers at 42 different places in three states. Anything for radio.

I gained five pounds during my quest, raised my cholesterol level about 200 points, and received one angry phone call from my cardiologist.

I visited fancy steak houses, corner bars, chain burger joints, and brewpubs. I tried to order the same thing at each place—bacon cheeseburger with either grilled onions or mushrooms. No Boursin, broccoli rabe, or goat cheese to confuse things. Just a basic all-American burger. Bring me a draft beer or black-and-white milkshake on the side.

Here were some of the best:

5. Del Frisco's 1426-28 Chestnut Street, Philadelphia. The Bar Burger ($14) is 10 ounces of prime beef from the Chicago stockyards that's got an 80/20 meat-to-fat ratio. Not sure I can say the same for my midsection, but that appears to be the perfect breakdown to give the burger maximum flavor. It's seared on a flat-top grill so that all those beautiful juices don't have a chance to escape. Throw it on a buttered brioche roll, melt some cheddar, and toss on iceberg lettuce, tomato, onion, and that ubiquitous special sauce. I've had many a steak at Del Frisco's over the years, but some of the best are those put through a meat grinder.

4. Shake Shack, multiple locations. This iconic NYC-based chain's burger starts as a ground beef tower (antibiotic and hormone free) that's smashed and flattened against a hot griddle. It's fun to watch it sizzle, but, more importantly, the cooking process means it comes to you seared on the outside and pink on the inside. Medium means medium, not—like at many fast-food joints—overcooked to the consistency of a sneaker insole. I haven't been to In-N-Out Burger for more than a decade, but I'll put our East Coast Shake Shack against their West Coast franchise. Just try not to look at the calorie counts, which are posted on the wall and use numbers way higher than the cost of your burger.

3. Spot Gourmet Burger, a food truck usually parked at 33rd and Market, Philadelphia. Who would have thought a tiny two-person food truck would be a finalist in my contest? But Spot Burger deserves its cult following. There's a waitress to take your order, a guy yielding the spatula, and a long line of devotees. Think Soup Nazi, except with a cheery demeanor. The Spot Burger—grilled to order—starts with 90-percent lean, fresh-ground sirloin butts. It's jammed into a delicious potato roll and topped with bacon, cheddar, dill pickle chips, coleslaw, and a savory nine-ingredient Spot Sauce. I can't figure out all the ingredients in the sauce, but all in all, it's a great melding of flavors. Give this tiny upstart a try. You won't regret it.

2. Dog and Bull, 810 Bristol Pike, Croydon. Go to Croydon, go to Croydon, the followers of my Great Burger Hunt kept telling me. There is a treasure there, they said. Worth the drive. So I did—26.2 miles from my home (same as a marathon, coincidentally), one hour and change to Dog and Bull, where the burger was . . . well worth the drive! It's a huge hand-formed patty, perfectly cooked outside and in, seasoned—but lightly enough that the Grade A beef can speak for itself. The Cheddar Ale Bacon Burger comes adorned with crispy fried onions, the kind people put on those infernal holiday-season green bean casseroles, only a lot tastier. Nice touch. Different.

1. Rouge, Rittenhouse Square, Philadelphia. Jeff Lurie has his gold standard, I've got mine. And this is the standard by which all great burgers must forever be judged. It's legendary, gaining acclaim from everyone from Oprah to legendary food critic Alan Richman, who listed it among "20 burgers you must eat before you die." I don't know about the other 19, but I could eat a Rouge Burger and then die happily.

It's made up of a 12-ounce custom beef blend patty, caramelized onions, and a nutty gruyère cheese on a buttery brioche challah bun. The first bite is bursting with flavor. So is the second, the third, and the fourth. Hall of Fame status.

Big Daddy says: Burger and fries. Does it get any more American? If I donated any of my organs to science (and who the hell would want them?), doctors would cut me open and thousands of burgers and fries would come falling out of my body. I am always—*always*—in the mood for a burger. When all else fails on a menu, you never fail with a burger. NEVER! There's no mood that doesn't fit a burger, is there?

I am going to get no fancier on my list than a bacon cheeseburger. That's as complicated as I like my burgers to get. And although I have eaten 467,348 Roy Roger's Double-R-Bar Burgers in my life, my list has no national chains. I also have to give a special shout-out to the defunct downtown H. A. Winston's that had the greatest burger this town ever produced.

Here are five of my favorites:

---

5. Thai Burger, 7 South Broadway, Pitman, N.J. I know what you're thinking. *Thai* Burger? You're reading that right. When a friend told me I had to check these bad boys out, I replied that I don't like Thai food, but he so insisted that he said if I went with him, he would buy. So I was in. Boy, was I glad I took my buddy up on his offer because I've been there at least 50 times since. Yes, they serve Thai food, but their burgers are as American as Pam Anderson and simply incredible. And the fries they serve are good old-fashioned regular fries. Not the newfangled, annoying, thin, curly kind all covered with seasoning. It's a small, unpretentious joint you'll just love. Call ahead.

4. P. J. Whelihan's, 799 DeKalb Pike, Blue Bell. Start off with eight ounces of Angus beef. Throw in two slices of yellow cheddar and two strips of smoked-apple bacon with a healthy dose of lettuce, tomato, and onions. It's all served up on a kaiser bun that's kind of "snowflaky." You've got a real winner. The 30-plus TV screens make it a great place to watch a game, and the servers ain't bad on the eyes either.

3. Krick Wuder, 2676 Bridge St., Philadelphia. This Bridesburg saloon and restaurant sits among all those I-95 refineries, but do not let its surroundings fool you. Seek it out. Inside, it's a gem with beautiful hardwood floors, and not only are their burgers tremendous, you simply must check out their scrapple sandwiches, which will just blow you away. So come with a great appetite and wolf down both.

2. Charlie's Hamburgers, 336 Kedron Ave., Folsom. Remember the "cheeseburger-cheeseburger" skit with John Belushi and the gang on *Saturday Night Live*? (By the way, I was in the real joint in Chicago.) That's the feel of Charlie's. It's one of those places where when you call them on the phone, the guy answers by saying, "Yeah?" The burgers are so tiny that you gotta eat about five of them, but believe me, these greasy suckers are worth it. They butter the bun, which is a unique touch. They've been around since 1935, and when I lived in Upper Darby, I must have gone to their old location off Baltimore Pike a zillion times. Fantastic shakes too.

1. New Wave Café, 784 S. 3rd Street, Philadelphia. First off, it's one of our favorite Queen Village watering holes. Nothing fancy, just a good old-fashioned tavern with a strong jukebox and cold beer. There's even a dartboard in the back. When we questioned the owner, Aly, if we could ask the chef what goes into these tasty babies, he replied, "Are you kidding? It's a secret!" But he did reveal that they're cooked with eight ounces of Angus beef that's hand formed, never pressed, never frozen, and cooked on a grated surface and not a flat grill. Not sure what that all means, but they sure taste great. Many unusual cheeses to choose from, and they're all served up on Vilotti Pisanelli bread (which, you might notice, I'm partial to). You must check these out.

Years back, on a slow summer night, I was trying to fill four hours of radio on WIP. I wondered aloud who made the best ribs in the Delaware Valley—more so because they're my favorite food than I was looking for a show topic. Well, all the lines lit up. Every caller had a strong opinion, emphatic that his favorite place was the only spot to go.

And so I came up with an idea. Over the next few weeks, I went out and tried ribs from about 20 joints. I picked my top six, and one night I invited in Temple coach John Chaney, my radio partner Ray Didinger, and two 320-pound Eagles linemen to help me pick the best on the radio. The winner was an upstart South Jersey barbeque named Fat Jack's.

Since then, my food hunts have grown. I pick a different item each year—"guy food," as I define it—and persuade WIP to give me the budget to go out and try 40 to 50 places. We end the shebang with a big event where the public gets to eat for free and help me judge the best of the best.

My life really is one big scam.

Anyway, here's a year-by-year history of my more recent food hunts, with the winners and other finalists. I can't promise you they're as good moving into the future as they were when I visited them. But I suspect you'll find some gems on this list that you've never sampled.

2018: Tacos

Winner: El Vez, Center City
Winner: Sancho Pistola's, Northern Liberties
Winner: Vida, Havertown, PA
Teresa's Next Door, Wayne, PA
Dos Gringos, Media, PA
Tortilla Press, Collingswood, NJ

2017: Meatballs

Winner: Ralph's Italian Restaurant, South Philadelphia
Winner: In Riva, East Falls
Altomonte's, Doylestown
Amis Trattoria, Center City
Little Nonna's, Center City
Villa di Roma, South Philadelphia

2016: Food Trucks

Winner: Rio Brazilian Steak Truck, Brazilian Steak Sandwich
Winner: Pie-Stand: Chocolate Cheesecake Pie
Chewy's Food Truck, Honey Sriracha Fried Chicken Wings
Mama's Meatball Truck, Mama's Meatballs
Sum Pig Truck, Smoked Pork Parfait
Undrgrnd Donuts, Doughnuts

2015: Bacon Creation

Winner: Harry's Blue Bell Taproom, Blue Bell, PA, Bacon-Wrapped Scallops
Winner: The Pop Shop, Collingswood, NJ, Shakin' Bacon Milkshake
Bieler's Doughnuts, Reading Terminal Market, Bacon Maple Doughnut
Cresheim Valley Grain Exchange, Philadelphia, Smoked Gouda Bacon Mac and Cheese
Grubhouse, Philadelphia, Bacon-Wrapped Jalapeño Tots
Khyber Pass Pub, Old City, Bacon Grease Popcorn

2014: Hot Sandwiches

Winner: Shank's Pier 40, South Philadelphia, Chicken Italiano
Carlino's Specialty Foods, Ardmore, Hot Roast Pork
Hershel's East Side Deli, Reading Terminal Market, Hot Pastrami on Rye
McNally's Tavern, Chestnut Hill, the Schmitter
Old Original Nick's Roast Beef, South Philadelphia, Roast Beef on the Outs
Pastificio Homemade Pasta Co., South Philadelphia, Meatball Sandwich

2013: Italian Hoagies

Winner: Paesano's, Fishtown
Winner: Sarcone's Deli, South Philadelphia
Abbruzzi and Giunta's, Mount Laurel, NJ
Carmen's Deli, Bellmawr, NJ
Pallante's, Richboro
PrimoHoagies, various locations

2012: Cheesesteaks

Winner: John's Roast Pork, Pennsport
Dalessandro's, Roxborough
Grey Lodge Pub, Northeast
Joe's Steaks and Soda Shop, Northeast
Sonny's Famous Steaks, Old City
Steve's Prince of Steaks, Philadelphia
Tony Luke's, South Philadelphia

2011: Pizza

Winner: Tacconelli's, Port Richmond
Celebre's, South Philly
Franzone's, Bridgeport
Lazaro's, South Philly
Mama Palma's Gourmet Pizza, Center City
Marra's, South Philly

My Favorite Philadelphia Restaurants :: Brandon Brooks

Right guard Brandon Brooks joined the Eagles as a free agent in 2016 and was a major factor in winning Super Bowl LII. He made the Pro Bowl in 2017 and 2018. The 335-pounder is a huge (literally) fan of this city and its food scene.

5. Harp and Crown, 1525 Sansom. I love everything on the menu, but my favorite is the Spicy Soppressata Pizza. It comes with shishito peppers, which are like jalapeños, along with provolone cheese and honey on top. It sounds a little strange, but it's delicious.

4. Del Frisco's Grille, 225 S. Broad Street. I started going to Del Frisco's Grille when I played in Houston (2012–2015) and was happy to find it when I moved here. I like their Double Eagle Steakhouses as well, but I've got to get dressed up for that; I can put on a T-shirt and head for the Grille. It's very laid back. If I'm a little hungry, I order the 16-ounce filet, medium-rare, maybe Oscar style or with béarnaise on top. And they've got a good bar scene. My drink? Johnny Walker Blue on the rocks.

3. Ralph's Italian Restaurant, 760 South 9th Street. I know it's the oldest Italian restaurant in the country, and I like that it's great and the food never changes. I usually get the veal in marinara sauce.

2. Baby Blues BBQ, 3402 Sansom Street. As I said, I played four seasons in Houston, so I got used to excellent barbecue. I was skeptical here. What barbecue would Philly have? But Jason Kelce took me here for the first time, and it was great. Ribs, shoulder tips, wings, beef brisket—they're all terrific.

> **Glen says:** I've been going to Baby Blues for years myself and was honored to have a menu item named after me. The Macnow Sandwich is a combo of pulled pork, sharp cheddar, coleslaw, and honey-soaked hot peppers. Try it next time you're there.

1. Butcher Bar, 2034 Chestnut Street. I've been to Village Whiskey, Rouge, and others, but to me, this is the best hamburger in the city. I order it medium or medium-rare, with everything but the pickles. Every menu item is good there. They have big guy-friendly stuff—like a thick-cut, maple-soaked bacon appetizer, homemade cornbread in a skillet, and a big cookie in a mini-skillet with ice cream. I'm hungry thinking about it.

Barchard, Shorr-Parks, and Seltzer make up the WIP "Go Birds" team, producing podcasts, radio shows, and blogs. They are a motley crew of Eagles fandom, journalism, strong opinions, and occasional fart jokes. You can follow their work at 94WIP.com.
They combined to write this list, putting their names by the entries each wrote.

10. Carson Wentz to Nelson Agholor on Opening Day (John). The first touchdown of the season was among the most special moments. Agholor (who had been doubted for two seasons) and Wentz (who had lots of doubters in the off-season) connected to make a joint statement. Fletcher Cox looked leaner and meaner in that opener; Brandon Graham looked faster than before. Everything felt different. This was special.

9. Jake Elliott's FG vs. Giants (Eliot). Thirteen seconds. That is how close the Eagles' special season came to never happening. After allowing 24 unanswered points in the fourth quarter, the Eagles got the ball back with 13 seconds remaining and the reality of falling to 1–2. Instead, Wentz found Alshon Jeffery 19 yards downfield to put the Eagles in Giants territory. Sixty-one yards later (and one promise by Wentz to give Elliott his game check) the Eagles had the moment they needed to solidify that this season would be unlike any other.

8. The Eagles tell the world they are for real against the Panthers (John). A lot of national pundits wanted this team to falter; they wanted to see where the holes were because, hey, this team can't be that good, right? I mean, the Birds only squeaked by those Giants, helped by a disallowed Odell Beckham Jr. TD. They looked terrible against the Chiefs and barely edged the Chargers. But on this Thursday night, Wentz, Zach Ertz, and Cox showed the world how good this team really was. They weren't considered pretenders by many after this one.

7. Wentz's coming-out party on *Monday Night Football* vs. Washington (John). "And Wentz will be . . . escaping!" Sean McDonough's voice will always be tied to this game for me. This was it. For those who had stuck by Carson Wentz's talent and had planted their flag, this solidified everything. Wentz's Houdini ability was one thing, but hitting his fourth read in Corey Clement for a touchdown in the red zone while getting hit in the process? That's Joe Montana stuff.

6. The celebrations (James). Philly's first time couldn't have been more special. Not only did this team overcome tremendous adversity and injuries to win in storybook fashion, but it also comprised a group of good guys who seemed to genuinely like each other. Nothing spoke to that more than the celebrations. From Torrey Smith's home run swing to both Electric Slides, this team had fun winning—and that made it fun for us, too.

5. Wentz goes down (Eliot). As Wentz walked into the blue medical tent at the Los Angeles Coliseum on December 11, there was a feeling among media at the game that his injury wasn't serious. He had, after all, just thrown a touchdown pass, breaking the franchise single-season record at 33. But less than an hour later, I watched Wentz stand in the back of a tunnel, trying to avoid media members before being carted away for good. Players celebrated the win, but deep down, the feeling that night was that the season was over. Enter, of course, Nick Foles.

4. The underdog masks (James). I guarantee Chris Long and Lane Johnson had no idea the impact they'd create by donning dog masks. But they captured the imagination of the fan base and became a galvanizing symbol of this team. The swagger and confidence they emanated somehow made us feel confident, too. Absolutely no one believed in a Foles-led Eagles team—except for us. As silly as they seemed, the dog masks were one big reason why.

3. Vikings get crushed (James). Patrick Robinson. That's all I need to say. Any Eagles fan hearing that name will immediately flash back with vivid accuracy to Robinson's Pick Six—the play that changed everything. In that moment, we knew the Eagles were heading to the Super Bowl. It took another 31 unanswered points for it to become official, but it was over the moment P-Rob took it to the house.

2. Philly Special (James). The best sound in a sports stadium is the silence of 60,000 people all taking a second to realize what just happened—followed by the entire place erupting. That is exactly what happened when Nick Foles caught a touchdown in the corner of the end zone. The play design, the guts to call it, the execution. There will be another Super Bowl champion. There will never be another Philly Special.

1. Super Bowl win. Eliot: I've been in many Super Bowl–winning locker rooms. None of them were like the scene that took place when the Eagles won. Players threw confetti in the air. Coaches hugged. Tears flowed as the trophy was passed around. Some players searched for their family to celebrate. I thought about my dad as well in that moment—the games we used to go to together and all the fans back in Philadelphia. The 2017 Eagles will be remembered for winning the trophy, but the team was special because of how they connected to fans. Oftentimes the championship doesn't mean as much to the players who win it as it does the fans who have waited years for it. When the Eagles finally won, it is safe to say everyone—from the players, to fans, to everyone in Philadelphia—felt the magnitude of the moment.

John and James: We were at the Fillmore in Philly with thousands of Eagles fans from across the world. The moment Brandon Graham strip-sacked Tom Brady, we both put our hands on our heads and held back tears until we no longer could. This is what it's supposed to feel like; this is when you know. Of course about 30 seconds later we had to snap out of it because the game wasn't over and Tom Brady had the ball. But after two more minutes of game clock, we walked 45 minutes to the celebration on Broad Street. We livestreamed that joyous flock of Eagles fans to the entire world. It was the best family reunion you've ever attended because everyone was hugging and crying for joy. This was finally our time.

Sometimes the most unexpected of mortals can reach up and turn in a magical moment. Here's a dirty dozen of otherwise-forgettable average Joes who we'll always remember for one great performance.

12. Steve Jeltz. The weakest of weak-hitting shortstops hit all of five homers in eight Major League seasons. Somehow, on June 8, 1989, he hit two in one game—one lefty and one righty. His fan club, all nine members, still talk about it.

11. Andy Delmore. Came up late in the 1999–2000 season to help the Flyers' exhausted defense. Played so-so in the regular season. Then, in the playoffs, he had a two-goal night against the Penguins. Two games later, he popped in three more. No rookie defenseman had ever scored a hat trick in the playoffs or five goals in one series. A year later, Delmore was gone.

10. Kim Batiste. The seldom-used infielder had just one postseason at bat for the 1993 Phils, but he made the most of it. In the bottom of the 10th in Game 1 of the NLCS, he beat the Braves, driving in John Kruk with a walk-off double. Career regular-season average of Kimothy Emil Batiste: .234. Career postseason average: 1.000.

9. Bobby Hoying. In his first three starts for the Eagles in 1997, he threw for 835 yards, with six touchdowns and just one interception. Some of us were seeing the next Van Brocklin. Unfortunately, in his next 11 starts, he tossed four touchdowns and 15 interceptions. Turns out he threw more like the next Van Morrison.

8. Darren Jensen. No player in sports ever had a tougher call-up assignment. Jensen, a career AHL goalie, had to start the November 14, 1985, Flyers game three days after popular star goalie Pelle Lindbergh died in a car crash. Against the Cup champion Oilers yet. Jensen had his moment, holding Wayne Gretzky and teammates to three goals in a winning effort. Jensen won just 14 more NHL games in his career.

7. Willie Burton. Just eight Sixers ever scored 50 points in a game. You could probably guess seven of them—Iverson, Wilt, Moses, guys like that. And then there's this career 10-point-per-game scorer who went off for 53 against the Heat one night in 1994. He did it attempting just 19 field goals, which is an NBA record for fewest attempts in a 50-point game. "He played tonight with the sparrow on his shoulder," said Coach John Lucas. We still don't know what *that* means.

6. Koy Detmer. When Donovan McNabb got hurt in Week 11 of the 2002 season, Eagles fans figured a promising season was ruined. Detmer stepped in against the 49ers on *Monday Night Football* and went 18-for-26 for 224 yards and two touchdowns. Then God appeared to wake up, see how ridiculously well Detmer was playing, and immediately dislocate his elbow before things really got out of hand. That, of course, led to . . . A. J. Feeley, who won four of the next five games and would be another valid name on this list.

5. Marty Bystrom. Probably the Phils' best-ever September call-up. Bystrom started five late-season games in 1980 and won all of them. Then he won a playoff game and another in the World Series against Kansas City. After that, well . . . imagine what it's like to have your career peak at age 21.

4. J. J. Daigneault. For many years he held an NHL record: Most Teams Played For, career (10). That mark has since been passed by Mike Sillinger, who hit 12 teams on his tour, including the Orange and Black. But Daigneault's two-season stop in Philadelphia will always be remembered for one of the most memorable goals in franchise history—his slap shot past Edmonton's Grant Fuhr with 5:32 left was the winner in Game 6 of the 1987 Stanley Cup Finals. It was his only postseason goal for the Flyers.

3. Robert Person. As a pitcher, he was a mediocrity, with a 4.64 ERA strung over nine seasons. As a hitter, he was a joke, with a .117 career average. But on June 2, 2002, at the Vet, this Person became a Superman, slugging a grand slam and a three-run homer against the Expos. In the rest of his at bats that season, Person went 0-for-22 with 17 whiffs.

2. Al Hill. Made his debut with the Broad Street Bullies on February 14, 1977. And what a debut it was. Hill set an NHL record by recording five points—two goals, three assists—in his first big-league game. We don't know if Gretzky lost sleep that night, but it turned out that the Great One's scoring records were never really in jeopardy.

1. Trey Burton. Truth be told, he might be too talented for this list—the $32 million, four-year deal he signed with Chicago when he left Philly speaks to that. But, hey, he was a third-string tight end here with just 63 catches over four seasons. And then came Super Bowl LII. And then came the Philly Special, with Burton, of all people, throwing the greatest touchdown pass in the history of the franchise. A statue ought to be built of everyone involved in that play.

Edward Malcolm Snider brought the National Hockey League to Philadelphia when he founded the Flyers in 1966 and was the driving force behind the franchise until he passed away in 2016. Mr. Snider wrote this chapter for us in 2006.

The Greatest

5. 1974 Semifinals, Game 7, Flyers vs. NY Rangers, May 5, 1974. We beat them, 4–3, at the Spectrum in a vicious, exciting contest. I really believe this game proved to us that we had what it took to win the Cup. The entire series was hard fought, and each team won every game at home. Thank God we had the home ice advantage.

4. 2000 Eastern Conference Semifinals, Game 4, Flyers at Pittsburgh, May 4, 2000. If Keith Primeau hadn't scored the winning goal in the fifth overtime, we would have had players crawling up and down the ice on their knees. I personally don't know how any of the players could withstand that long of a playoff game—6 hours and 56 minutes—under that kind of pressure. The game ended around 2:00 a.m., with us winning, 2–1. My friends and I flew home and had breakfast at the Melrose Diner at dawn.

3. 1975 Stanley Cup Finals, Game 6, Flyers at Buffalo, May 27, 1975. We won it in Buffalo, 2–0, on goals by Bill Clement and Bob Kelly, and, of course, more great goaltending by Bernie Parent. Then we came back for another humongous parade—two million people.

2. Flyers vs. Soviet Army Team, January 11, 1976. The Soviet Army Team was, in reality, the Soviet All-Star team. They had won all of their games against NHL teams to that point, and it was up to us to show that *we* were the cold warriors. We beat them emphatically—so much so that they walked off the ice during the game and refused to come back until (NHL commissioner) Clarence Campbell and I told them they weren't going to get paid. They came back on the ice but were little competition for what I think was our best team ever. We beat them 4–1, and the game wasn't really that close. If Parent hadn't gotten hurt, there is no doubt that we would have won our third consecutive Cup in '76.

1. 1974 Stanley Cup Finals, Game 6, Flyers vs. Boston, May 19, 1974. The most incredible game ever, not only because we were the first expansion team to win the Cup but also because Bernie Parent played the greatest game I have ever seen a goalie play against one of the most high-powered offenses ever—Bobby Orr, Phil Esposito, et al. No one wanted to go back to Boston for Game 7, and the 1–0 lead against that team kept everyone on edge for every second of action. I've never seen anything like the celebration when the final buzzer sounded. For that matter, I've never seen anything as amazing as the parade that brought two million people out onto Broad Street. The parade was the largest crowd I've ever seen in professional sports history and remained so until the next year.

The Worst

3. 1980 Stanley Cup Finals, Game 6, Flyers at New York Islanders, May 24, 1980. That season we went 35 games without a loss, setting the all-time professional record. If we won Game 6 on Long Island, there is no doubt in my mind we would have won the Cup back home in Game 7. But during the game, Islanders defenseman Denis Potvin clearly and illegally batted the puck into the net from over his head. The refs counted the goal. Then, to add insult to injury, Leon Stickle made his infamous noncall on a pass that was two feet off-sides, which led to the Islanders' tying goal. That game is etched in my memory. I'll always believe it cost us the Cup in 1980.

2. Flyers vs. Chicago, January 30, 1969. The worst loss ever, as the Blackhawks beat us 12–0. Our fans couldn't believe it. I wanted to crawl under the stands when the game was over. I wondered that night if we would ever win another game.

1. Flyers vs. St. Louis, November 7, 1968. We lost to St. Louis, 8–0, on our own ice. If that wasn't bad enough, Red Berenson, their great left winger, had six goals, just one short of the all-time record. St. Louis, believe it or not, was our biggest rival and archenemy at the time. What a humiliation.

Jim Jackson has been the Flyers play-by-play broadcaster since 1993, first on radio and then TV—ably calling more than 2,000 games. Jim has also been a part of Phillies broadcasts since 2007. He agreed to pick up this list in 2001, where Ed Snider ended his.

The Greatest

5. 2012 Eastern Conference Quarterfinals, Game 2, Flyers at Pittsburgh, April 13, 2012. Any time the Flyers beat the Penguins in a playoff game, it has to be listed among the greatest. This game pitted the upstart Flyers against a Penguins team many expected to roll. Jake Voráček's overtime goal shocked the Pens and their fans in Game 1, and then came this game, when the Flyers proved once and for all that they were going to be a tough out for Sidney Crosby and his gang.

It didn't start well, as Crosby scored a goal and set up another to help the Pens to a 3–1 lead after the first period. But then the Flyers absolutely went off. Claude Giroux and 19-year-old Sean Couturier both recorded hat tricks in an eventual 8–5 victory. The Flyers spoiled the Penguins' first playoff venture in their new arena and went on to win the series in six games to the surprise of many.

4. Flyers vs. Ottawa, March 5, 2004. This was absolute chaos, and the fans loved it. The Flyers and Senators combined for an NHL record 419 penalty minutes in a game that just became one brawl after another in the third period. It started with expected combatants Donald Brashear and Rob Ray squaring off, escalated into goaltenders Robert Esche and Patrick Lalime going toe to toe, and ended with nonfighters like Patrick Sharp and Shaun Van Allen dropping the gloves. What I remember most is the empty benches by the end of the game, with most players having been ejected. That, plus the volume level of the fans with each fight that broke out. By the way, the Flyers won, 5–3.

3. 2004 Eastern Conference Semifinals, Game 6, Flyers at Toronto, May 4, 2004. This one makes the list because of one sequence I consider as exciting as any I have had the opportunity to call as a voice of the Flyers. No fan of the Orange and Black will forget the huge overtime hit by Darcy Tucker on Sami Kapanen, followed by the dazed Flyer forward simply trying to get his bearings and return to the Philadelphia bench. As Keith Primeau literally reeled him in, Robert Esche made several huge saves to keep the Flyers' hopes alive. Moments later, Jeremy Roenick jumped over the boards into a two-on-one and beat Ed Belfour to send the Flyers on to the Eastern Conference Finals. I was out of breath by the time JR scored and just barely had enough voice to get through the call.

2. 2010 Eastern Conference Semifinals, Game 7, Flyers at Boston, May 14, 2010. If an author or playwright penned the story of this Flyers-Bruins series and, in particular, the final game, they would have been turned down because it was just too hokey. The Flyers fell behind in the second-round series three games to none and were dead to rights. Then, they pulled an amazing feat by winning the next three. In Game 7, they fell behind, 3–0—and were *still* able to overcome that? Impossible, right? I would have said so if I hadn't seen it with my own eyes. I'll always remember Peter Laviolette applying the magic touch with one of his timeouts with the score 3–0, and back came the Flyers. Simon Gagne's third-period goal was the difference, and the Flyers became just the third NHL team to overcome a three-game deficit to win a series. It's always fun to be part of history.

1. Flyers vs. New York Rangers, April 11, 2010. Another made-for-Hollywood script. I put this at the top because of the simplicity of it all. After struggling down the stretch of the season, the Flyers faced one of their most heated rivals, the Rangers, in a true win-ner-take-all scenario. The winner went to the playoffs; the loser went home. It was like Game 7, except it was the culmination of an 82-game season instead of a seven-game series. Then it came down to a shootout, and the Flyers had to find a way to beat one of the all-time best shootout goalies in Henrik Lundqvist. Danny Briere and 22-year-old Claude Giroux solved King Henrik, while Brian Boucher made enough saves at the other end. Pandemonium broke out in South Philly. I know a lot of people don't like the shootout, but it made for high drama and an epic conclusion in this instance.

The Worst

3. 2001 Eastern Conference Quarterfinals, Game 6, Flyers at Buffalo, April 21, 2001. The largest playoff loss in Flyers' history. After five closely contested games, the Sabres took apart the Flyers, 8–0, in Game 6 in Buffalo. I was not broadcasting that day as the network had an exclusive. I remember it as being the only time I was actually happy I was not calling a game. I usually hate sitting and watching, but as the Sabres piled on in this one, I found myself sympathizing for radio play-by-play man Tim Saunders.

2. 2009 Eastern Conference Quarterfinals, Game 6, Flyers vs. Pittsburgh, April 25, 2009. Once again, I wasn't broadcasting this one. The Flyers entered this one down three games to two in the series. As the Flyers built a 3–0 lead on goals by Mike Knuble, Joffrey Lupul, and Daniel Brière, I was getting excited at the thought of calling a Game 7 showdown in Pittsburgh. Our building was rocking and the Penguins were reeling. Then Dan Carcillo dropped the gloves with Pittsburgh's Max Talbot and everything seemed to change. Evgeni Malkin and Sidney Crosby took over, and the Penguins rallied back to win, 5–3, on their way to the Stanley Cup. The Game 7 showdown never happened, and what an empty feeling it left.

1. 2010 Stanley Cup Finals, Game 6, Flyers vs. Chicago, June 9, 2010. Two wins from the Cup after a miraculous run that included the shootout win against the Rangers on the final day of the season and the historic comeback against the Bruins, the Flyers were still a confident bunch even though they trailed three games to two in the series. But then it went to overtime . . . and I'm still looking for the puck that Patrick Kane put in the goal. Getting that close to the ultimate prize and falling short on such a bizarre goal was a bitter pill for the team and its fans. The Flyers have not been close since, but a young nucleus of impressive talent backstopped by the promising Carter Hart gives hope. Hey, there's always hope.

The Best Team Nicknames

Sure, players get catchy nicknames, but sometimes a team is worthy as well. Or even a part of a team. Here are the 10 best in Philadelphia history.

10. Dream Team. Okay, we're touching a nerve with this disaster. It was backup quarterback Vince Young who looked at all the free agents Joe Banner was signing in 2011 and declared, "From Nnamdi (Asomugha) to Dominique Rodgers-Cromartie to Jason Babin to myself, this is kind of a dream team." Nightmare was more like it.

Dishonorable mention: The short-lived Sixers FEDS of 2017—for Fultz, Embiid, Dario (Šarić), and Simmons.

9. LCB Line. It wasn't as catchy as Buffalo's "French Connection" of the same period, but it was more potent. Among them, Reggie Leach, Bobby Clarke, and Bill Barber collected 141 goals and 181 assists in 1975–1976. Still, for us, the name always calls to mind the Pennsylvania Liquor Control Board.

8. Mighty Mites. We're going way back on this one, so if you remember Coach Bill Ferguson's undersized St. Joe's basketball teams, you're well into collecting Social Security. The Mites consisted of 6-foot-4 passing guru Matt Guokas Sr. plus four guys who didn't reach the "you must be this tall" line for most carnival rides. Still, they compiled a 54–17 record over four seasons in the mid-1930s.

7. Four Aces. Every kid in the Delaware Valley had that *Sports Illustrated* cover of the 2011 Phillies rotation tacked on his or her bedroom wall. Together Roy Halladay, Cliff Lee, Cole Hamels, and Roy Oswalt went 59–33 with a 2.70 ERA, leading the Phils to a franchise-record 102 wins. Of course it was the "other guy," fifth starter "Fat Joe" Blanton, who launched that homer in the World Series.

6. Gang Green Defense. Buddy Ryan's defense demanded a worthy nickname. With their all-black shoes and nasty swagger, the players behaved like a street gang. So Gang Green fit nicely. Funny thing is, the unit had its best season in 1991, after Buddy left and Bud Carson took over the defense. That season they finished first in the NFL against the rush and the pass, first in sacks, and first in takeaways.

5. Legion of Doom. No one recalls Jim Montgomery of the Flyers, but everyone remembers his contribution to history. Watching Eric Lindros, John LeClair, and Mikael Renberg bully their teammates in practice one day, Montgomery was reminded of the group of super-villains who regularly battled Superman.

"They look like the Legion of Doom out there," Montgomery remarked. The trio—with an average size of 6-foot-3 and 228 pounds—combined for 305 goals from 1994 to 1997. Then, of course, personality issues turned the Flyers into a real-life Bizarro World.

4. Macho Row. It was the perfect handle for that swarthier-than-thou squad of Darren Daulton, Lenny Dykstra, Dave Hollins, John Kruk, and the rest of the '93 Phils. Lots of testosterone in that clubhouse—some of it reportedly from hypodermic needles.

3. Whiz Kids. By some accounts, the 1950 NL Champion Phillies were the youngest pennant winner ever assembled. We can't verify that, but consider this nucleus—Richie Ashburn, 23; Robin Roberts, 23; Curt Simmons, 21; and Del Ennis, 25. Perhaps the most amazing thing is that the group never won the pennant again.

2. Wheeze Kids. In this case, the sequel nickname beats the original. The 1983 Phils were, in fact, a last-gasp collection of aging mercenaries. Pete Rose was 42, Joe Morgan 39, and Tony Perez 41 when they tried to reassemble the Big Red Machine in Philadelphia. On a side note, isn't this the most forgotten league champion our city has ever seen?

1. Broad Street Bullies. Give credit to newspaperman Jack Chevalier of the defunct *Bulletin* for being the first to come up with the nickname of Bullies of Broad Street. The name reflected a team that regularly prompted opponents to come down with the Philly flu—a mysterious illness that struck just as the team bus turned onto Broad Street. The Bullies won back-to-back Stanley Cups and produced three Hall of Famers, but the highlight was probably the 4–1 thrashing of the Soviet Red Army team on January 11, 1976.

10. The fact that fans put up with tied games as long as they did. I must admit that as a kid it really bothered me and contributed to me not embracing the game. I hate ties! They say they are like kissing your sister, but they are way worse than that. They're more like having sex with Roseanne Barr.

9. How, if you bumped into Bobby Clarke walking down Chestnut Street and asked him for directions to Atlantic City, he would *still*, to this day, find a way to bitch about the Lindros family. And Lindros is long retired.

8. Tim Peel. Seriously, does he ref every single game?

7. Guys skating around with no sticks. They resemble Herman Munster on skates out there. Who cares if your stick is broken or if you dropped it? Pick it up!

6. The face-off dance. "You put your right skate in, you put your left skate out . . ." Drop the stinkin' puck already. I know jump balls in basketball are also ridiculous, but there's only a couple of those a game.

5. Players with no vowels in their names. I know I'm sounding like some ugly North American here, but please, bring back players like Gordie Howe and Keith Jones (two players never confused for each other). Names I could pronounce. And what's up with the three little non-capital letters that begin James van Riemsdyk's last name? Why isn't the *v* capped?

4. Records like 16–12–8 OTL? What the hell is an OTL, Glen? Oh, I'm sorry, it's not a new home shopping network, it's the network that carries the NHL. Or is that the OLC? Who the hell knows?

3. Third-period officiating. How ridiculous is it that hockey refs swallow their whistles during the third period? Basketball refs don't ignore a shooter getting hacked during the fourth quarter. If they did, there would be no scoring down the stretch. Why can't hockey refs call the entire game the same way?

2. Switching lines during play. Okay, let's get this straight, Glen. If basketball played with this insane rule, a great defender could block a shot, run out of bounds, and be replaced by a great shooter on the other end, without ever calling a timeout. It's proof that Canadians love their beer, because they must have been hammered when they came up with this ridiculous rule.

1. The Columbus Blue Jackets. Why? Just why?

Ten Things Glen Doesn't Get about the NBA

First off, let me address a few of your lamer points, Big Daddy. You miss the days when hockey players had easy-to-pronounce Anglo-Saxon names? Okay, try these NBA tongue twisters on for size—Giannis Antetokounmpo. Sviatoslav Mykhailiuk. Thabo Sefolosha. Whatever happened to Joe Smith?

Then you rip the officiating in the NHL, which, I'll admit, is not good. But, seriously, are you going to defend a league that employs both Scott Foster *and* Lauren Holtkamp?

And feel free to tease the Columbus Blue Jackets. But then explain the Utah Jazz. There's a franchise that A) plays in a city that fits the lifestyle of exactly *zero* NBA players and B) is named for what? That swinging sound coming from the Mormon Tabernacle Choir?

Now that I've cleared that up, here are a few things that I don't get that didn't quite crack my list: the slam dunk contest, the draft lottery (fix!), why fans can't keep balls that go into the stands, and how come they call them "shorts" when they go below the knees. More like culottes.

Here are my top 10:

10. The rules make no sense. Like being able to call time out while flying out of bounds. Like the "advance-to-half-court-on-a-timeout" rule. That's my favorite. I want to put that in football so the Eagles can gain an extra 10 yards before attempting a game-winning field goal.

9. Why does the first round of the playoffs take forever? Seriously, when the Sixers beat the Heat a few years back, they opened the series on an April Sunday, rested three days to put Game 2 on TNT, gave the players time off for good behavior, traveled to Miami for Game 3, broke a week for Easter, and wrapped things up under Independence Day fireworks.

8. The Disgruntled Superstar Bingo. Every season, a few top players in the league get fed up with their franchise and start whining that they want to move on. In 2018–2019 it was Anthony Davis, Kristaps Porziņģis, and Kyrie Irving, who announced to Boston fans in January, "I don't owe anybody shit." Well, he probably owes a few bucks to all those loyalists who bought his jersey in green, even if they are Celtics fans.

7. The league has more deadwood than *Gilligan's Island*. If you underperform your contract in baseball or hockey, they can send you to the minors. In the NFL, they just cut you. In the NBA, you just keep hanging around.

6. Why can't a $23-million-a-year player make half his free throws? The basket isn't moving, no one's defending you—explain all the bricks and air balls. My 15-year-old niece sinks 70 percent from the so-called charity stripe, so how did Andre Drummond manage to miss 23 in a single game? Maybe this is why NBA players feel the silly need to congratulate teammates after every free throw attempt, make or miss.

5. Why does the last minute take an hour to play? Hey, Coach, your team is down 14, there are milliseconds left. Stop fouling! You're not coming back! Please, just let us go home already.

4. The NBA assaults its fans with more bright lights and screaming barkers than the Las Vegas strip. After some baskets, Miami's PA announcer draws out calls, "Jusssss-tiiiiice Winsssssssss-low for twoooooo, from Gorrrrrrr-annn Draaaaaagic!" that take longer than some teams' possessions. Why does it take 20 minutes and a laser light show to introduce the home team?

3. The cap. Nobody can explain it. Because, really, no one understands it. There are exceptions, exemptions, and enough pie charts to confound a Penn math professor. The NFL and NHL salary caps have ceilings and floors, and basically, that's it. In the NBA, there are special cap rules for injured players, retired players, and slovenly indolent wastes of space—also known as *Geigers*. There literally have been guys counted against the NBA salary cap who were dead.

2. The NBA encourages and rewards tanking more than any sport. Regardless of whether you supported the Process, you must agree that forcing a franchise to deliberately lose for four straight seasons in order to become competitive is beyond ridiculous.

1. I honestly believe that many, many NBA players care more about style points than winning. Getting your dunk on *SportsCenter* becomes more important than getting to the playoffs. Hockey is all about the sport; the NBA is all about selling sneakers.

That's it. Now, get off my lawn!

My Favorite Moments from the Phils' Great Run from 2007 to 2011 :: Joe DeCamara

Joe DeCamara cohosts the Midday Show *on 94-WIP with Jon Ritchie. Joe grew up in Huntingdon Valley and has been a fan of the Philadelphia sports teams his entire life.*

The greatest era of Phillies baseball is 2007–2011. Up until 2007 the Phils had only made the playoffs nine times in 124 seasons. Then they won five straight division crowns, reached the World Series twice, and won one of the only two World Series titles in franchise history. And they gave us a lot of thrills. With that in mind, let's look at what I believe are the top 10 moments from the 2007–2011 Phils.

10. September 27, 2008. Clinching the division on an amazing double play. This was nuts. Brad Lidge was already 40-for-40 on the season but in serious trouble with the bases loaded in the top of the ninth versus Washington. Knowing that a Nationals win would trigger hair-raising angst for Game 162 and simultaneously force Charlie Manual to use Cole Hamels on Sunday, Lidge induced a ground ball, which was spectacularly picked by Jimmy Rollins, who flipped it to Chase Utley, who relayed the ball to Ryan Howard to end the game and clinch a playoff spot for the Phils.

9. October 2, 2008. Shane Victorino's grand slam off CC Sabathia. This was the moment I remember thinking: "Wow, this really might be the year!" Sabathia was seemingly unhittable down the stretch for Milwaukee in 2008, but with one swing of the bat Victorino obliterated that narrative, giving the Phillies a 5–1 lead early in Game 2 of the NLDS. The Phils were on their way.

8. August 27–30, 2007. The four-game sweep of the Mets. It seemed this would not be the Phillies' year—again. Just five games above .500 entering this late-August series, we viewed the 2007 Phils as a squad not good enough or not hungry enough to get to the playoffs. And then, in four games, they turned it all around and jump-started the greatest era in Phillies history. The fact that the final win came in thrilling come-from-behind fashion against Mets closer Billy Wagner . . . well, that was icing on the cake.

7. December 13, 2010. Signing Cliff Lee. This was jubilation! The Phils made some major acquisitions from 2007 to 2011, but no others stirred our hearts as fans quite like Cliff Lee choosing to come back for the 2011 season. The Four Aces of Halladay, Hamels, Oswalt, and Lee was born, but more importantly our hearts were whole again after the pain of seeing Lee unceremoniously dumped following his spectacular 2009 run.

6. March 29, 2010. Roy Halladay's perfect game. What a roller coaster of a night. First, the Flyers lose Game 1 of the Stanley Cup Finals. Then Roy Halladay stamps himself as a Philadelphia sports legend. It had been an odd first few months for Halladay because the pall of Lee's departure hung over Halladay's acquisition by the Phils. But with 27-up and

27-down in Florida, Doc cemented himself as one of the best we have ever seen and as a player we loved to root for. The love affair between Halladay and Philadelphia was on.

5. October 13, 2008. Shane Victorino and Matt Stairs hit home runs in Game 4 in LA. Victorino always gets short-changed on this one. And it's just not right. Stairs's homer "into the night" is one of the most important in franchise history, but Victorino's was critical too, as it turned an eighth-inning two-run deficit into a tie game just a few batters before Stairs. With these two mighty blows, what seemed like a soon-to-be 2–2 series turned into a 3–1 Phils' edge and the pathway to the World Series.

4. October 19, 2009. Jimmy Rollins's walk-off two-run double with two outs in Game 4 of the 2009 NLCS. Jimmy! How close this one came to being a 2–2 series. But Rollins had other plans. With a gapper to right-center field, Rollins turned Citizens Bank Park into Pandemonium Park as runners rounded the bases, giving the Phillies the win and a commanding 3–1 series lead. At that moment I vividly remember thinking: "It is fun to be a Phillies fan!"

3. September 30, 2007. The Phillies *finally* make it back to the playoffs on the last day of the regular season. This was so key. For 14 seasons the Phillies had been shut out of postseason play. But with a surge down the stretch they were on the doorstep, yet still tied with the Mets entering Game 162. Then New York pitcher Tom Glavine got rocked by the Marlins in his early afternoon start, setting the stage for scoreboard watching and baseball watching at CBP. What ensued was three of the most fun hours of Phillies baseball we have ever seen. And when Brett Myers recorded the final out and heaved his glove high in the air, wow, the celebration was on!

2. October 6, 2010. Roy Halladay's postseason no-hitter. It's hard to imagine a no-hitter topping a perfect game on a list. But, then again, it's hard to imagine a no-hitter in the playoffs. This was magic. For nine innings Halladay's stuff was electric, and considering that the future Hall of Famer was doing this in his first postseason start after so many years of toiling in the brutal AL East made it all the more special. It was Doc's definitive masterpiece—and with a huge assist from Carlos Ruiz on that incredible play from behind the plate to throw Brandon Phillips out at first to secure the no-hitter.

1. October 29, 2008. The Phillies win the 2008 World Series. Could there be any other choice? Twenty-five years. That's how long it had been since one of the four Philly teams had won a title. To say we were starving for a championship would be an understatement. To say the Phillies almost won the World Series in a rain delay would have been the most Philadelphia thing *ever*. Fortunately, that did not happen. Instead the stage was set for Game 5 of the World Series, Part II. Geoff Jenkins's double. Utley's decoy play nailing a Rays runner at home. Pat Burrell's double. Pedro Feliz's RBI single. And, of course, Brad Lidge striking out Eric Hinske, a moment crystalized in our collective conscious. "World Champions of Baseball."

Honorable mention:

Wilson Valdez pitching the 19th inning in a Phillies victory in 2011.

Joe Blanton's World Series home run in 2008.

Carlos Ruiz's walk-off single to win Game 3 of the World Series in 2008.

Breaking news at Citizens Bank Park of the death of Osama bin Laden in 2011.

Ryan Howard's ninth-inning two-out RBI double to give the Phils the lead in Game 4 at Colorado in 2009.

Brett Myers's marathon at bat versus CC Sabathia in 2008.

Ten Greatest Pro Coaches in Philly History

It's interesting to learn that the average Philadelphia pro coach here lasts just slightly longer than three seasons. Most leave for illness or fatigue—which is to say we get sick and tired of them. More fail than succeed in the long run.

But for every gaggle of Kotites and Kellys, every sack of Sandbergs and Simpsons, occasionally we come across a real gem.

Apologies in advance for leaving favorites like Mike Keenan, Pat Quinn, and Buddy Ryan off the list. All were popular and can make an argument for inclusion. We also skipped Alex Hannum, who ran up a 68–13 record and won a title with the 1967–1968 Sixers but only stuck around for two seasons.

10. Dick Vermeil. It kills us to rank him so low, but as you'll see, we reserve the top slots for coaches who won championships. Still, the Dick Vermeil era of Eagles football remains so popular that, to this day, his face smiles down from dozens of billboards scattered throughout the Delaware Valley. Dick came along after 10 losing Eagles seasons. Within two years he had the Birds in the playoffs. They stayed there for four straight seasons, including an appearance in the 1980 Super Bowl. With a driving work ethic and tremendous loyalty, he was the right guy at the right time. We're getting all choked up just writing about him.

9. Larry Brown. He drove us nuts, too. The creator of all that is basketball. He knows the game, and you don't. The ultimate carpetbagger. But remember, before Brown arrived, the Sixers didn't make the playoffs for eight straight years. And after he left, they had just two winning seasons in the next 14. Brown pushed his team to five straight playoff appearances, including that great run to the Finals in 2001 with Allen Iverson and four guys named Moe. It killed us when he landed in Detroit and won a World Championship.

8. Dallas Green. We're half reluctant to include Dallas because he only managed two full seasons with the Phils and was lucky enough to have one of the more loaded teams in this town's history. When you factor in his spotty record as a manager after he left, it makes you wonder. But for 1980, Dallas, you'll always have a special place in our heart. It was the first of just two World Championships this franchise ever produced. RIP, old buddy.

7. Andy Reid. Say what you want about those boring postgame news conferences, but you can't argue with the success of Reid's Eagles. He made the playoffs nine times in 14 seasons, won a franchise-record 19 playoff games, got to five NFC titles games, and, of course, appeared in Super Bowl XXXIX. He went on to Kansas City, where he continues to make the playoffs and confound the fans. Only seven coaches in NFL history have more than Andy's 195 wins. "Time's yours."

6. Doug Pederson. True confession: we laughed aloud when the rumor first came out that Jeff Lurie was considering Pederson as head coach. *That* mediocrity of a backup quarterback? It seemed the Eagles owner was just searching for a yes-man after his brutal three years with Chip Kelly. Boy, are we glad to have been wrong. Pederson, of course, combined the guts, creativity, and people skills to direct this franchise to its first-ever Super Bowl win in the 2017 season. We expect him to stay here for years to come, which means he has the biggest opportunity to move up—or down—on this list.

5. Charlie Manuel. Another hire for whom we had a wrong first take. Manuel seemed a confused bumpkin during his first season with the Phils, earning the cruel nickname, "Elmer Befuddled." But country hick doesn't always mean dumb, and while it took Manuel a while to master the double-switch, he sure knew how to run a clubhouse and push players' buttons. Uncle Charlie won a franchise-record 780 games, plus 27 more in the playoffs, plus two pennants and that magnificent 2008 World Series. Also turned out to be one of the nicest guys we ever met.

4. Billy Cunningham. The Kangaroo Kid. Our last championship in 1983. Who will ever forget a "slightly" inebriated Billy C. gingerly walking down those airplane steps, with the NBA championship trophy in one hand, a cigar in the other? Tough as nails. Took a giant collection of egos and went to the playoffs eight straight years. Three trips to the NBA Finals. Also, without a doubt, the greatest player on this list. How's this for a regular-season record? 454–196. Are you kidding me? He remains funny and a class act.

3. Fred Shero. "The Fog." Sure, he coached the Flyers to two Stanley Cups. Yes, he remains the winningest Flyers coach in history—308 regular-season wins plus 48 more in the playoffs. Yes, he's a brilliant tactician and a cunning motivator. But we'll always remember Fred as the architect of the two greatest parades this city has ever had. When he died on November 24, 1990, we all thought back to that glorious time and quietly (the way Shero would have) shed a tear or two.

2. Connie Mack. He managed the A's for 217 years before stepping down at the age of 240. Who was gonna fire Cornelius McGillicuddy? He was the owner. Seriously, Mr. Mack didn't stop managing until age 88. However—and this is a big however—he won nine pennants and five World Series with those teams filled with guys like Home Run Baker and Stuffy McInnis (God, those names are great), and later Jimmie Foxx and Mickey Cochrane. You've got to respect those numbers. Plus he wore a suit in the dugout. How cool is that?

1. Greasy Neale. After coaching the Eagles to losing seasons in his first two years, Greasy and the Eagles ripped off seven straight winning seasons, including NFL Championships in 1948 and 1949. His overall record in 10 seasons is 71–48. He gains extra points for having the coolest name on this list. My man, Greasy!

The Best Trades in Philadelphia History

By "history" here, we mean the last 50 years. So we won't get into two golden oldies—the Eagles' 1958 highway robbery of the Rams to acquire Norm Van Brocklin and the Sixers' 1965 theft of the Warriors to bring back Wilt Chamberlain.

10. Eagles get a first-rounder from Minnesota for QB Sam Bradford, 2016.
This was the shocker that came down eight days before the season opener. It followed a series of draft-day moves that spring in which GM Howie Roseman worked up to the number two pick to select Carson Wentz.

Everyone expected the rookie Wentz to watch the season on the sidelines. And then, Vikings QB Teddy Bridgewater shredded his knee in late August. Minnesota's pain was the Eagles' gain, as the Vikings desperately swapped their top 2017 pick in return for Bradford, who led them . . . nowhere, before moving on to Arizona two seasons later. Meanwhile, Wentz had a solid rookie season and emerged as a star in his second year. Oh, and that draft pick turned into defensive end Derek Barnett.

9. Flyers get forward John LeClair, defenseman Eric Desjardins, and forward Gilbert Dionne from the Canadiens for forward Mark Recchi and a third-round draft pick, 1995.
Recchi was no slouch, but he scored 40 goals three times before this trade and never again afterward. LeClair and Desjardins (forget Dionne, who was a throw-in) were keys to the resurgence that pushed the Flyers 178 games above .500 over the next decade. Desjardins was named the Flyers' top defenseman seven separate seasons, and LeClair surpassed 50 goals three times.

8. Phillies get pitcher Curt Schilling from Astros for pitcher Jason Grimsley, 1992.

> **Glen says:** Working for the *Inquirer* back then, I was the only reporter around spring training the day Schilling first arrived from Houston with a reputation as an underachiever. I watched as pitching coach Johnny Podres taught him a big roundhouse curve, which Schilling mastered in about five minutes.
>
> "He's gonna be a good one," Podres said to me as he walked away.
>
> What an understatement. Schilling won 101 games as a Phillie—the most of any right-hander since Robin Roberts. He was a three-time All-Star here and MVP of the 1993 League Championship Series against Atlanta. Rumor has it that he did a few things after leaving town, but that's for another list.

7. Eagles get quarterback Ron Jaworski from Rams for tight end Charles Young, 1977.
Young, a tight end, made three Pro Bowls as an Eagle—and none after he left here. Jaworski, meanwhile, became the quarterback that the Birds had been searching for since tossing aside Sonny Jurgensen in 1964. Jaws set a ton of team passing records, was the NFL Player of the Year in 1980, and, of course, led the Eagles to the Super Bowl that same season.

6. Phillies get pitcher Roy Halladay from the Blue Jays for prospects Travis d'Arnaud, Kyle Drabek, and Michael Taylor. Phils GM Ruben Amaro Jr. coveted Halladay for years and came close to getting him at the 2009 trade deadline. When the Jays held a fire sale that winter, Amaro showed up, swapping away three upper-level prospects, none of whom amounted to much. Meanwhile, Doc went on to win the 2010 NL Cy Young Award, throw a perfect game and postseason no-hitter, and give the Phils a few solid seasons of pitching and great leadership. He was elected to the Baseball Hall of Fame in 2019; Drabek made his high school's Distinguished Alumni list soon after that.

5. Sixers trade guard Lloyd Free to Clippers for a future first-round pick, 1978. Free—in his pre–World B. days—went on to become a very good scorer for some very bad clubs. He averaged more than 20 points per game for eight straight seasons—although his team failed to make the playoffs in seven of those seasons.

So how is this trade a good one for the 76ers? Well, the pick didn't pay off for six full years. But when it did in 1984, the Clippers—as usual—had a lottery spot, and the Sixers used it to draft Auburn forward Charles Barkley.

Free was a nice player and fun to watch. But Sir Charles—along with Wilt, Iverson, and Doc—is in the pantheon of all-time great Sixers.

Every trade from this point on directly contributed to a Philadelphia team winning a championship.

4. Flyers get winger Reggie Leach from the California Golden Seals for Larry Wright, Al MacAdam, and a first-round pick (Ron Chipperfield), 1974. MacAdam became a nice scorer after the trade; the other two guys never panned out in the NHL. But Leach—possessor of a 115-mile-an-hour shot—flourished as Bob Clarke's right winger on the famed LCB line (with Bill Barber) of the mid-to-late '70s. He scored 61 regular-season and 19 playoff goals in the Cup year of 1975–1976, both still franchise records.

3. Sixers get center Moses Malone from Rockets for center Caldwell Jones and a first-round pick (Rodney McCray), 1982. You all know this story: Doc couldn't do it alone for years . . . Magic jumps center in the '80 Finals and embarrasses Darryl Dawkins . . . "We Owe You One" . . . "Fo', Fo', Fo.'"

The trade was hastily hammered out after the Sixers signed Malone to a free-agent offer sheet. Jones was nothing more than a nice defensive player; McCray was a decent pro—though certainly not the player he was expected to be coming out of Louisville.

Moses, inarguably, is the guy who delivered the Sixers' last championship in 1983. He was the league MVP, and he destroyed Kareem Abdul-Jabbar and the Lakers in the Finals. He is, perhaps, the best offensive rebounder in the last 40 years. We just wish he'd stuck around longer.

2. Flyers get goalie Bernie Parent and forward Larry Goodenough from Maple Leafs for goalie Doug Favell and a first-round pick (Bob Neely), 1973. Bernie had been with the Flyers once before. They traded him in 1971 in a three-way deal that brought scoring punch in the form of Rick MacLeish. He was a decent goalie the first time around here, a little better in Toronto, and seemingly disinterested after defecting to the Philadelphia Blazers of the WHA.

When he returned to the Flyers after two-plus years elsewhere, he was a changed goalie. He credited Leafs great Jacques Plante with teaching him the position. He wound up as the backbone of two Stanley Cup teams, twice winning the playoff MVP award. He retired as one of the 10 best goalies ever and, for our money, the best player *ever* to wear the Flyers uniform.

1. Phillies get pitcher Steve Carlton from Cardinals for Rick Wise, 1972.

One of the greatest heists in sports history. The amazing thing is that it was proposed *to the Phillies* by St. Louis general manager Auggie Busch. John Quinn, the Phils GM, probably had to restrain himself from kissing Mr. Busch.

Carlton won 20 games his final season in St. Louis. That was a mere precursor. His first season as a Phillie—27–10, 310 strikeouts, 1.97 ERA, all for a last-place club—remains one of the greatest accomplishments in baseball history. Four Cy Youngs and 13 postseason wins for the Phils. Only Warren Spahn has more career wins by a lefty than Carlton's 329.

8. Sixers trade Andre Iguodala, Nikola Vučević, Moe Harkless, and a first-round pick for Andrew Bynum and Jason Richardson, 2012.
This stink bomb deal actually involved four teams and included Dwight Howard, but the Sixers were the biggest loser.

Sixers' ownership was so proud of obtaining former All-Star Bynum that they held an introductory news conference at the National Constitution Center, where hundreds of fans greeted him with chants of "We love you." Not for long. The former All-Star arrived with enough injury baggage to fill a Louis Vuitton shop, and he blew his knee out again while bowling during his rehab. One year later, the team let him walk as a free agent and fired the coach and GM to boot.

Vučović, meanwhile, became a solid rebounder and scorer for Orlando, and Iguodala (never liked in Philly) was a solid cog in Golden State's dynasty.

7. Phillies trade Cliff Lee to Seattle for Tyson Gillies, Phillippe Aumont, and J. C. Ramirez, 2009.
We praised GM Ruben Amaro in the previous chapter for acquiring Roy Halladay. That joy was short-lived for Phillies fans, when Amaro turned around and traded away the popular Lee *on the very same day.* Amaro rationalized that he needed to restock the team with young up-and-coming players. Problem was, none of the trio he got from the Mariners fit that description. Aumont—the *best of the bunch*—went 1–6 with a 6.80 ERA over parts of four seasons for the Phils.

This deal would have ranked higher had Amaro not atoned for his gaffe by re-signing Lee as a free agent one season later. Whew.

5. Flyers trade Sergei Bobrovsky to Columbus for a second-round draft pick and two fourth-rounders, 2012.
One year into the $51 million Ilya Bryzgalov disaster, the Flyers traded Bob, who had shined as a 22-year-old rookie two seasons earlier. It's not like there weren't already hints that Bryz would self-immolate.

Bobrovsky went on to become one of the league's top goalies with the Blue Jackets, winning two Vezina trophies and running up a 13–3–1 record against the Flyers through 2018–2019. The Flyers, meanwhile, continued their 30-year search for a competent goalie, which, as of this writing, finally looks to be solved with young Carter Hart.

4. Phillies trade pitcher Curt Schilling to the Diamondbacks for pitchers Omar Daal, Nelson Figueroa, and Vicente Padilla and first baseman Travis Lee, 2002.
An Ed Wade special. We'll always recall how the Phils GM said of Schill, "One out of every five days he's a horse, and the other four he's a horse's ass." Maybe so, but the horse went on to win the World Series with both the D-backs and Red Sox—making Wade look like the ass. Schilling also led both leagues in wins and has our support for eventual induction into the Hall of Fame.

Padilla was hit with the cliché "million-dollar arm and 25-cent head" so often that it seemed to become his legal ID. Lee was a truly despicable player who could sleepwalk through an entire season. Daal and Figueroa never panned out to anything.

4. Sixers trade forward Charles Barkley to the Suns for guard Jeff Hornacek, forward Tim Perry, and center Andrew Lang, 1992. Charles kind of forced his way out of town, but was this the best Harold Katz could get in return? Perry, a Temple alum, was a tall guy who couldn't shoot, couldn't pass, couldn't rebound. Lang was downright worthless. Hornacek was more infuriating—he was a good player before he got here and after he left, but he had no interest in performing for the Sixers.

Barkley took the Suns to the 1993 NBA Finals. He had five more great seasons until his knees betrayed him. He is one of the 25 best players ever in the NBA and someone who should have spent his entire career as a 76er.

3. Chip Kelly's double whammy, trading LeSean McCoy to the Bills for Kiko Alonso; and Nick Foles, a second-round pick, and a fourth-rounder to the Rams for Sam Bradford, 2015. All of this happened with no forewarning on a shocking March afternoon as our friend Ray Didinger described Chip on live TV as "a mad scientist blowing up the house." Certainly, Kelly dynamited his own career that day. McCoy was among many players Kelly didn't get along with, so the franchise's all-time leading rusher was exiled to Buffalo for Alonso, a linebacker most notable for A) cutting his jersey off above his navel and B) missing 75 percent of the tackles he attempted.

Meanwhile, Kelly was in a line of many NFL types who falsely believed in Bradford, a thief who made $129 million in career earnings but never played in a postseason game. Sammy Sleeves did his check-down thing here for a year before Howie Roseman got rid of him (see previous chapter).

Foles? Hmm, not sure whatever became of that guy.

2. Phillies trade shortstop Larry Bowa and second baseman Ryne Sandberg to the Cubs for shortstop Iván DeJesús, 1982. The Phils considered this merely a swap of veteran shortstops. Sandberg was regarded as a minor league third baseman whose path was blocked by Mike Schmidt.

But Dallas Green—who left Philadelphia for the Cubs in 1981—knew a little bit about the Phils' farm system. While Sandberg produced a Hall of Fame career as Chicago's second baseman for 16 years, the Phils ran out seven guys to man the position, including Tom Herr and Mark Lewis.

1. Sixers trade center Moses Malone, forward Terry Catledge, and two first-round draft picks (Anthony Jones and Harvey Grant) to the Bullets for Jeff Ruland and Cliff Robinson. At the same time, the Sixers also trade first-overall draft pick (Brad Daugherty) to the Cavaliers for Roy Hinson, 1986. June 16, 1986—the Mother of All Bad Days in Philadelphia Sports History. We combined these two deals because they were made within minutes of each other—on a day when someone should have stuffed Harold Katz in a duffel bag. One wonders what the Sixers might have been had Barkley's front-line teammates entering the '90s been Daugherty and Malone rather than Armen Gilliam and Rick Mahorn.

Rickie Ricardo is the Spanish radio voice of the Eagles and the New York Yankees, and he served as the Phillies' Spanish radio voice from 2007 to 2013. He is famous for his viral play-by-play calls, such as, "No, señor! No, señor!"

The "I stayed long enough to have a cheesesteak" category

5. Willie Hernandez, Phillies reliever (Puerto Rico)
4. Ron Rivera, Eagles coach (Mexico and Puerto Rican descent)
3. Greg Dobbs, Phillies infielder (Peruvian mom)
2. Kiko Alonso, Eagles linebacker (Cuban and Colombian descent)
1. Mark Sanchez, Eagles quarterback (Mexican descent)

The "came up just a little short" category

5. Von Hayes, Phillies outfielder (Puerto Rican mom)
4. Pedro Martínez, Phillies pitcher (Dominican Republic)
3. Willie Montañez, Phillies first baseman (Puerto Rico)
2. Juan Castillo, Eagles coach (Mexican descent)
1. Jeff Garcia, Eagles quarterback (Mexican descent)

My Top 10

10. Cookie Rojas, Phillies infielder (Cuba). The "Days of Wine and Rojas"—need I say more? He played nine seasons in Philadelphia, 16 in the Major Leagues. Made the All-Star Game in 1965, a year in which he played seven different positions.

9. Danny García, boxing (Puerto Rico). A North Philly local boy makes good. He was a world champion in two weight classes and maybe just a step away from Floyd Mayweather.

8. Carlos Ruiz, Phillies catcher (Panama). Chooch was part of the glue from that golden era of Phillies baseball. He was a clutch hitter and the mastermind behind the plate for Roy Halladay's perfect game and postseason no-hitter.

7. Ruben Amaro Sr., Phillies shortstop and scout (Mexico and Cuba). A groundbreaker; a pioneer for Latinos playing in Major League Baseball at a time when many fans didn't understand that Hispanics and people of color could be the same thing.

6. Ruben Amaro Jr., Phillies outfielder and GM (Mexico and Cuba). He picked up where Pat Gillick left off. His teams ran into some postseason buzz saws or they would have won another championship. Ruben put together one of the all-time great starting rotations. I think he'll be more appreciated as time goes on.

5. Manny Trillo, Phillies second baseman (Venezuela). One of the quiet leaders from the Phillies' first championship era. He could give you the clutch hit, and he was solid defensively and a huge part of that clubhouse. The Phils wouldn't have won the 1980 World Series without him.

4. Tony Taylor, Phillies second baseman (Cuba). Like Ruben Sr., he was one of those darker-skinned pioneers. Tony always had a big smile and a great demeanor. He enjoyed being a Phillie, showing personality and living here. He brought a little mustard to that hog dog.

3. Juan Samuel, Phillies second baseman (Dominican Republic). As Dominicans came to prominence, Sammy was one of the first real stars—a mix of speed, power, and defense. He had some flash, some pizzazz, and that Jheri curl going. He helped lay the foundation for Dominican players of today, and they stand at attention when his name and Julio Franco's are mentioned.

2. Bobby Abreu, Phillies outfielder (Venezuela). Bobby was a bit underappreciated and misunderstood by fans in both Philadelphia and when he went to the Yankees. He didn't love running into fences, and that became the only thing some people saw about him. But you don't know what you have until it's gone, and the Phillies had a big hole in right field for years after they traded him. A terrific player.

1. Steve Van Buren, Eagles running back (Honduras). Some people forget about him because he played before the Super Bowl, but he helped lead the Eagles to two NFL championships. And what a story: he was born in Honduras and then adopted and brought to the United States after his parents died. He got to the height of stardom here in his second country. When you look at the history, Steve Van Buren is worth much more respect and admiration than he gets.

Top 10 Most Hated Personalities in Football

We didn't include any former Eagles here, although the likes of Jason Babin, Nnamdi Asomugha, and Sam Bradford warrant inclusion. Hmmm . . . maybe that's a list for later in the book.

10. Jeremy Shockey. A loudmouth showoff. A pompous jerk. Not that we wouldn't have wanted the big tight end for our own squad.

9. Tiki and Ronde Barber. In 22 career games against the Birds, Tiki gained 2,591 rushing and receiving yards (although he did cough up the ball a few times). Ronde—we don't need to say aloud what he did with a fluttery Donovan McNabb pass in the 2002 NFC title game. The twins were so damned good looking and so polished; it made us loathe them even more.

8. Bill Belichick. Of course we share this opinion with the rest of the football world. Eagles fans will forever believe Coach Hoodie and his sidekick, Tom Terrific, cheated to steal the 2004 Super Bowl. That we got them back 13 full seasons later will always be the sweetest revenge.

7. Michael Strahan. Sure, he was talented. But broadcasters ridiculously puffed him up as the next Reggie White. It was a sham when Brett Favre laid down to allow Strahan to break the NFL sack record. We enjoyed it more when Jon Runyan would punch him in that gap-toothed mouth.

From this point on, every name is a Dallas Cowboy. And trust us; we could have expanded the list.

6. Bob Lilly. And Chuck Howley and Roger Staubach and Jethro Pugh and every player from those smug Dallas squads in the 1970s who had the nerve to call themselves America's Team. Hey, America started in Philadelphia, Bub. And the eagle—not the star—is the national symbol.

5. Hollywood Henderson. As much of a showboat as the nickname suggests. Henderson was never a great player, but CBS (the Cowboys Broadcasting System) loved to show him on the sidelines, waving to his mom or, perhaps, making a quick coke deal. Last we heard about Henderson, he won $28 million in the Texas lottery. Nothing in history ever served as greater proof that life isn't fair.

4. Deion Sanders. In the first Eagles game that Glen ever took his son to, in 1998, Sanders took an interception back for a touchdown and proceeded to dance like he had just discovered oil under the Vet Stadium end zone. "Someone should deck that guy," said Ted Macnow. That's my boy!

3a. Tom Landry, and 3b. Jimmy Johnson. Landry was a Bible-thumping hypocrite who loved to rub it in against bad teams. We always wanted to knock that Stetson off his head. We never got that chance, but we did muss up Johnson's perfect hair with a few snowballs back in 1989. Current Cowboys coach Jason Garrett doesn't make this list because he's more laughable than despicable, standing on the sidelines clapping like a seal.

2. Michael Irvin. We single him out, but he represents every preening, diva Cowboys wide receiver over the years—Drew Pearson, Dez Bryant, and even the post-Eagles Terrell Owens. As for Irvin, yes, we'll admit we cheered as he lay sprawled on the Vet turf, his career over. We didn't know he was hurt that bad. We're sorry. Sort of.

1. Jerry Jones. The lizard-skinned, drawling representation of all that is evil. The viscous, conniving personification of Satan. Hey, he's luxury box buddies with Chris Christie. Need we say more?

Top 10 Most Hated Personalities in Baseball

10. José Reyes. Let's own up here. We hate the Mets. We are fond of saying the only thing worse than a Mets fan is a Mets fan who hasn't been born yet. Why Reyes in particular? Because this hot dog actually escaped the organization and went back!

9. The Steinbrenner sons. Their dad was no day at the beach, but at least he hated to lose and won multiple championships. What have these doofuses accomplished? The only World Series they've won, despite spending money like Elton John, was over the Phils 10 years ago. And someone please tell Hank the crewcut went out with Johnny Unitas and Biff from *Back to the Future*. (By the way, did you know Tom Wilson, who portrayed "Biff," is from Philly?)

8. Ryan Braun. Instead of just taking his PED punishment like a man, Braun lied and blamed innocent people for improperly "handling" his samples. D-bag.

7. Marlins Man. We're not going to be hypocrites here. Who wouldn't want to be rich enough to travel the country partying at one awesome sporting event after another? But of all teams and jerseys in the USA, you pick the Marlins? His real name? Laurence Leavy.

6. Joey Votto. A great player, but a troll who revels in taunting Phillies fans. A few years back, the Reds first baseman fake-tossed the ball toward a group of children in the seats at Citizens Bank Park, only to put it back in play. When he was asked later why he did that, Votto said, "I have no problem with the Philly fans, except the Philly fan kids. All the kids. I can't stand the kids here." A genuine heel.

5. Tony La Russa. Baseball has practically been ruined with all the pitching changes. And we have this self-proclaimed genius to blame. Come to think of it, he also helped start the ridiculous number of defensive shifts we suffer through today as well.

4. Ryne Sandberg. Quick, name another Philly manager who ever *quit* during the season. Not fired, but quit.

3. Jonathan Papelbon. We're begging here. We need another Phils reliever to step up and overtake this annoying cockroach, because as of this writing he is the all-time saves leader for the Phils.

2. Curt Schilling. If his constant bellowing about his political leanings weren't enough, the man ripped off a state. (We know it's small, but Rhode Island is still a state.) Who rips off an entire state?!

1. Pete Rose. The only remaining name from this list in the first book, and the latest allegations are too slimy to print. Gains (loses?) more points for his horrible haircut. We will tell you this. There was a time when if you had even the tiniest negative word to say about Rose on the air, his supporters would light up the phone lines to attack you. But not no more. The Hit King has no fans.

10. Mike Milbury. We despised him during his 12 years as a second-rate defenseman and third-level goon for the Bruins. But our rancor has really increased in recent years watching his ugly puss as a broadcaster. Oh, to see Keith Jones lean over and sock him just once.

9. Jaromír Jágr. Consider this a group entry and add Ron Duguay, Garry Unger, and any other pretty-boy visitor who sashayed onto Philadelphia ice over the years. How great was it when the sound system would play Aerosmith's "Dude (Looks Like a Lady)" whenever one of them skated out for warm-ups? Of course, we adored Jágr when he played in orange and black late in his 72-season career.

8. Dale Hunter. He was a great and tough player, but we'll always remember him for 19 years of cheap shots. We were once at a game where Hunter fought two Flyers—Valeri Zelepukin and Roman Vopat—and tuned up both. Neither of those players was a noted tough guy, but that was the thing about Hunter. He'd pick a fight with Lady Byng if she laced them up. Amassed 4,294 penalty minutes over his career and probably deserved twice that amount.

7. Martin Brodeur. For 21 seasons he was always there, brilliantly guarding the net for the Devils. He beat the Flyers 63 times, including playoffs. Nothing about his personality was annoying; it's just he was so damned good.

6. Matthew Barnaby. The ultimate pest. This undersized, grinning ninny had the persona of a pro wrestling heel who would smack someone with a roll of nickels and then sidle away with an angelic look on his face. "Who, me?" You always wanted to see Barnaby get thrashed, but he seemed to weasel his way out of fighting the tough guys. In fact, the only time we ever saw Chris Therien drop the gloves was against Barnaby—which pretty much affirms the previous sentence.

4. Scott Stevens. The anti-Barnaby. When Stevens hit people, there was nothing furtive about it. And his victims often didn't get up. Just ask Eric Lindros.

3. Claude Lemieux. He transformed from Droopy Dog in the regular season to Superman in the postseason. Three of the Flyers' most notorious playoff moments involved this jackass—the pregame skirmish in the 2000 Conference Finals, the fluttering goal he scored over Ron Hextall's shoulder to clinch the 1995 Conference Finals, and, of course, the 1987 pregame brawl he initiated that had some Flyers running on the ice in shower slippers to take a shot at his ugly puss.

2. Tie Domi. Remember the time that fat slob from Havertown fell through the glass behind the penalty box trying to get at Domi? It's still worth a chuckle.

Other hated goons: Sean Avery, Keith Magnuson, Tiger Williams, Terry O'Reilly, Steve Durbano.

1. Sidney Crosby. Like Brodeur, he's a Hall of Famer whose talent must be respected. Unlike Brodeur, he's a jerk—an Alfred E. Neuman lookalike who would whine to the refs one second and spear a Flyer in the groin as soon as that ref turned his back.

Honorable mention: Billy Smith, Dominik Hašek, Chris Chelios, Darius Kasparaitis, Matt Cooke, Darcy Tucker, Zdeno Chára, Clark Gillies, the Plager Brothers, every Soviet in 1976. Really, Flyer fans tend to hate every opponent.

Top 10 Most Hated Personalities in Basketball

10. Andrew Bynum. But he is a terrific bowler if the Sixers ever join a league.

9. Franklin, the Sixer mascot dog. Seriously? This is a town with Hall of Fame mascots like the Phanatic, the endlessly flapping St. Joe Hawk, and Gritty. This is the best the Sixers could come up with?

8. LeBron James. That farce he helped perpetuate that he was coming to play for the Sixers? That was *never* happening. I was never a LeBron hater, but something happened since the Decision (which Commissioner David Stern begged him not to do) and he's become so full of himself with his bragging tweets.

7. Every Boston Celtic who ever lived. That about covers it, doesn't it? But let's give a special shout-out to Danny Ainge who is never freakin' going to go away and stuck us with number two on this list.

6. Dr. Mark Schwartz. It's not his fault, but they always booked him on *Philly Sports Talk* to discuss some Sixer's injury. He'd have a fake knee with fake tendons and x-rays and whatnot, but whoever was hosting would endlessly point out that even though he's explaining the latest Joel Embiid injury, "He is not Embiid's actual doctor." Then why is he on? We want to hear from the actual doctor of the actual injured Sixer they're discussing.

5. Villanova haters. Look, Big Daddy's from rowhome Southwest Philly. So, yeah, Villanova (not just the school but the town too) will always be perceived as snooty and rich. We also excuse your hatred if you are a St. Joe's alum because of that terrific rivalry. But enough already. Jay Wright is a cool guy running a clean program with quality players who never get in any trouble—and they've won two more national championships, for crying out loud. Stop and applaud them.

4. Tim Donaghy. Look, if pro sports were fixed, someone would have been caught by now, or blabbed on a talk show, or written a book. But every single time we express that belief on the air, some degenerate gambler calls within seconds and exclaims, "Oh, yeah, how about that Tim Donaghy?" Yeah, Donaghy was an NBA ref who was nailed by the FBI fixing games, and we wish he never existed. The only ref or ump caught doing so in decades. To make matters worse, he had to be from our area, Delaware County.

3. Rick Pitino. He's never coached a Philly team, but we went up against him enough, be it college or pro. How he is respected and revered is beyond us, because he's a flat-out disgrace. If you believe he knew nothing about the prostitutes used as bait for Louisville recruits, then we've got a beat-up 1972 Pinto to sell you. And don't forget the man had sex with a woman who wasn't his wife inside an Italian restaurant *on campus.* That's first class, eh? Charles Barkley may be correct that you shouldn't be expected to be a role model just because you're in the world of sports, but c'mon. You're a coach who gets paid a fortune on top of your salary to give motivational speeches, as well as writing those stupid self-help books. What a fraud.

2. Markelle Fultz. So, one night you're playing NBA ball, and the next game Coach Brett Brown (who has stuck by you through thick and thin) decides to insert T. J. McConnell instead because of matchup concerns. No big deal, right? It's not like you're Allen Iverson. So the next day you invent some mysterious injury that prevents you from playing for another couple months. Way to go, kid. Eventually, the Sixers just gave up and traded him to Orlando for pennies on the dollar.

1. The Colangelos. Bryan takes center stage because of that whole social media mess with his wife, but don't forget it's his holier-than-thou dad, Jerry, who brought him into the organization. Plus, we can't excuse the Sixers owners for allowing NBA commissioner Adam Silver to force Jerry down their throats. C'mon, guys; show some moxie.

Ten More Hated Nonathletes

10. Joe West. A surly, vindictive man who once body-slammed Phils reliever David West during an on-field rumble between players—no easy feat considering West's pear-like physique. Also once tossed Lenny Dykstra for simply complaining that West—umping second base that day—was interfering with Dykstra's view of the pitcher's delivery.

9. Joe Buck. We crowdsourced this list by asking our Twitter followers to provide names. More than 900 suggestions later, no one was called out more than this Fox broadcaster for baseball and the NFL. Thing is, fans in every city seem to believe Buck has it out for them. His own Twitter profile says, "I love all teams EXCEPT yours."

8. Clarence Campbell. The fossilized NHL commissioner openly rooted against the Broad Street Bullies, saying aloud that their nasty play was destroying the NHL. He didn't seem to mind on one day—when the Orange and Black defeated the Russian Army team in 1976.

7. Mike Lombardi. In September 2017, this former Joe Banner lackey wrote that Doug Pederson "might be less qualified to coach a team than anyone I've ever seen in my 30-plus years in the NFL." He further compared the Eagles' head guy to Roy Rubin, who once led the Sixers to a 4–48 record. Five months later, of course, Pederson was bathed in confetti at Super Bowl LII. You think we're going to forgive and forget that take, Mike?

6. Drew Rosenhaus. Never in the history of mankind has one man so mishandled a delicate situation. While we never exonerated Terrell Owens for his immaturity, we still think his divorce from the Eagles could have been avoided had Rosenhaus exhibited a shred of common sense. Our lasting memory will be Rosenhaus, with his lavender shirt and slicked-back hair, wearing that smug grin and repeating his mantra—"Next question"—while T.O.'s reputation slipped even further away that November 2005 afternoon in New Jersey.

5. Leon Stickle. Edges out Kevin Collins and Don Koharski as our least favorite hockey official. Infamous, of course, for the case of brain-lock that caused him to miss an obvious offsides call in the 1980 Stanley Cup Finals, costing the Flyers a goal, the game, and the Cup.

4. Skip Bayless. There's a roster of braying TV blowhards (Colin Cowherd, Michael Wilbon, etc.) who get their jollies tweaking the Philadelphia fan base. But no one does it more nakedly than this Jerry Jones sycophant. And we apologize if the previous sentence made you conjure up an image of Skip Bayless naked.

3. Pete Morelli. The recently retired NFL ref spent 22 years wandering the field with a cane and sunglasses. He always seemed to have an anti-Eagles agenda. Don't believe us? Consider these numbers: in the last four Eagles games he officiated (which included the

Super Bowl season), Morelli whistled the Birds for 396 penalty yards, their opponents for just 74.

2. Carl and Bonnie Lindros. They were the original helicopter parents, pampering and protecting their son. Problem was, Eric was pushing 30, and they were still carpooling him to play dates. There's plenty of blame to go around for 88's infamous rift with Flyers management, but we start with Daddy and Mommy Dearest.

1. Cris Collinsworth. Like Joe Buck, he's a network broadcaster resented by fans in every NFL city. But there's genuine cause for Eagles partisans to feel this way. His biased color analysis of Super Bowl LII was a disgrace, as he pushed the "Tom Brady Miracle Comeback" angle right up until the final play. You can literally hear Collinsworth groan as that last Hail Mary falls to the ground.

Honorable mention: Johnny Most, Jim Gray, Dan Dierdorf, Pierre McGuire, Scott Boras, Bruce Froemming, Kevin Collins.

The ABCs of Philly Pro Sports—Part 1

It seemed like a silly premise at first. Who are the greatest Philly athletes in alphabetical order? What one player would represent, for example, the letter *F*?

But when we threw it out on the airwaves and social media, people went nuts participating. It ended up being a ton of fun.

There are few rules. All that counts is how a player performed in a Philadelphia uniform. How he played in another city at a different point of his career counted for nothing. And if, like Dolph Schayes, almost all his career was in a Syracuse uniform, well, then he didn't make the cut even though the franchise later moved to Philly and became the Sixers.

On the other hand, if an old Philadelphia Athletic or Warrior kicked butt, we did count that. You'll see a special note or two.

One other thing: when we refer to "the Hall" we mean that sport's Hall of Fame, not an individual team Hall.

So fill in your answers here. No cheating by going to the back of the book until you're done. When you've got it all filled out, turn to page **254**, and you'll see the players we chose for each letter and each team. Enjoy.

A

Eagles _____
Phillies _____
Sixers _____
Flyers _____

B

Eagles _____
Phillies _____
Sixers _____
Flyers _____

C

Eagles _____
Phillies _____
Sixers _____
Flyers _____

D

Eagles _____
Phillies _____
Sixers _____
Flyers _____

E

Eagles _____
Phillies _____
Sixers _____
Flyers _____

F

Eagles _____
Phillies _____
Sixers _____
Flyers _____

G

Eagles _____
Phillies _____
Sixers _____
Flyers _____

H

Eagles _____
Phillies _____
Sixers _____
Flyers _____

I

Eagles _____
Phillies _____
Sixers _____
Flyers _____

J

Eagles _____
Phillies _____
Sixers _____
Flyers _____

K

Eagles _____
Phillies _____
Sixers _____
Flyers _____

L

Eagles _____
Phillies _____
Sixers _____
Flyers _____

M

Eagles _____
Phillies _____
Sixers _____
Flyers _____

N

Eagles _____
Phillies _____
Sixers _____
Flyers _____

O

Eagles _____
Phillies _____
Sixers _____
Flyers _____

P

Eagles _____
Phillies _____
Sixers _____
Flyers _____

Q

Eagles _____
Phillies _____
Sixers _____
Flyers _____

R

Eagles _____
Phillies _____
Sixers _____
Flyers _____

S

Eagles _____
Phillies _____
Sixers _____
Flyers _____

T

Eagles _____
Phillies _____
Sixers _____
Flyers _____

U

Eagles _____
Phillies _____
Sixers _____
Flyers _____

V

Eagles _____
Phillies _____
Sixers _____
Flyers _____

W

Eagles _____
Phillies _____
Sixers _____
Flyers _____

X

Okay, we'll skip X.

Y

Eagles _____
Phillies _____
Sixers _____
Flyers _____

Z

Eagles _____
Phillies _____
Sixers _____
Flyers _____

The Best Assistant Coaches

The head coach (or manager) gets all the acclaim—and more often, all the heat. But we've been fortunate over the years to have some great minds by their side. Here are some of the best:

10. Davey Lopes. The 2007 Phils stole 138 bases in 157 tries. That 88 percent success rate is the highest in MLB history, and the praise goes to this 16-year big leaguer who was the Phils' first base coach through their great run. Remember when he'd pull out that stopwatch during games to time opposing pitchers' deliveries?

9. Mike Nykoluk. Fred Shero hired him in 1972 as the NHL's first full-time assistant coach. Nykoluk gets credit for the strategy that helped the Flyers beat the Bruins in the 1974 Finals. "Everyone would say keep the puck away from Bobby Orr," Nykoluk said. "After watching films, we came up with a different theory. Every time we shot the puck into the Boston zone, we'd fire it into Orr's corner. We figured we'd tire him out.'"

8. John Harbaugh. He coached Eagles special teams from 1998 to 2005 (and one year of defensive backs) before winning a Super Bowl as Baltimore's head coach. Think of all those great highlights from that era—onside kicks to start the season, David Akers's trick plays, Miracles at the Meadowlands. This guy was behind all of them.

7. Jim Maloney. Because a college coach deserves to make this list. Maloney spent 23 years at Temple as lieutenant to Don Casey and John Chaney. He was a talented recruiter who specialized in developing backcourt players. All those great Temple guards over the years—Eddie Jones, Aaron McKie, Mark Macon, Rick Brunson, Terence Stansbury, Nate Blackwell, and Howie Evans—learned under him. So did his son, Matt, who starred at Penn.

6. Frank Reich. Hey, he helped win the Super Bowl. As offensive coordinator on a team with an offensive head coach (Doug Pederson) who also called the plays, it's tough to measure Reich's contribution. By all accounts, he was crucial in developing the Eagles' downfield passing game and was a big part of scripting the first-15-plays strategy for each game. The offense dipped when he left in 2018. Reich became head coach of the Colts, who zoomed to the playoffs.

5. Bobby Wine. By his own admission, Dallas Green knew little about managing when he took over the Phils late in 1979. Same thing with Paul "the Pope" Owens when he grabbed the reins in '83. Both relied heavily on a bench coach so baseball savvy that he eked out a 12-year playing career despite a .215 average. Wino (great nickname, eh?) stayed in the sport as an advance scout until he was 75.

4. Jack McMahon. He was a 12-year assistant coach for the Sixers, as well as super scout and personnel director. McMahon gets credit for discovering Mo Cheeks, drafting Charles Barkley, and convincing Harold Katz not to bring in Len Bias for a tryout before the 1986 draft. "The smartest thing I ever did," said Billy Cunningham, "was lean on Jack McMahon. He was a human white board."

3. Bud Carson. His 1991 Gang Green defense finished first against the run, first against the pass, and first in turnovers under Rich Kotite. Truth be told, Carson took Buddy Ryan's defense and made it several notches better. This was years after he was defensive coordinator of the famed Steel Curtain defense in Pittsburgh. There is the Dr. Z award given for lifetime achievement as an assistant coach in the NFL. Carson is among the 10 who've ever won it—as is the guy who tops this list.

2. Johnny Podres. The masterful Phillies pitching coach under Jim Fregosi. In 1993, the Phils had five starters with 12-plus wins, the only time that's occurred in franchise history. Here's three things you probably didn't know about this Buster Keaton lookalike: (1) He was MVP of the 1955 World Series, pitching for the Dodgers; (2) his wife was a bombshell who skated for the Ice Follies; and (3) a plaque of his image hangs at the National Polish-American Sports Hall of Fame in Troy, Michigan.

1. Jim Johnson. If not for Jim Johnson, said Brian Dawkins, "I would still have had a good career. But I wouldn't have made it to the Hall of Fame." The smartest hire Andy Reid ever made, Johnson was the architect of a defense that led the NFL in sacks from 2000 to 2007 and was third in turnovers and fourth in points allowed. Eagles defensive players went to 26 Pro Bowls during his tenure. Guys like Hugh Douglas and Jeremiah Trotter speak of him reverentially.

Honorable mention: Marion Campbell, Jon Gruden, Doug Scovil, Larry Bowa, John Vukovich, Jimy Williams, Mo Cheeks, Chuck Daly, Jimmy Lynam.

For every Moses (Malone) who leads us to the Promised Land, there are too many false prophets. Here are 10 of the most infamous.

10. Von Hayes. He's all over this book, so we needn't go into detail here. Suffice it to say, that "Ted Williams swing" may have been a bit of an exaggeration.

9. Chris Gratton. A fascinating case of an emerging young star who got the huge bucks and became a Shrinky Dink under the spotlight. Would have been terrific as a third-line center. But billed as "the Next Lindros," he looked like the next Barney Fife.

8. Dom Brown. In 2011, he was baseball's number three overall prospect—behind only Mike Trout and Bryce Harper. The 6-foot-5 outfielder was pegged to be the first of the next generation of Phillies stars moving up as the '08 nucleus moved on. Brown hit 27 homers in 2013 (all of them, it seemed, over one month), made an All-Star team, and then regressed into being a lackadaisical, slow-wristed Dallas Cowboys–loving slug. Not that we're bitter.

7. Markelle Fultz. Okay, maybe calling him a potential savior is too strong. But fans of the Process crowed that Fultz was the missing point guard who would lead the Sixers to a title when the franchise traded up to make him the top pick of the 2017 draft. The kid was immature, injury prone, and still being told what to do by his mommy. Gone and hopefully soon forgotten.

6. Roman Gabriel. When he showed up in 1973 (replacing John Reaves), he was quickly nicknamed the Messiah. Gabriel predicted a championship within two years—and who was going to doubt a three-time Pro Bowl QB and former league MVP? Still, despite Gabriel's strong play (he returned to the Pro Bowl as an Eagle in 1975), the team never managed a winning record in his five seasons here.

5. Andrew Bynum. The Sixers hired a brass band and rented out the National Constitution Center in 2012 to boast how they'd paid dearly in talent and money for this 24-year-old big oaf coming off a 19-point, 12-rebound season in LA. By his first practice his knees became Turkish Taffy. He blew off rehab (beyond bowling) while collecting $50 million from owner Josh Harris. If nothing else, Bynum was the big spike that drove the franchise toward packing it all in and starting from scratch.

4. Lance Parrish. Remember the cringe-inducing bumper stickers in 1987? "Lance us a pennant." Not only did they sound contrived, but the muscle-bound catcher, who was supposed to protect Mike Schmidt in the lineup, couldn't lance a boil, let alone a pennant during his two years in Philadelphia.

3. Ilya Bryzgalov. Ed Snider got so frustrated by his franchise's inability to fill the gaping five-hole at goalie that he gave this Russian nutcase a nine-year, $51 million deal in 2011. Two years later, Snider handed Bryz $23 million just to walk away. Always entertaining with outrageous quotes about the galaxy or his fear of bears, @bryzgoalie30 remains a tremendous Twitter follow.

2. Shawn Bradley. Some basketball experts who we really respect predicted this 7-foot-7 stick figure would "revolutionize" basketball. The only revolt going on took place in the Spectrum stands after fans got to see how little effort the Great White Nope put into his game.

1. Chip Kelly. The ultimate charlatan. Chip arrived with a flourish, directing a high-speed offense that caught the NFL off balance. For a season, he was great. And many (including us, we admit) bought into Chip as the next Bill Walsh. Problem was, he never had any Plan B to initiate once defensive coordinators caught onto the gimmick. His book of great ideas had exactly one page. Meanwhile, Kelly wrestled control of the franchise away from Jeff Lurie and Howie Roseman—then made a series of disastrous personnel moves. A faker. A fraudulent Wizard of Oz hiding behind a curtain. A nasty, petulant son of a bitch who disrespected everyone inside and outside of the Eagles. Hey, have a smoothie in his honor.

Ten Athletes or Coaches We Were Wrong About :: Joe Giglio

Joe Giglio hosts the 94-WIP Evening Show, where he's been known to take a stand outside of the conventional wisdom.

We're all wrong—a lot. No one likes to admit it, but it's true. Every sports fan has a gut feeling or take on something every day. And often, we've all been, well, totally wrong.

Here are 10 times we (myself included in many of these) were wrong about a Philadelphia sports figure.

10. Eric Lindros. The word "soft" was used way too often to describe Lindros's inability to stay on the ice. If we knew then what we know now about head injuries and concussions, Lindros would have been looked at as a "what if" star rather than a "should have been" throughout his career.

9. Terry Francona. Two things have become apparent since Francona left town: he's become a better manager, and his situations have allowed him to do it. Francona was New School when it was still in vogue to be Old School. Cooperstown will await him when he retires, something few in Philadelphia could have envisioned when he left town with a .440 winning percentage.

8. Mike Schmidt. It's hard to imagine now, but Schmidt was often booed during his career, especially in the early days. It's unfair to say Phillies fans were wrong about Schmidt's talent, but it's fair to wonder if anyone would have predicted him becoming the best third baseman ever and beloved all-time Phillie.

7. Charlie Manuel. The West Virginia drawl and Uncle Charlie feeling to this World Series–winning manager wasn't present when he got the job over a proven winner like Jim Leyland. In time, Manuel figured out the double switch, had 25 guys playing hard for him, and led the Phillies to a parade down Broad Street.

6. Joel Embiid. Here's one all the doubters like to forget, myself included. I questioned the idea of taking a big man with back issues and then doubted he'd ever stay healthy enough to play. Now we're watching the best big man in the NBA and a superstar on and off the court.

5. Sam Hinkie. Ah, the man behind the most overt tanking job in NBA history. As the Sixers slogged through some of the most (purposeful) bad years we've ever seen, the man behind the curtain had a plan to take advantage of the NBA's broken structure. It worked—regardless of where this franchise goes from here.

4. Howie Roseman. At some point, Roseman earned the ultimate respect from this town by becoming the one thing he never was. No, not a Super Bowl champion. Roseman became a "football guy." The executive who rose from the ranks of law school, then fell to the other side of Chip Kelly's broom closet, put together the first Super Bowl–winning Eagles team ever.

3. Nick Foles. It's in vogue to act as if Foles was never doubted, but we all know that's not the case. Foles always had the hearts of Philadelphia, but many minds pointed out his flaws and almost no one got excited when the team brought him back as a backup QB before the 2017 season. Now? We're talking about the most beloved quarterback in Eagles history.

2. Chip Kelly. No one fooled this town quite like Kelly. The buzz and excitement for his hiring was unlike anything we've seen on the coaching ranks. Many blindly supported his quirky ways and disregard for what typically wins in football because, well, we wanted to believe the next Bill Belichick arrived. He didn't, and Kelly's dismissal set the stage for us to be spectacularly wrong (in a good way) about the next guy on this list.

1. Doug Pederson. The search was ridiculed. The hiring was mocked. The process was criticized for months. After Pederson's first year (a 7–9 season with ups, downs, and the integration of a rookie quarterback), some cited the former longtime backup quarterback as the biggest concern moving forward. Two years later, Pederson has proven to be one of the NFL's best coaches, an excellent offensive mind, a leader, and the man most responsible for finally bringing a Lombardi Trophy to Philadelphia.

Honorable mention: Gabe Kapler (jury is still out, but he already made it longer than some thought he would), Carson Wentz (anointed too quickly), Brandon Graham (he wasn't a bust), Zach Ertz (not as "soft" as we thought), Michael Carter-Williams (remember all the triple-double hype?), Bobby Hoying (Kevin Kolb before Kevin Kolb), Domonic Brown (the one prospect Ruben Amaro can't trade!).

The Greatest Clutch Performers

8. Terrell Owens. Arrived with a reputation as a big-moment player—he had caught a legendary game-winner with three seconds to go in a playoff game for the Niners. He only got one postseason chance for the Eagles, playing the 2004 Super Bowl on a broken leg, although doctors wouldn't clear him. He snagged nine passes for 122 yards. Even in a losing effort, he deserved to be the MVP.

7. Bobby Jones. An elite sixth man who made the all-NBA defensive team eight times. His measurables don't stand out—in the 1983 Finals he averaged 12 points, 4.8 rebounds, two steals, and 2.3 blocks. But Jones seemed to shut down Magic Johnson or Jamaal Wilkes or even Kareem Abdul-Jabbar every time a big stop was needed.

6. Rick MacLeish. The thing is, MacLeish would often sleepwalk (sleepskate?) his way through regular-season games, infuriating coach Fred Shero. Then, he'd bolt awake for the playoffs. MacLeish is the franchise's all-time leader with 53 playoff goals and the only Flyer with 10 game-winning goals in the postseason. He scored two playoff OT game-winners and three postseason hat tricks.

5. Lenny Dykstra. Nails might be the biggest creep ever to pass through our town, but give the Devil his due. He had 15 hits, including six homers, in the 1993 postseason. His .348/.500/.913 slash line in that World Series is among the best ever. And in the seventh inning of Game 6, his three-run homer pulled the Phils back into the game. If only he could have also pitched in relief that night.

4. Danny Briere. Solid in the regular season, Briere saved his best for the postseason. He set the Flyers record with 30 points in the 2010 playoffs—just one short of Wayne Gretzky's NHL mark. In the unforgettable Game 7 comeback against Boston in the Eastern Conference, he snuck around the net and slipped one past Bruins goalie Tuukka Rask to tie the game at 3–3. And yeah, we'll give Simon Gagne an honorable mention here as well for scoring the magnificent game-winner that night.

3. Curt Schilling. Of course he's most famous for the "Bloody Sock" game with Boston. But Schilling was a clutch player here first. In Game 1 of the 1993 NLCS, he tied a record by striking out the first five batters. Two weeks later, in Game 5 of the World Series, he kept the Phils alive by tossing a complete game shutout against the Jays—who had scored 37 runs in the first four contests. In his career, Schilling pitched five elimination games for the Phils, Diamondbacks, and Sox. Every time he took the mound, his team won.

2. Nick Foles. When he stepped in for Carson Wentz in December of 2017, most fans feared the season was lost. But Foles, after a few shaky regular-season starts, was the number one reason the Eagles got to—and won—Super Bowl LII. In postseason games against the Falcons, Vikings, and Stinkin' Pats, he completed 76 percent of his throws, averaged 9.2 yards per attempt, and threw six TDs and just one interception. Caught a nifty Super Bowl TD as well. He almost repeated the feat in 2018, taking the Eagles back to the playoffs and beating the Bears before the magic ran out against New Orleans.

1. Bernie Parent. The Flyers captured just two Stanley Cups in their long history. Both times, Bernie received the Conn Smythe Trophy as playoff MVP. The greatest goalie in franchise history stepped up his game with a goals-against average of 2.02 in 1974 and 1.89 in 1975. He registered six shutouts in those two playoff years, including both Cup-clinching games. "Pressure? I didn't feel pressure," Bernie told these authors many years later. "The pressure would have been sitting at home trying to watch other teams play for the Cup."

Okay, you likely noticed we didn't include a single member of that great Phillies team that won five straight divisions and the 2008 World Series. They were so good under pressure that we decided to give them their own countdown.

8. Matt Stairs. Game 4, 2008 NLCS. Tie game, bottom of the eighth. Joe Buck: "Stairs rips one into the night. Deeeeep into right. Wayyyyy out of here. Philadelphia gets a pinch-hit, two-run shot and the Phillies lead, 7–5, in the eighth." It earned the 40-year-old Stairs a World Series ring and a lifetime of free beer in town.

7. Shane Victorino. He hit the homer to tie that Dodgers game that Stairs won. Also hit a grand slam off CC Sabathia in the '08 postseason. The Flyin' Hawaiian was a fan favorite for his energy, his bubbly personality, and his terrific defense.

6. Jason Werth. More than 2,100 men have played for the Phillies over the years. You know which one owns the franchise record for postseason homers? It's this guy, who slammed 11 in 37 games. But, yeah, we booed him when he came back as a Nat.

5. Brad Lidge. By definition, nearly every appearance by a closer is a clutch situation. Lights Out Lidge went 41-for-41 in those games during the 2008 regular season. Then he rolled seven more in the postseason. Struck out Tampa's Eric Hinske on a nasty slider to win it all.

4. Carlos Ruiz. In the two World Series, he hit .353/.488/.706. He nailed a few homers and also trickled a walk-off, check-swing 60-foot dribbler that drove in the winning run of Game 3 of the 2008 World Series. "Señor Octobre!"

3. Jimmy Rollins. Charlie Manuel called him "a red-light player. He loves when the lights are on and the game is on the line. He wants to be up there." Indeed, Rollins thrived putting the pressure on himself. In 2007 he declared the underdog Phils "the team to beat" in the NL East. For five straight seasons, he backed that up.

2. Cole Hamels. Check out this 2008 postseason timeline: He pitched eight innings of two-hit ball to beat the Brewers in the playoff opener. Then he beat the Dodgers, 3–2, in the

NLCS opener. Then he clinched that series in Game 5, allowing one run over seven innings. Then he beat Tampa in the World Series opener. Finally, on October 27, 2008, Hamels held the Rays to two runs over six as the Phils won that (much-delayed) game to capture their first title in 28 years.

Totals: Five starts, four wins, 35 innings, 23 hits, 31 strikeouts, nine walks, 1.80 ERA. MVP of both the NLCS and the World Series. Can't do any better than that.

1. Chase Utley. He tied an MLB record with five homers in the 2009 World Series. Made the great fake throw to deke out Jason Bartlett at home in the seventh inning of Game 5 of the '08 Series. Considering that the Phils won the Series two innings later, that run-saver qualifies as the best defensive play in franchise history.

"World F—in' champions."

Not-Clutch Philadelphia Sports Figures

8. Pat Burrell. Sure, he hit that key double off J. P. Howell in the seventh inning of Game 5 of the 2008 World Series. Pinch runner Eric Bruntlett then came around with the winning run. More often, Burrell disappointed in key moments. He was a career .186 hitter in the postseason, with just five homers and a lusty 37 whiffs in 114 postseason plate appearances. He did much better in the clutch around 2:00 a.m. in Old City.

7. John LeClair. The big guy averaged .51 goals per game during the regular season—prorate that, and it's 42 goals over an 82-game season. During the playoffs? He managed .30 goals per game, or 25 projected over a full season. Yes, it was an era when opponents clutched, grabbed, and essentially tackled LeClair without penalty. Still, we could have used a bit more production.

6. Bobby Abreu. The stat geeks go powder blue in the face arguing Abreu actually *was* a clutch player by citing his BABIP with two runners on and two outs in September games started by left-handed pitchers from west of the Mississippi. Bull, we say. (Actually, Bull Luzinski was a decent clutch hitter.) We just remember too many dreadful summer nights when we'd be heading for the Vet Stadium exits with the Phils trailing 7–1, only to look over our shoulder to see Abreu hit a meaningless homer.

5. Donovan McNabb. He's not higher on this list because he won nine playoff games, converted 4th-and-26, and staged some early-career game-winning drives. But fans didn't call him McChoke for nothing. From 2005 through the end of his Eagles career, the team went 7–18–1 in games he played decided by less than a TD. He couldn't connect late in that 2008 NFC title game at Arizona. And of course . . . Super Bowl XXXIX. We don't care whether he barfed. It's less important that he couldn't keep it down than it is that he couldn't get it done.

4. George McGinnis. A terrific regular-season player during his three seasons here in the '70s. In the postseason? He was "Honey, I shrunk the power forward." Consider these comparisons as a Sixer: points per game—21.6 in the regular season to 15.2 in the playoffs; rebounds—11.5 to 9.9; assists—4.1 to 3.5; steals—2.1 to 1.2. Sometimes he looked like he was just trying to hide behind Darryl Dawkins.

3. Andy Reid. At the end of 2018, Reid had more career wins than all but seven coaches in NFL history. He took his team to the playoffs 14 seasons. Alas, each time ended the same: frustration. There were squeakers, blowouts, blown leads. You know the numbers with the Eagles—nine times in the playoffs, no Super Bowl wins. At the end of each loss, the camera would catch Big Red standing behind his enormous play chart, eyes blinking, mustache twitching. A great coach, but never a finisher.

2. Every Flyers goalie since 1987. There was Bernie and then Pelle and then baby Hextall. And then a parade of pretenders giving up inopportune goals at the toughest of moments. Hextall version 2.0 letting in a center-ice floater from Claude Lemieux. Sean Burke and Garth Snow going back and forth to see which one had a more expansive five-hole. Roman Čechmánek imploding in 2003. Michael Leighton's "where's-the-puck" Cup loser in 2010. With the exceptions of John Vanbiesbrouck in 1999 and Brian Boucher in 2000, it's been a parade of Mr. Softies. Here's hoping young Carter Hart breaks the string of futility.

1. Gene Mauch. Perhaps the most legendary choke job in pro sports history. The 1964 Phils had a 6½-game lead with 12 to go. Then came the Phold. There were many contributors, but crusty manager Mauch was most to blame. He shortened his bullpen, giving up on closer Jack Baldschun, who was having a fine season. And, most infamously, he shortened his rotation to two starters—Jim Bunning and Chris Short. Not surprisingly, both ran out of gas. Mauch managed 27 years in the Majors and never, ever got to a World Series. How he hung on 22 seasons after this stinkeroo defies logic.

Guys Who Were Both

It's possible, of course, to fall on your face one year and shine in the showcase the next. Here are seven who gained both reputations. We left the eighth spot blank for a reason. So far, Carson Wentz hasn't risen to the big moment; we're confident he eventually will.

7. Ron Hextall. We already mentioned him, but the details are worth discussing. As a 23-year-old rookie, Angry Ron stunned the hockey world by frustrating the powerful Edmonton Oilers. He won the Conn Smythe Trophy, even in a losing effort. Gretzky called it "the greatest effort I've ever seen by a goalie." After that? Well, in two stints with the Orange and Black, Hexy never was that guy again. His goals-against average in the playoffs was over 3.00, and he always seemed good for one disheartening cheapie a night.

6. Brian Dawkins. Sacrilege you say? Sure it is. But let's examine it. Dawkins's NFC title game against the Falcons in 2004 is a signature game: the crumpling hit on Alge Crumpler, the smackdown of Mike Vick, a crucial interception. That kind of game deservedly puts Dawk in Canton. The OT win against Green Bay in 2003 was special as well, culminating in his interception of Brett Favre's pop-up desperation pass. But there were conference championship games where he did little—the crushing loss to Tampa and the next year's loss to Carolina, in which he produced a stat line entirely of zeroes.

5. Reggie White. More sacrilege. Reggie played five postseason games with the Eagles. They lost four, and he wasn't much of a factor. Dallas OT Erik Williams once performed the magic trick of making the Minister of Defense appear invisible. But in the one win, White was magnificent. Against the Saints in 1992, he brutalized QB Bobby Hebert for a safety that was part of a 26-point Eagles' run after they fell behind 26–10.

4. Cliff Lee. Lee pitched one of the great postseasons ever in 2009—4–0 in four starts, 1.56 ERA, two magic nights humiliating the Yankees. We had already picked out a spot for his statue by Citizens Bank Park. Then came 2011 and Game 2 of the NLDS against St. Louis. The Phils staked Lee to a 4–0 lead. Then he blew it—allowing five runs in six-plus innings. That stung. It stung more when Lee was asked how he felt about the loss. All we got was a nonchalant shrug and the unforgettably bad quote: "That's baseball."

3. Keith Primeau. For most of his career, the guy was historically bad in the postseason. Through age 31, he managed nine goals in 110 playoff games—including just three in 40 with the Flyers. One of those he scored in the fifth OT period against Pittsburgh. Maybe that flipped on his clutch gene. In the 2004 Cup run, Primeau scored nine times in 18 games. Against Tampa in the conference finals, he created shorthanded goals, power play goals, and a Game 6 game-tying goal with 1:47 left to keep the season alive. All in all, he erased his old reputation.

2. Mike Schmidt. We'll just quote the Hall of Famer from a 1990 interview: "Going into 1980, I was the highest paid player, but I wasn't the clutch guy. Sure I had the awards, but there were better hitters under pressure than I was. I didn't deliver the way a Steve Garvey or Greg Luzinski did. The rap on me was I hit a lot of early homers, none in the clutch.

"Well, 1980 was when I finally became comfortable in the clutch role. I hit seven home runs down the stretch that we needed badly and a couple in the World Series that helped out, too. I really helped my image. I felt comfortable in pressure spots after that. I think if there was any question of who they wanted up there with the game on the line, it was answered in 1980."

Yep.

1. Ryan Howard. Two moments. It's the 2009 playoffs in Colorado and the Phils trail by two in the ninth. Howard, scheduled to be the fifth hitter of the inning, tells his teammates, "Just get me to the plate, boys." They do. With two outs, two on, and two strikes against him, he powers a ball to the right-field wall that leads to the win.

Now, it's 2010, bottom of the ninth of Game 6 of the NLCS—an elimination game against the Giants at Citizens Bank Park. Two men on, Howard up with the Phils down one. San Francisco closer Brian Wilson's seventh pitch, a slider, catches the corner of the plate. Howard stands meekly with the bat on his shoulder. Season over.

Howard was, alternatively, the MVP of the NLCS, and a guy who hit .213 with 36 strikeouts in his last 75 postseason at bats. The toast of the town and a slice of stale bread. We'll choose to remember the good times.

Best One-on-One Rivalries

Within the team game, we've been treated to some terrific individual rivalries over the years. Here are 10 of our favorites.

10. Joel Embiid vs. Russell Westbrook. Or Embiid vs. Hassan Whiteside. Or Embiid vs. Andre Drummond. The Sixers star center loves the trash talk and personal grudges. He has aggravated Westbrook, scuffled with Whiteside, and dominated Drummond, saying, "I own real estate in his head." The one rival Joel never fared well against was Al Horford. We assume when Horford moved from the Celtics to the Sixers in July 2019, Embiid greeted him with a nice meal and a few rounds of Shirley Temples.

9. Bobby Taylor vs. Michael Irvin. When Ray Rhodes drafted the rangy Taylor in 1995, it was specifically with the idea of covering the 6-foot-2 Cowboys receiver. Good plan. Taking away Taylor's rookie season (which we'll call a learning experience), the two men matched up six times. Irvin had just 22 catches for 315 yards and a single touchdown.

8. Andrew Toney vs. Dennis Johnson. Another case of a team adding a player just to stop its rival's star. In this case, the Celtics traded for DJ in 1983 after Toney torched them throughout the Sixers' championship season. Hey, they didn't call him the Boston Strangler for nothing.

7. Steve Carlton vs. Johnny Bench. This was one of those Hall of Fame matchups of the 1970s that always caused you to stop what you were doing and intently listen to Harry Kalas describe each pitch. Unfortunately, Bench often got the best of Lefty. Twice, the Reds catcher hit three home runs in a game against Carlton.

6. Claude Giroux vs. Sidney Crosby. This one wasn't business—it was personal. Asked why he once slashed Giroux across the wrists, Crosby simply said, "Because I don't like him." Sid the Snotty Kid usually got the best of his Flyers' counterpart, with those Cups and all. But Flyers fans could always point to that 2012 playoff game when Claude blasted Crosby five seconds into the game, forced a turnover, and scored the early game-winning goal.

4. Chuck Bednarik vs. Chuck Noll. The NFL was a nastier game back in the 1950s, and nothing was as intense as the hatred between Bednarik and Noll, then a guard for the Browns. One memorable contest ended with those two slugging it out on the 50-yard line as the network credits ran over them on the TV screens of America.

5. Jon Runyan vs. Michael Strahan. They matched up 13 times between 2000 and 2005, and Strahan had 13 sacks. To be fair, Strahan dominated the rivalry early, but Runyan adjusted and came to hold his own (*and* the Giants' defensive end's jersey). Strahan described the matchup as "wrestling with a dancing bear." At his Hall of Fame induction in 2014, Strahan asked Runyan to stand up and said, "You were the toughest man I ever faced . . . You made me a student of the game."

3. Julius Erving vs. Larry Bird. Of the dozens of times they met, all everyone remembers is the famous fight of 1984, with Doc's long fingers enveloping Bird's throat. Doc always said he was embarrassed by the incident—but Sixers fans loved it.

2. Dave Schultz vs. Terry O'Reilly. Certainly a lot of Boston hate on this list, eh? No one recorded how many times these two NHL heavyweights fought, but it seemed to occur every game between the Flyers and Boston Bruins—often more than once per. Said Schultz: "I'm not sure I can call any guy the toughest, but me and Terry went at it more than anyone else." Said O'Reilly: "Dave had Game 7 anger in him every night."

1. Wilt Chamberlain vs. Bill Russell. You expected anything else? This is probably the greatest one-on-one rivalry in the history of team sports. We love the stories of how the Celtics would play every Thanksgiving in Philadelphia—and Wilt would try to slow Russell down by loading him up with his mom's home cooking. Another great story was how Wilt signed a $100,000 contract in 1965—and Russell threatened to retire until the Celtics gave him $100,001. Unfortunately, you know how this ends: Russell's Celts won seven of their eight playoff series against Chamberlain's teams. They were 4–0 in seventh games.

Honorable mention: Reggie White vs. Erik Williams, Chris Therien vs. Jaromír Jágr, Tommy Hutton vs. Tom Seaver, Tie Domi vs. Donald Brashear.

The Classiest People in Philadelphia Sports History :: Bill Campbell

Bill Campbell, the dean of Philadelphia sports, had a career in broadcasting spanning seven decades. He served as the play-by-play announcer for the Eagles, Phillies, and Sixers. He also helped invent sports-talk radio in this city.

Beyond that, Bill personified class and dignity. Here is his list, written in 2006, of the classiest people he dealt with over the years. Bill passed away in 2014. We still miss him.

10. Bob Clarke, Flyers center and general manager. He's a real man, a genuine guy. What I always liked is that he wouldn't try to duck out of the blame when he made a mistake.

9. Paul Arizin, Villanova and Sixers forward. He was the greatest competitor I've ever seen in any sport. I remember him as a young kid, starting out at Nova. He would come to the Warriors game and study Joe Fulks, watching his great jump shot, to get better. Paul became a great college player and then a great pro.

8. Mo Cheeks, Sixers point guard and coach. As a player, he was such a good guy. He's the last one I would have projected to become a coach, because I thought he was too nice to be tough enough. Honestly, his success has surprised me.

7. Tony Taylor, Phillies second baseman. One of the first Latin players in town, which couldn't have been easy for him. But Tony fit in, and he commanded everybody's respect. You never heard anyone say an unkind thing about him.

6. John Vukovich, Phillies infielder and coach. Just a good guy. I know what it has cost him emotionally not to coach third base anymore because he's really an on-field guy. But he has handled the change with dignity. (Note: Vukovich passed away from cancer in 2007.)

5. Merrill Reese, Eagles broadcaster. He follows the rule that was taught to me by Byrum Saam when I started with the Phils: you can't be a decent broadcaster if you don't prepare. Merrill does that, and nobody deserves success more than he because he worked so hard to get it.

4. Julius Erving, Sixers forward. The most gracious and accommodating guy to the media and fans. With as much notoriety as he had, he was always open. And he was always great with kids.

3. Connie Mack, A's manager and owner. I was a 23-year-old kid coming out of the service when I met Mr. Mack. He always called everyone "Mister," even his players. You can't imagine what it was like having the patriarch of baseball, in his eighties, calling a punk kid like me "Mister."

2. Norm Van Brocklin, Eagles quarterback. I was broadcasting the Eagles when he came in 1958. We did a weekly TV show together, and in preparing it, he and I would listen to my play-by-play from the previous game. He'd listen to my work and say, "Bill, you're the worst damned broadcaster I've ever heard. Get the damn play right." It was kind of jarring at first, but after a while I learned from him.

One other thing about Dutch: he was at a party at my house once. He was talking to my daughter, Chris, who was about five, and asked her, "Little girl, why don't you have a dog?"

"Because my daddy won't let me get one," she said.

Months passed. We all forgot about it. Then, on the morning of July 24—her birthday—the doorbell rang at 7:00 a.m. I answered the door in my pajamas, and there was this big quarterback with a small puppy in his arms. Chrissy had that dog for years.

1. Robin Roberts, Phillies pitcher. He never changed. Even at the end of his career, he was the same guy as when he started. No pretense, just a completely genuine guy.

10. Larry Bowa. He was 5-foot-10 and about 145 pounds of battery acid when he came up to the Phils. We recently dug out his 1971 baseball card, on which he looks like an escapee from the high school junior varsity team.

9. Pelle Lindbergh. The math doesn't compute—a 5-foot-9 guy covering 24 square feet of open space—but the Swedish import did it masterfully. Lindbergh would work and sweat so hard in games that he often finished them 15 pounds less than his stated weight of 180. Ahh, what might have been.

8. Darren Sproles. We always got a kick seeing him standing in the huddle next to one of the massive linemen like Lane Johnson or Jason Peters. And we loved when Merrill Reese referred to him as "Mighty Mouse." Sproles stands 5-foot-6, has legs like tree trunks, and could run through linemen as much as run around them. One of those guys you wish spent his entire career here.

7. Bobby Shantz. Sportswriters of the day referred to him as the Elfin Southpaw or the Little Sampson of the Mound. They sure don't write like that anymore. The 5-foot-6, 140-pound lefty out of Pottstown won the 1952 American League MVP Award pitching for the Philadelphia A's. There are old heads who swear they saw a gust of wind blow him off the Shibe Park pitcher's mound.

6. Smarty Jones. How many times did you hear him called "the little colt from Philadel-phia"? Or "the small horse with the big heart"? We'll always remember Smarty running away from Rock Hard Ten in the 2004 Preakness. It looked like a mouse scampering from a rhino.

5. Jameer Nelson. A 6-foot-nothing point guard out of Chester High, Nelson was college basketball's top player in 2003–2004. He left St. Joe's as the Hawks' all-time leader in points, assists, and—most importantly—wins.

4. Wilbert Montgomery. They listed him at 5-foot-10 and 190 pounds, but who's kid-ding? He lasted to the sixth round of the NFL draft in 1977 because scouts thought he was too small to make it in the pros. When he left eight seasons later, he was the Eagles' all-time leading rusher. And that doesn't even count the 194 yards he put up against the Cowboys in the 1980 NFC title game.

3. Tommy McDonald. The smallest player in the Pro Football Hall of Fame. The amaz-ing thing about McDonald—who stood 5-foot-9 and weighed 170—was his durability. He missed just three games in a 12-year career. His 35-yard touchdown catch in the 1960 NFL Championship Game remains a highlight in Eagles history.

2. Jimmy Rollins. His original scouting report said, "Small package, big skills." By his own account, the 5-foot-8 MVP said, "I was short and skinny, but when I picked up a ball and a bat, there was nothing people could say. After that, they didn't care. They'd just say, 'He can play.'"

1. Allen Iverson. The ultimate little giant. Twenty years from now, our lingering memory of AI will be of that scrawny little body—all elbows and knees—yo-yoing a crossover dribble into the land of the giants and scooping a feathery layup just before some 7-footer pounded him to the ground. He always got up again.

The Five Greatest Receivers in Eagles History :: Tommy McDonald

Tommy McDonald is the Eagles' only Hall of Fame receiver; he helped lead the team to the 1960 championship.

This is the list Tommy wrote for us in 2006. He passed away in 2018, before we decided to update this book. We asked Tommy's friend, Ray Didinger—playwright of *Tommy and Me*—if he felt the list warranted change from 12 years earlier.

Said Ray: "You could add DeSean Jackson and Zach Ertz at the bottom, but neither of them cracks the top five. I think Tommy's original list still stands."

And so here it is, in McDonald's words:

5. Pete Retzlaff. A great receiver, he just didn't get thrown to a lot. Back then if you got thrown to two or three times in a game, that was a lot. Plus, he agreed to play tight end, which cut down his receptions even more. Nowadays it's easier for somebody to catch a lot of balls. The game is different.

4. Pete Pihos. Well, I didn't get to see him play, but his stats speak for themselves. Almost 400 receptions and 61 touchdowns back in the early days of the NFL. For that era, those were great numbers.

3. Mike Quick. An unbelievably reliable receiver. He always got the job done. With Quick, you didn't hope he'd catch it. You knew he'd catch it.

2. Tommy McDonald. Hey, I scored 84 touchdowns myself (66 for the Eagles). In 1960, I only caught 39 balls, but 13 of them went for touchdowns. Say this about me: God made me little, but he gave me a big heart.

1. Harold Carmichael. A receiver has one object, that's to get in the end zone. His 79 TDs are the most in franchise history. That says a lot to me. So big, so smooth. How could anyone cover him?

And what about Terrell Owens? Well, it's hard for me to grade him because he didn't spend very much of his career with the Eagles. But he's awesome. I'd put him up there with Marvin Harrison and Randy Moss and Keyshawn Johnson as the best guys around.

Greatest Mcs and Macs

Well, Big Daddy is Irish, and Glen is a true Mac, so who better than us to deliver a fun All-Mc and All-Mac list you can refer to on that grandest of holidays, St. Patrick's Day?

10. T. J. McConnell. Starting with the Process, and continuing through the additions of Jimmy Butler and Tobias Harris, there was one thing you could always count on if you bought a ticket to see the Sixers. And that was that the hustling and scrapping McConnell was always going to leave everything he had on the court.

9. Tim McCarver. As an announcer he got on your last nerve, but he gave the Phillies nine good seasons. And where would Steve Carlton have been without his "personal catcher" for all those years?

8. George McGinnis. The Sixers' return from the dead in the '70s truly begins with Big Mac.

7. LeSean McCoy. Yeah, he wasn't a nice guy—to say the least. But he is the Eagles' all-time leading rusher, and he just can't be left off the list.

6. Donovan McNabb. Well, he comes from Chicago where they dye the Chicago River green on St. Patty's Day. That puts him on this list, doesn't it?

From this point on, this list is reserved for champions.

5. Dwayne McClain. April 1, 1985. The greatest college basketball game ever played, for our money. Nova beat Georgetown, 66–64, for the NCAA Championship. Guess who was the leading scorer, with 17 points? Dwayne went to the NCAA Elite Eight three out of his four years with Nova. And the man could slam.

4. Bake McBride. An oft-forgotten member of the World Champion 1980 Phillies, but not by us. Take Bake off those Phils and you can forget about the first championship the franchise ever won. A clutch, money right fielder, with a great 'fro to boot.

3. Rick MacLeish. Two Stanley Cup Championships, and who can forget the sight of Rick gliding down the ice with his long hair flowing? Damn, it was fun when they played without helmets, wasn't it? He leads all Flyers with 10 game-winning goals in the playoffs and rightly earned a spot in the franchise's Hall of Fame. Rick stayed in the area, and we used to see him down the Shore hanging at the Deauville Inn in Strathmere.

2. Tommy McDonald. Not only the top receiver on the Eagles' 1960 Championship team but also a member of the NFL Hall of Fame. And a nicer, funnier guy you never met.

Big Daddy says: Remember playing touch football as a kid? You'd argue over who was going to be what player. "I'm Mike Quick." "I'm Wilbert Montgomery." Well, the first player I wanted to be when I was going deep was Tommy Mac. Telling McDonald about that many years later was a real thrill for me.

1. Tug McGraw. We don't know where to begin. He captured the hearts of this city, first as a World Champion pitcher and years later while going through his courageous battle against a brain tumor. He stayed funny and engaging right to the very end. We miss you, Tugger.

Big Daddy special mention: Mac and Mac. Glen and Jody McDonald don't work together anymore, but their show was terrific. Nowadays, Glen's show with Ray Didinger is "don't miss" radio. And when I get in my car to drive to the station and Jody McDonald is on, I smile, because Jody always brings it, and I know I'll have a sizable built-in audience waiting for me.

Ten Eagles Players That Fans Never Liked :: Jon Marks

Jon Marks cohosts the 94-WIP Afternoon Show with Ike Reese. He was raised in Willow Grove. His first favorite athletes were Lonnie Smith, Wilbert Montgomery, and Maurice Cheeks.

John says: "This isn't a most hated Eagles list. This is a specific list for Eagles players who fans *never* liked. And they aren't necessarily bad players or busts—although that helps. Some were productive but disliked for other reasons."

10. Danny Watkins. Fans scratched their heads when the Eagles drafted the 26-year-old Watkins with the 23rd overall pick in 2011. Watkins was supposed to start at right guard from Day One, but that didn't happen. Simply, Watkins didn't enjoy playing football. A volunteer firefighter growing up in Canada, Watkins didn't prepare hard like his teammates because, well, he was hanging out at the firehouse.

I did some player shows on the radio with Watkins during his rookie season. He always came to the broadcasts with a group of guys from a local firehouse. He was a nice guy, smiling and more than willing to sign autographs and talk to fans. But it became clear in his second season that the NFL wasn't going to work out. He just wasn't into it. So when Andy Reid was fired by the Eagles, Chip Kelly released Watkins during the following training camp.

9. Donovan McNabb. Unlike others who were disliked by the majority of the fan base, Donovan had many supporters. After all, his number is retired and he's considered the best QB in franchise history. However, those fans who disliked him—well, they *really* disliked him. They were loud about it. And it started the night he was drafted. Is it deserved? Probably not. Is it reality? Yup.

Even with McNabb's success, many will only remember him for his passive aggressiveness, goofiness, and coming up small when the light was shining the brightest.

8. Cary Williams and Bradley Fletcher. The lone duo of the list. They started and ended their Eagles careers together, playing 2013–2014. Williams was a somewhat talented guy who played hard, but his Eagles career was doomed before he even played a game. Williams missed his first OTAs with the team and gave the famous "had to check on my sconces" excuse. It didn't get better from there. Williams was plagued by mental mistakes and aloof comments.

Fletcher, meanwhile, was signed to start at corner but was exposed early and often, giving up more yards and TDs than almost anyone else at the position. It was compounded by an unqualified defensive coordinator (Bill Davis) who constantly left Fletcher on an island by himself.

7. Todd Pinkston. When you are known by most as "Stinkston," it's safe to say you make this list. The fans probably beat up on Todd Pinkston more than any receiver in the Andy Reid era. Remember Rickie Manning Jr. roughing up Pinky during the 2003 NFC Championship Game? How about the following season, when he mysteriously "lost the ball in the lights" at FedExField?

6. Mike Mamula. He coined the term "workout warrior" after his performance at the 1995 combine. He was the first player who trained for its drills and tests. His performance was so impressive that Eagles coach Ray Rhodes traded two second-round picks to Tampa Bay to move up five picks in the first round to select Mamula. The Bucs, meanwhile, took Warren Sapp with the pick they got from the Eagles. Sapp went on to have a Hall of Fame career; Mamula never lived up to expectations and was out of the league after five seasons.

Mamula was actually a decent player, hardly a bust—but tell that to Eagles fans. The times I brought up the question for this list, Mamula was mentioned as often as anyone.

5. Izel Jenkins. His nickname was Toast because he was burnt so many times. His five years with the Eagles also coincided with the best Eagles defenses of the modern era. Unfortunately, he was the weak link. If there was a deep pass to an opposition wide receiver, number 46 was probably a step or two behind.

4. DeMarco Murray. Former Cowboys haven't had much luck here, and Murray is a prime example. Chip Kelly thought he struck oil when Murray, coming off two Pro Bowl seasons in Dallas, was available on the free agent market in 2015.

Needless to say, the move never worked out. Murray only managed 702 rushing yards, and compounded his poor stats by sliding down on a 3rd-and-1 to avoid contact from a cornerback. Then after getting just eight carries in a game at New England, Murray reportedly complained to owner Jeff Lurie about his role in the offense during the flight back to Philadelphia.

3. Nnamdi Asomugha. Perhaps the best example of the failed Dream Team. When he was signed by the Eagles, Asomugha was considered the second-best corner in the NFL. It didn't take long to see he wasn't close to that—or even an adequate starter.

Like many Eagles players from this period, there was a level of disconnect on and off the field for Nnamdi. He never fit in with the team or the city. He was more comfortable talking about economics or his postcareer aspirations than hanging with teammates in the trainer's room. Famously, it was reported that Asomugha ate lunch by himself in his 1997 Nissan Maxima.

2. Jason Babin. He played for the Eagles in 2009 and then returned with a star's reputation in 2011. With him came Wide Nine Guru Jim Washburn, and the sacks kept coming. Babin had 18 sacks, third most in franchise history, and made the Pro Bowl. But his arrogance and selfishness made him the least popular player in the locker room. He cared only about his sack numbers, refusing to play the run.

Babin was released halfway through the 2012 season, mostly because his act had grown old with teammates—and also Andy Reid. After being released, Babin said he had heard vile things from Eagles fans during games and called the Eagles organization a "big socialist system."

1. Sam Bradford. Sammy wasn't a bad guy like others. He was just a mediocre player on a Chip Kelly–built team full of mediocre players. The best thing Bradford ever did in the NFL was earn money. Lots of it.

I never believed he had the intangibles to be a successful NFL quarterback. So when Kelly traded Nick Foles *and* a second-round pick to the Rams for Bradford, Eagles fans were only going to warm to him if he led the team on a playoff run. Which was never going to happen.

I almost felt bad for Bradford at times; he had that deer-in-the-headlights look. He looked bad in the uniform, sleeves too long. Quarterbacks are supposed to be the alpha males of offense, able to manage the rigors of an NFL season while balancing media obligations and the spotlight. And that sure wasn't Sam.

As we write this chapter, Bryce Harper is just beginning his first season with this Phillies, having signed a 13-year, $330 million deal. We can only envision that the next time we update this book, he will be right at the top of this list.

The memory plays tricks. Neither Doc nor Moses came to Philly as a free agent. The Sixers bought Julius Erving from the Nets, and Moses Malone arrived via a trade.

Nor was Terrell Owens a free agent. He became an Eagle in a swap with the Ravens (remember that?). Otherwise, T.O. would make both of these lists. His one-and-a-half-season career here was spectacular—but the fallout was devastating.

We also didn't qualify undrafted rookie free agents—like Tim Kerr with the Flyers. Just veteran players who came from another team. Anyway, here we go:

The Best

10. Jeremy Roenick, Flyers, 2001. One of the most engaging athletes ever to pass through Philadelphia. Roenick was on the downside of his Hall of Fame career when he joined the Flyers, but he still led the club in scoring his first two seasons. He played through concussions and broken jaws. Among many classy guys on this list.

9. Ricky Watters, Eagles, 1995. Yeah, we know, "For who? For what?" Some fans will remember Ricky only for those four foolish words. But you shouldn't forget the 3,794 rushing yards he put up from 1995 to 1997. No running back in franchise history ever surpassed that total over three seasons. In fact, no one else in franchise history ever had three straight years surpassing 1,000 yards.

8. Cliff Lee, Phillies, 2011. He came back on a five-year, $120 million deal a year after GM Ruben Amaro foolishly traded him to Seattle. Lee blew out his elbow in year four of the deal, but, boy, those first three seasons were special. That 2011 rotation—with Roy Halladay, Cole Hamels, and Roy Oswalt—was among the best in baseball history. Lee was a joy to watch. He worked fast, never walked anyone, and you could be home from the ballpark before the 10 o'clock news.

7. George McGinnis, Sixers, 1975. His three seasons here—in which he averaged 21.6 points and 11.6 rebounds per game—are kind of forgotten. But McGinnis and Doug Collins formed the foundation that helped the Sixers rise in the mid-'70s, forming the bridge between the 9–73 era and the team that eventually won the title. The knock was that his scoring always went way down in the postseason. Eventually traded for Bobby Jones, which helped the franchise as well.

6. Jon Runyan, Eagles, 2000. A rock at right tackle who didn't miss a game in six seasons. Do you remember how it all started? Andy Reid was wooing Runyan at a Center City steakhouse, when Temple's John Chaney (who was dining separately) sprinted to their table and shouted, "Don't come here. Don't ever come here for these fans." Gee, thanks, Coach.

5. Danny Briere, Flyers, 2007. When the skilled but undersized forward hit the open market at age 29, everyone in hockey expected him to sign with his hometown Montreal Canadiens. Give Paul Holmgren credit for sneaking in the first day of free agency and inking Briere to an eight-year deal. Briere was solid during the regular season (he twice led the Flyers in goals), but he saved the magic for the postseason. In 2010, he broke the franchise record with 30 points in the playoffs. Another class act who knew how to treat fans with respect.

4. Troy Vincent, Eagles, 1996. Many people forget how good he was in his eight years in green. Vincent and the oft-maligned Bobby Taylor gave the Birds a pair of top-flight cornerbacks season after season. Vincent made five straight Pro Bowls as an Eagle. Just two players in franchise history—Reggie White and Pete Pihos—ever topped that streak.

3. Malcolm Jenkins, Eagles, 2014. In his first five seasons in green, Jenkins played in an amazing 98.4 percent of the Eagles defensive snaps—often covering ground for inexperienced or untalented partners in the secondary. An iron man, a smart player, a leader on the team and in the community. Give GM Howie Roseman credit. Several free agent safeties (Jairus Byrd, T. J. Ward) drew more attention and more money when they signed in 2014, but none performed as well over time as Jenkins.

2. Pete Rose, Phillies, 1979. At the time, his $800,000 annual salary was so exorbitant that Phils ownership convinced Channel 29 to help foot the bill. At age 38, Rose arrived with one assignment: convert a team of talented underachievers into a champion. In 1980, he delivered. Rose was not quite the white-hot talent that he was in his earlier years in Cincinnati. But there never would have been a parade without him.

1. Nick Foles, Eagles, 2017. You know the story: Foles had early success with the Eagles, bounced around the NFL, considered retiring, and returned here to back up young Carson Wentz. At the time, we viewed him as just a slight upgrade over Chase Daniel. Eleven months later, he was brushing confetti out of his hair as the Super Bowl MVP. A year after that, he performed late-season magic and pulled the Birds into the playoffs again. Nick Foles shouldn't have to pick up a meal tab in Philadelphia for the rest of his life.

Honorable mention: *Brandon Brooks, Jim Eisenreich, William Fuller, Scott Hartnell, Raúl Ibañez, Alshon Jeffery, Steve Mix, Asante Samuel, Jim Thome, Jayson Werth*

The Worst

10. Chris Boniol, Eagles, 1997. When he came here, he boasted the highest field-goal percentage in NFL history. We snickered at stealing one from the Cowboys. The joke was on us. A more gutless player never wore Eagles green. Boniol couldn't kick outside of wind-shielded Texas Stadium, and he certainly couldn't perform under pressure. Our everlasting impression is of him scooping up the snap that Tommy Hutton botched against the Cowboys and dancing around like Urkel on crack.

9. Scott Williams, Sixers, 1994. General manager John Lucas gave Williams a *seven-year*, $18 million deal, figuring that the 6-foot-10 stiff had something to do with all those Chicago Bulls championships. Umm, maybe that was more because of guys named Jordan and Pippen. Over four-plus years here, he averaged a lusty 5.3 points per game and 6.8 muscle pulls per month.

8. Danny Tartabull, Phillies, 1997. He'd rank higher on this list if he had signed more than a one-year deal at the (relatively) cheap price of $2 million. Tartabull fouled a ball off his foot on Opening Day, struggled for three games (0 for 7), and then went on the disabled list—forever. Cost per at bat: $285,714. Cost per hit: Infinity.

7. Chris Gratton, Flyers, 1997. If you can remember back, he really was a dynamic young player for a horrible Tampa team who was going to supplement (or perhaps replace) Eric Lindros at center. No one envisioned how much he would shrink in the spotlight of playing for a fan base that actually paid attention. He got a $9 million signing bonus, a $16 million contract, and an immediate case of what Roberto Durán used to call "manos de piedras"—hands of stone.

6. Byron Maxwell, Eagles, 2015. Maxwell thrived in Seattle's "Legion of Boom" defense, where the secondary was loaded with Pro Bowlers. But change his role from supporting actor there to lead cornerback here, and he just withered. Chip Kelly gave Maxwell a six-year, $63 million contract, and he wound up being graded the NFL's 80th best cornerback in 2015. Just a year later, after Kelly was bounced, Maxwell was shipped to Miami along with other detritus for a draft pick that was eventually converted into Carson Wentz. So at least he's got that going for him.

5. Matt Geiger, Sixers, 1998. Signed a six-year, $48 million contract and—within weeks—declared that "basketball doesn't mean that much to me." Also sniffed his annoyance at Philadelphia weather, whining that shoveling snow "hurts my back." The Vanilla Gorilla had one great moment as a 76er, when he planted bratty Reggie Miller on his keister during the 1999 playoffs. Other than that, he mostly sat on the bench nursing arthritic knees and styling in $1,200 sunglasses. We're not sure if he's actually come off the Sixers' salary cap yet.

4. Vincent Lecavalier, Flyers, 2013. Everyone in hockey knew the four-time All-Star was cooked at age 33, when his production fell to just 10 goals. Everyone, that is, except Flyers GM Paul Holmgren. Homer gave him a five-year, $22.5 million deal, explaining that coach Peter Laviolette's up-tempo system was the tonic to rejuvenate old Vinnie. Then Holmgren fired the coach three games into the new season. Replacement coach Craig Berube had no use for the offense-first old centerman.

3. Lance Parrish, Phils, 1987. Expectations were high when Bill Giles bucked other Major League owners in the Era of Collusion by signing the muscle-bound, strong-armed catcher away from the Tigers. Parrish had won three Gold Gloves and five Silver Slugger awards in Detroit. In the Vet, it all turned to rust. He raged at the fans, sulked through minor injuries, and counted the days until he could escape back to the American League.

2. Ilya Bryzgalov, Flyers, 2011. Another Holmgren disaster that placed the franchise in salary cap hell, although you can blame this one partly on owner Ed Snider, who had been searching for a franchise goalie for a quarter-century. "Bryzgoalie" was alternately fun and infuriating, spectacular and stupefying. One factor that pushes him up this list is that the Flyers traded backup Sergei Bobrovsky to avoid the possibility of a goalie controversy. Bobrovsky went on to win two Vezina Trophies in Columbus; Bryzgalov went on to the far side of the moon.

1. Nnamdi Asomugha, Eagles, 2011. GM Joe Banner conceived the so-called Dream Team, signing big-name free agents Vince Young, Ronnie Brown, Jason Babin, Dominique Rodgers-Cromartie, and Steve Smith (not the good one). It was an amazing collection of overpriced stiffs, and none exemplified it more than Asomugha, who made it to the cover of *Sports Illustrated* with the caption "Philly Lands the Biggest Prize." Soon enough, he was getting burned every Sunday by run-of-the-mill wide receivers. A year later he was so disconnected from teammates that he would sneak out during practice and eat lunch alone in his car.

Glen says: I was at Eagles training camp at Lehigh on July 30, 2011, the day the Eagles signed Asomugha. It also happened to be the same day the Phillies traded for outfielder Hunter Pence. I went on WIP and predicted dynasties for both franchises. Oh well, 0-for-2.

Dishonorable mention: *Stacy Andrews, David Bell, Elton Brand, Adam Eaton, Tim Harris, Dhani Jones, Carlos Santana, Kenny Thomas, John Vanbiesbrouck*

John Clark grew up a Philadelphia sports fan in Delaware County. He has been a sports anchor/reporter for NBC-10 and NBC Sports Philadelphia since 2001.

Clark has earned the nickname Johnny Airport with his uncanny ability to track down athletes for exclusive interviews as they arrive in town. It's a combination of hustle and intuition that lands him the big fish.

"And time," Clark added. "Lots of time. I've hit some dead ends, too. We don't show you the ones that don't work out."

Clark said his goal is not to confront or embarrass subjects. "I have the same interests as the Philadelphia fan wanting to hear what the new athlete in town has to say about coming to our city."

Here are 10 of his favorite times:

10. Cliff Lee signs with the Phillies, December 2010. Everyone thought he was going to the Yankees. But he surprised the world by coming to the Phils. I learned that he was flying into the private airport at PHL the next day. Usually, people there just drive off the tarmac in an SUV, so I didn't think I'd get a chance. But Lee had a long private flight from Arkansas, and he had to go to the bathroom. Luckily, he went into the airport lobby. I followed him into the lobby and talked to his wife and his agent. When Cliff came out of the bathroom, we had a nice, exclusive interview that ended up running around the country. Fans all over were shocked to see him come here. I was just lucky Cliff had to use the men's room.

9. Alshon Jeffery signs with the Eagles, March 2017. One thing sticks out. He was a big-time receiver, and I asked him, "How come you chose to join the Eagles?" He said, "Because I think Carson Wentz can be MVP of the NFL." This was just after Wentz's rookie season, so I thought that said a lot. Alshon foresaw something, didn't he?

8. Bryan Colangelo gets in trouble, June 2018. The news had broken about his burner accounts, and I learned he was coming back from LA. I wanted to give him a chance to tell his side to everyone in Philadelphia. He was not happy to see me and asked that we turn off the camera. We did, but I said people wanted to hear what he had to say. He looked me in the eye and told me, on the record, that he didn't know what was going on with the accounts or who was posting on them. It was a few days later that the Sixers determined it was his wife. I didn't get any video, but he gave me some on-the-record quotes that shed light before people really knew what was up with the story.

7. Carson Wentz joins the Eagles, April 2016. We were covering the draft in Chicago. Word was out that the Eagles wanted him at Pick 2. He flew in from North Dakota, and I was able to track down the flight, so we got the first interview as Wentz arrived to be drafted. He had on glasses; he looked like the student part of student-athlete. What a good, humble kid. You could really see his decency.

6. Jimmy Butler gets traded to the Sixers, November 2018. I tracked him down coming into Philly on a private plane. He got out with Sixers owner Josh Harris and GM Elton Brand. Harris had a helicopter next to the plane to whisk him off. Butler was leaving in a big, dark SUV, but when he saw us, he stopped, rolled down the window, and chatted. He was fun. Justin Patton (a minor player in the trade) was with him, and Jimmy kept telling us to talk to Justin. Lots of charisma, very upbeat. He didn't have to stop for us, but I think it helped him make a very good initial impression on fans.

5. Torrey Smith leaves the Eagles, March 2018. I was in AC at the Maxwell Club banquet where they were honoring Doug Pederson and Dick Vermeil. I got a call that Torrey had been traded to Carolina and was coming back to get his affairs in order. I left the banquet and met his plane at the airport. He was obviously hurt by leaving the team that had just won the Super Bowl. You could see it. He loved it here, had some family here. He said some really profound things about that.

4. Pedro Martinez joins the Phillies, August 2009. He had flown in from the Dominican Republic, and either the Phils or the police saw us and were trying to help Pedro avoid us. They took him through a back way at the airport to avoid the media. I thought, "Oh, well." But then I saw some police gathered around a car on the lower level. My cameraman and I walked down there, and there was Pedro in the front seat. He was friendly as can be. He gave us a hilarious, fun, engaging interview. Nice as hell and thrilled to be joining a team with a chance to win another World Series.

3. Jeremiah Trotter blows off steam, March 2002. Things were getting ugly when the Eagles slapped a franchise tag on him. He said he didn't want to play under that tag, and he and Andy Reid had an argument in Andy's office. We'd heard he was going to be at the airport and went to try to understand what was going on. He sees me and says, "How'd you know I'd be here?" He told me in the interview he wanted to stay an Eagle—but not under the tag. Then he said he had to catch the shuttle to economy parking. He had his whole family with him, returning from vacation. Of course, we ended up giving him a ride to parking.

2. Allen Iverson returns, December 2009. This was when GM Ed Stefanski brought him back. Classic AI—he missed two flights from Atlanta. A source told me he was on one plane, but he missed that. Then it happened again. I was at the airport for at least four hours before he finally made it. Funny thing is, while I was waiting, notable people kept walking by. First, Eric Snow, who was in town to announce the game. Then wrestler King Kong Bundy. He was easy to recognize. Then, a guy with a very recognizable head walks by the gate, and I said, "I think that's Plácido Polanco." It was; we interviewed him, and he was in town taking a physical to join the Phillies. So we went there to catch Iverson and ended up breaking another story.

1. Hugh Douglas signs in Jacksonville, March 2003. I was in Clearwater for spring training, eating midnight pancakes with my producer, when we got a tip that Hugh was flying to Jacksonville to leave the Eagles and sign with the Jags. That was a big deal. I said to my producer, "You want to do something nuts? Let's drive up there through the night, nap at the airport, and wake up to greet Hugh's plane in the morning." So we did—three-plus hours. Hugh's agent, Drew Rosenhaus, saw us and wouldn't let us talk to Hugh, even after we drove across the state. But he told us to drive to the Jags' office and he'd let us talk to Hugh afterward. Well, we interviewed him right after he signed the paperwork. We had the exclusive, live from Jacksonville at 6:00 p.m, then turned around, drove back to Clearwater, and did another live hit for the 11:00 p.m. news.

Ten Best Philadelphia Sports Beards

With Bryce Harper joining the Phillies in 2019, we thought, who had the most impressive beards in Philadelphia sports history? Let's start with Harper, who first grew his glorious beard during a playoff run with the Washington Nationals. Here's hoping it carries him to several World Series titles in Philadelphia.

We're not ranking awesome moustaches, like Larry Andersen's, or famous goatees, like Wilt Chamberlain's or Julius Erving's. It's got to be the whole nine yards.

Our ranking here is based less on whiskers than the wearer's importance to his franchise. That leaves off Howard "Wolfman" Eskin, since he barely got off the bench at Burger King Community College.

10. Brett Brown. We could not think of a single Sixers player who was ever well known for wearing a beard, so the coach will have to do for now.

9. Bill Flett. The Cowboy! This Flyer earned this nickname not just because of his legendary beard, but because he actually had a real rodeo career. One of the few players in the NHL at the time to sport a beard, he's also one of the last NHL members to not wear a helmet. That's a tough guy.

8. Jayson Werth. If this Phils right fielder were to walk down a Philly street back in the day, one of the old heads would have taken one glance and said, "What are you doing? Posing for a Holy Card?"

7. Jason Peters. Both of your cherished writers of this book would look idiotic with this "just below the jaw"–style beard, but Jason rocks it.

6. Bill Bergey. Did you know that this three-time Eagles MVP was once the highest-paid defensive player in the league?

5. John Kruk. The Krukker sported a goatee as often as he sported a beard, but his full beard is on display on the cover of his awesomely titled autobiography, *I Ain't an Athlete, Lady*.

3. Garry Maddox. The Phillies' Secretary of Defense looked smooth as silk in his Marvin Gaye–style beard. The Vietnam vet grew the beard because exposure to chemicals during the war left his skin sensitive.

2. Steve Bedrosian. How many of you remember that Bedrock actually won a Cy Young in 1987 for the Phils?

1. Jason Kelce. The Eagles center is listed at 295, but 30 pounds of that is his beard. Because of that legendary Super Bowl parade speech, Jason will be ranked number one on any list for the rest of his life.

Big Daddy's Favorite Things about the Jersey Shore—2019 Edition

Since the first edition of this book came out, I continue to spend my summers down the Jersey Shore. The original list was so popular that I started "performing" them live every Memorial Day weekend on the now-canceled *Daily News Live* and *Philly Sports Talk* TV shows.

I would record that segment on a Thursday, and when it would actually air Friday at 5:50 p.m., I'd watch it at the Sand Bar in Beach Haven with a gaggle of drunks already hammered, although the weekend had barely begun.

That led to a gig writing for the *Sea Isle Times,* where I list 10 new "favorite things about the Jersey Shore" every Memorial Day. The list is now over 60 items long. Here are 15 new ones.

15. Binoculars. Always carry a pair in your beach bag. They will be needed to properly check out the "sights." The trick in not getting busted by your wife is occasionally dropping a line like, "I'm pretty sure that's a Grady-White," or, "Boy, that guy out there is a little deep on that board."

14. Walking and riding bikes. At home, I have to drive everywhere I go. But at the shore, I rarely get in my car. Just getting anywhere without driving is cool enough, but it also reminds me of growing up in my Southwest Philly neighborhood where I walked and biked everywhere because (1) I could and (2) I didn't have a car.

13. "There's no one on the lease." I used to love attending a giant house party and the cops would show up and ask who was on the lease. Even though there were 78 people squeezed into a two-bedroom condo, nobody would actually claim to live there. It's like this huge mob was strolling down the street and went, "Oh, that looks like a terrific place to throw a kegger. Let's just break in and throw a party."

12. Bumping into old friends. The cool thing about the shore is that it's a vacation destination that attracts folks from all over. When you drop by your neighborhood bar at home, there's a good chance everyone you bump into is from that same neighborhood. But down the shore, you can hook up with someone you went to high school or college with who you rarely see.

11. Live music. I see more live music between Memorial Day and Labor Day than I do the rest of the year. Most bars offer music (an acoustic act) starting at 4:00 p.m. at their outdoor bar. Then, around 9:30 p.m., a band kicks up inside. So there's music seven days a week from 4:00 p.m. to 4:00 a.m., depending on what beach you are partying at.

10. Outdoor showers. Dag, I love them. Who doesn't? Ever stop to wonder why your house at home doesn't have one? Seriously, there are plenty of beautiful days between April and October when you could shower outdoors. Well, guess what? I have an outdoor shower at my home in Mullica Hill, it didn't cost much, and I use it all the time. There's just something about looking up at that blue sky.

9. Skee-Ball. You can't walk a hundred yards down the shore without bumping into one. And what vacation is complete without taking home a spider ring?

8. Thursday and Sunday nights. Is there a better feeling than making that last-minute decision to turn a regular weekend into a three-day extravaganza? You'll be in work Thursday afternoon and get a phone call from a friend:
"I just took Friday off. Let's go down tonight."
"I can't. I have an extremely important meeting tomorrow that I just can't miss."
"Oh really, I just found out the 58th St. girls are throwing a party."
"Really? What time can you pick me up?"
Or you'll be on the beach on Sunday afternoon.
"You know, it's supposed to be this nice tomorrow. Let's take Monday off."
"I can't. I have an extremely important meeting tomorrow that I just can't miss."
"LeCompt's playing tonight."
"Well, actually, I do feel a 24-hour flu coming on."
Just make sure there are no seagulls screeching above you when you call in sick, or busted you'll be.

7. Dudes sitting on their deck playing an acoustic guitar. And they're always playing James Taylor, Neil Young, or Cat Stevens.

6. Pizza. What is it about pizza down the Shore? Is it the salt air that makes it taste so terrific? Or the six shots of tequila? I'll go with the latter. Ever check out the curbside trash? Stacks and stacks of empty pizza boxes.

5. Pickup basketball. Before I had four back surgeries, I lived to play pickup basketball. Now I wasn't any great shakes, but I knew *how* to play. If the talent level was particularly high, I contributed by playing D, setting picks, and grabbing rebounds. I was the last scoring option. And pickup ball down the shore is wildly unpredictable because you never know who's going to show up because of vacations. Over the years I have played with countless Big 5 players, Division 3 players, and even some pros. Steve Mix was a regular in Sea Isle, and Tim Legler and Franny O'Hanlon were staples on the Avalon courts.

My squad, "Big Daddy Graham: The Team," won the Sea Isle Men's Championship one season despite having a guard by the name of Joe Dempsey who once went two-and-a-half games without once passing the ball. To this day when I'm on a bike ride, I never pass up swinging by those courts. I'll watch a league game. Men. Boys. Girls. It doesn't matter. I just love pickup ball down the shore.

4. The beach at night. Okay, I know. It's technically against the law to go on the beach at night. But it's so damn beautiful. Even if there's just a sliver of a moon shining down, it's spectacular. I never get tired of it. We'll be sitting on the deck, and my wife will say, "Let's go down to the beach," and she never gets an argument from me. We don't go in the water with the sun down (not since *Jaws,* anyway), but we'll kick off the flip-flops and dip our toes. And for the record? The first time I ever kissed my wife was at night on the Sea Isle City 66th St. beach. 'Nuf said.

3. No-shower happy hours. This is difficult to admit, but I'm not the "close the bar" party animal I once was. Heck, I'm "Big Granddaddy Graham" now because my daughter Keely had twins, Jameson and Lucy. But these late afternoon–early evening jams fit me like a glove. And every club has one now with excellent entertainment. You have some beers, bump into old friends, make new ones, and you're home watching Netflix by 10:00 p.m. Love it.

2. Listening to the Phils on the beach. It's a gorgeous Sunday and the Phils are up by a run in the fourth when you decide to go for a walk. You don't have to miss a pitch because there are countless radios tuned in to the game. You'll hear a group let out a little yell.

"Hey! What happened?"

"Bryce Harper just hit a three-run homer!"

It unites the beach, doesn't it? It's so cool.

1. Chicks, chicks, and more chicks. Yeah, I'm aware of the justified #metoo movement, but this will always stay number one for this red-blooded American male.

Did you know the Hooters celebrated their 40th anniversary in 2019? Forty years! Philly has a long, cool musical history—from Mario Lanza to Meek Mill—and what a band for Philly to be proud of.

We reached out to legendary drummer David Uosikkinen of the Hooters for his take on his favorite drummers. Don't you find it interesting who a great quarterback or standup comic thinks are the best in the field? We do.

So here they are. By the way, David describes himself as a "four-for-four" Philly sports fan. Okay, maybe he roots a little harder for the Eagles.

The song listed after David's salute is the one he thinks you should check out to fully hear how great that drummer is.

10. Jim Keltner. He's played with all the Beatles and generations of important artists. A living legend who still is playing at an incredible level. I can listen to him for hours. "Memphis in the Meantime," by John Hiatt.

9. Clyde Stubblefield. The dude played on some of the nastiest funky grooves ever. His work is probably sampled more than any drummer on the planet. "Sex Machine," by James Brown.

8. Vinne Colaiuta. He's an absolute freak of a player. Can virtually play anything and any style. Swings like a beast. "Seven Days," by Sting.

7. Steve Jordan. If Charlie Watts ever left the Rolling Stones, Steve would make the perfect replacement. Flat out the best feel drummer on the planet. Makes every record sound great. Minimalist with a flare. "Locked Away," by Keith Richards.

6. Mickey Curry. The greatest drummer I ever toured with. Watching Mick is like watching poetry in motion. So damn fluid, and his approach rocks a song to its core. He's the man. "Cut Like a Knife," by Bryan Adams.

5. Richie Hayward. He's the second-line king. He takes what Zigaboo does and makes it rock. He's also the boogie-woogie king. "Teenage Nervous Breakdown," by Little Feat.

4. Ringo Starr. The greatest song drummer of all time. He's the heartbeat of the Beatles. Great drummer. "Drive My Car," by the Beatles.

3. Charlie Watts. Charlie dictates the feel of the Stones. Everyone thinks it was Keith. It's Charlie who does that. Coolest cat to walk the planet. "Paint It Black," by the Rolling Stones.

2. Steve Gadd. On everyone's list of the great drummers of all time, including mine, and he just keeps getting better. Probably recorded more than any drummer alive. "50 Ways to Leave Your Lover," by Paul Simon

1. Buddy Rich. Buddy was fierce. He had arguably the greatest chops of any drummer ever. He was the king of swinging it. Played with all the greats of his day and still a legend. Where is the bio-pic of his life? "Caravan," by the Buddy Rich Band.

The Best—and Worst—Renditions of the Pregame Anthems :: Lauren Hart

Lauren Hart has beautifully sung the US national anthem ("The Star-Spangled Banner") and sometimes the Canadian national anthem ("O Canada") before Flyers games since 1997. The daughter of Hall of Fame Flyers broadcaster Gene Hart, her version of the anthem was featured in the Disney movie Miracle. *The singer-songwriter has released seven albums of her own work. You can learn more about her at her website: www. laurenhart.com.*

Let me start by saying singing the national anthem is no easy thing. Technically it's a beast: all eyes on the singer, no room for error, and if you get it wrong it's a hardcore fall that doesn't end. Getting it right is a rush: it gives you a great sense of pride, charges up the fans, and then is mostly forgotten a few minutes later when the game begins. It's been more than 20 years since I sang my first one for the Flyers. It never gets easy; it's always a challenge, and the butterflies are going each and every night. But when all is said and done, I've loved every minute of it.

Respect to all those voices brave enough to take the leap.

The Best

8. Marvin Gaye's National Anthem at the 1983 NBA All-Star Game. A great day. Doctor J was the game's MVP, and Marvin actually made the anthem sound sexy.

7. Jose Feliciano's National Anthem at the 1968 World Series in Detroit. Perhaps the first time someone put that much individual style into the anthem. Very controversial at the time.

6. Jimi Hendrix's National Anthem at Woodstock in August 1969. Wailing, piercing music. No one who heard it will ever forget.

5. Aretha Franklin at Barack Obama's 2009 inauguration. Aretha singing "My Country, 'Tis of Thee" is a moment that will forever be etched in history. She brought the power and the symbolism, proving once again why she was the Queen.

4. Ray Charles's "America the Beautiful"—whenever he sang it. It's the sweetest song of all, and his rendition was perfection. The land, the people, the soul—no one did it better than Ray.

3. Lady Gaga at Super Bowl L in 2016. She may not have been the obvious choice, but man, did she deliver. Straightforward, powerful, simple piano, and that giant voice. She sang from the heart, and fans all over the world felt it. Lady Gaga is the real deal.

2. Kate Smith's "God Bless America" at Flyers games, 1973–1974. In one of the most unusual marriages ever, an aging radio and film star became a good-luck charm for one of the toughest teams ever—the Broad Street Bullies. Prior to 9/11, no anthem ever meant more to a team, a building, and a city.

1. Whitney Houston's National Anthem at Super Bowl XXV, 1991. Hands down, my favorite anthem performance ever. Powerful vocals, great arrangement, a beautiful performance. At the time, Whitney was still one of the greatest talents on the planet.

The Worst

6. Caroline Marcil at the 2005 World Hockey Finals, USA vs. Canada, in Quebec. This is my worst nightmare. She has a great voice, but . . . first, she forgot the words and left the ice. She came back for another try, forgot the words again, and left a second time. Returning a *third* time, she slipped and fell to the ice on her back. To her credit, she sang it beautifully the next day on national TV. Ouch, I feel your pain.

5. John Michael Montgomery at NASCAR's Golden Corral 500 in 2005. Slurred, stumbling, off-key, *and* he used a cheat sheet. Did he actually sing "Pennzoil's red glare" during the song?

4. R. Kelly at the Bernard Hopkins vs. Jermain Taylor world middleweight championship fight, 2006. Please. Just stop.

2b. (tie) Roseanne Barr's National Anthem at a San Diego Padres game in 1990. Just gross.

2a. (tie) Fergie at the 2018 NBA All-Star Game. One of the best pieces of advice I ever got from my dad was "keep it straight; it's all about the song." And when thinking of "The Star-Spangled Banner," sex isn't the thing that comes to mind. But in this rendition, Fergie was in full-on seduction mode. I'm not sure what she was thinking, but the ramparts just ain't a sexy thing. To add insult to injury, the cameras panned to the players and fans giggling, laughing, and looking embarrassed. This one's gotta hurt, and I feel for her. But when in doubt, keep it classy.

1. Carl Lewis at a New York Nets game in 1993. Midway through the song, he actually promised it would get better. It never did. You can run, Carl, but you cannot hide—because this has to be the all-time worst-ever rendition.

Ten Eagles Who Were Better Than You Thought :: Ray Didinger

Ray Didinger's coverage of the Eagles over the years has earned him a spot in the Pro Football Hall of Fame and the Philadelphia Sports Hall of Fame. Didinger wrote about football and other sports for the Philadelphia Bulletin *and* Daily News *for 27 years. He is currently a football analyst for NBC Sports Philadelphia and cohost with Glen Macnow on WIP's weekend morning shows. He is also the author of 11 books on football, including the 2018 best seller* The Eagles Encyclopedia: Champions Edition.

In writing *The Eagles Encyclopedia,* I went through thousands of pages of research dating back to the first season, 1933. In poring over all that material, I developed a new appreciation for certain players. I wouldn't call them forgotten players because in most cases their names were familiar. But these were the 10 players who, upon further review, made me think: "I knew he was good, but I didn't realize he was *this* good."

10. Marion Campbell, defensive end, 1956–1961. Most Philadelphia fans only remember Campbell as the head coach who won just 17 games in three seasons after succeeding Dick Vermeil. The Swamp Fox is not given enough credit for what he accomplished as a player. He was the best defensive lineman on the 1960 championship team, and he played most of the season on a bad ankle.

9. John Bunting, linebacker, 1972–1982. He was underrated his entire career, beginning with his selection as a 10th-round draft pick. But he was one of the most consistent performers on a defense that allowed the fewest points in the NFL from 1979 through 1981. His jarring hit on Ron Springs on the first series set the tone for the Eagles' 20–7 win over Dallas in the 1980 NFC Championship game.

8. William Thomas, linebacker, 1991–1999. Watching the Eagles game with Seth Joyner in the NBC studio each Sunday is always an education. During the 2018 season Seth said, "The Eagles haven't had a big-play linebacker since William Thomas." It was an interesting observation coming from Seth, who specialized in making big plays. So I went back to check the stats and realized, yeah, Willie T was an impact player. He had 33 sacks and led all NFL linebackers with seven interceptions in 1995.

7. Andy Harmon, defensive tackle, 1991–1997. Thanks to Fletcher Cox, we developed a greater appreciation for Harmon. Each game Cox adds to his sack total, we note where he ranks among all-time Eagles interior linemen—and the name Andy Harmon is right there. We know how good Cox is, so that means Harmon was pretty special too. He had 39½ sacks in seven seasons. Cox finally passed him (41½) in 2018 in his seventh season.

6. Chuck Weber, linebacker, 1959–1961. To this day, most fans believe Chuck Bednarik was the middle linebacker on the 1960 championship team. Not so. Weber, the other Chuck, played the middle. Bednarik played outside. Weber, a West Chester State grad, also called the defensive signals and was second on the team with six interceptions. He also recovered the fumble after Bednarik's legendary hit on the Giants' Frank Gifford.

5. Rodney McLeod, safety, 2016–2018. Most Eagles fans probably didn't realize how valuable McLeod was until he went out with an injury four weeks into the 2018 season. The first game he was sidelined was the overtime loss to the Titans when Marcus Mariota riddled the Eagles secondary for 344 yards. There were numerous breakdowns in coverage, and the tackling suffered without McLeod, who had more than 200 tackles in his first two seasons with the Eagles.

4. Harold Jackson, wide receiver, 1969–1972. I was blown away when I looked back at Jackson's numbers. In four seasons with the Eagles, he led the NFL in receiving yardage twice, and that was with Norm Snead, Rick Arrington, Pete Liske, and John Reaves throwing him the ball. He played 56 games with the Eagles and went over 100 yards receiving 13 times. Nicknamed the Roadrunner, he was 5-foot-10 and 170 pounds with explosive speed. He was like a DeSean Jackson but without the diva act.

3. Norm "Wildman" Willey, defensive end, 1950–1957. Glen Macnow rolls his eyes when I talk about Willey having 17 sacks in one game against the Giants. It sounds far-fetched, but it did happen. Quoting a newspaper account from 1952: "Willey awed inhabitants of the Polo Grounds by dumping (quarterback) Charlie Conerly 17 times while he was attempting to pass." Sacks did not become an official statistic until 1982, so there is no mention of Willey in the record book and most fans never heard of him. But he was one of the best defensive players of his era.

2. Tommy Thompson, quarterback, 1941–1942, 1945–1950. Hall of Fame halfback Steve Van Buren was the star of the championship teams of 1948 and 1949, but Thompson did a superb job running the T-formation. In 1948, a 12-game regular season, Thompson led the NFL with 25 touchdown passes. Sammy Baugh of Washington was second with 22. No other quarterback in the league had more than 14.

1. Bobby Walston, tight end and kicker, 1951–1962. Walston's 881 points ranks second to David Akers in the club's all-time scoring list. He was overshadowed on the '60 championship team by wide receivers Tommy McDonald and Pete Retzlaff, yet he averaged 18.8 yards per catch, outstanding for a tight end. Walston also provided one of the biggest plays of that season, kicking a 38-yard field goal in the final seconds to lift the Eagles to a 31–29 win over Cleveland. General manager Vince McNally called Walston "the best draft pick I ever made," and he selected more than 400 players in his 15 years with the Eagles.

Few things are quite as exciting as adding a key player to your team during a stretch drive. Here are 10 times it really worked out for Philadelphia.

10. Bake McBride. Shake and Bake was traded to the Phils in June 1977, essentially for a sack of marbles. He hit .339 for the rest of the season, stole bases, and helped elevate the team to 101 wins. Even blasted a homer off of Rick Rhoden in that year's NLCS. McBride hung around for four seasons after that, gaining some MVP votes in 1980.

9. Dikembe Mutombo. There are critics who argued this wasn't a great pickup for the 2001 Sixers, given that they were 40–14 before the swap (for Theo Ratliff, Toni Kukoč, and some spare parts) and just 16–12 after it. Perhaps, but Mt. Mutombo was named the NBA's Defensive Player of the Year that season and was crucial to the team making it to the Finals. The only mistake was Billy King re-signing him after the season to a four-year, $68 million deal.

8. Joe Blanton. Fat Joe came from Oakland in July 2008 for some anonymous minor leaguers. The Phils went 9–4 in his starts (he was 4–0), and he won two postseason starts, even bashing a homer in the World Series. Despite looking like a guy who lived at the Golden Corral buffet, Blanton pitched to the age of 36.

7. Jay Ajayi. Well, it was fun while it lasted. Eagles GM Howie Roseman grabbed Ajayi for a fourth-round pick seven games into the 2017 season, after the 24-year-old running back feuded with his Miami Dolphins coach. Ajayi averaged 5.8 yards per carry for the Birds. Then he gained 254 yards in the postseason, which, of course, ended at the Super Bowl parade. Alas, his Eagles career was ended by injury five games into the next season.

6. Garry Maddox. He began his career as Willie Mays's centerfield replacement in San Francisco. In 1975 he came to the Phils in exchange for fan favorite Willie Montañez. He won the Gold Glove that season, the first of eight consecutive years. A classy guy who often clashed with manager Dallas Green. It was Ray Didinger who wrote, "Two-thirds of the Earth is covered by water, the other one-third by Garry Maddox."

5. Mark Recchi. The rebuilding Flyers traded franchise icon Rick Tocchet and a whole lot more for the 23-year-old winger late in the 1991–1992 season. The following season Recchi scored 123 points—still a franchise record. He helped ease Eric Lindros's entry into the NHL and scored 232 goals in two stints in black and orange. His name will soon again turn up on this list for another reason.

4. Cliff Lee. Phils GM Ruben Amaro loved acquiring ace starters during the Phils' great run from 2007 to 2011 (and, no, we're not counting Blanton in that elite group). Lee won the 2008 American League Cy Young Award, but by the following July had a falling out with the Cleveland Indians. Amaro grabbed him for four prospects, only one of whom (Carlos Carrasco), went on to have a productive career. All of us will remember Lee's dominance over the Yankees in the '09 World Series, punctuated by his dismissive catch of a Johnny Damon pop-up and a flashier snag behind his back on a comebacker by Robinson Canó.

3. John LeClair and Eric Desjardins. They arrived together from the Montreal Canadiens in February 1993 in exchange for . . . Mark Recchi. LeClair immediately clicked with Lindros, scoring 25 goals in 37 games. He went on to top 50 goals each of the next three seasons. Desjardins steadied the Flyers' defense and became a smart power play quarterback. Between them, they made eight All-Star Games for Philadelphia. Both are in the Flyers Hall of Fame.

2. Wilt Chamberlain. It's a rare list in this book where Wilt isn't number one, but regard that as no slight to the greatness he brought to the Sixers when he returned to town midway through the 1964–1965 season. The Dipper led the NBA in scoring that season (as well as the next three) and carried the Sixers to Game 7 of the Eastern Division Finals where (stop us if you've heard this before), they lost to the Celtics. Two years later he would lead them to a title, averaging 24.2 rebounds and hitting an amazing 68 percent of his field goal attempts.

1. Reggie White. When the USFL collapsed in 1985 (thank you, Donald Trump), the Eagles bought out his contract with the Memphis Showboats and signed him to a four-year, $1.85 million deal. Most Eagles fans didn't know who he was, but White announced his presence with authority in the season's fourth game, ringing up 2½ sacks and 10 tackles in his debut against the Giants. He was the Defensive Rookie of the Year with 13 sacks in 13 games. Arguably the top player in franchise history.

Special note: Although the 1989 Phillies finished in last place, we'll give a nod to GM Lee Thomas, who had a productive summer, picking up Lenny Dykstra, John Kruk, Terry Mulholland, Roger McDowell, and Charlie Hayes. Much of that rebuilding paid off four seasons later.

Special note 2: In October 2011, the Eagles swapped running backs with Detroit, getting Jerome Harrison for the worthless Ronnie Brown. During Harrison's physical, Eagles doctors discovered a brain tumor. Harrison underwent career-ending surgery. Although the trade didn't pay off for the Eagles, it was a great one for Harrison, in that it likely saved his life.

As a splendid wide receiver for the Eagles from 1982 to 1990, Mike Quick got to compete against some of the NFL's best cover men each day in practice. And since 1997, he has served as the Eagles' radio color commentator.

10. Bobby Taylor. He was better than a lot of people give him credit for. Maybe not a great hitter, but he could tackle people around the knees, and he had very good cover skills. He was talented at getting his hands on guys at the line of scrimmage and throwing them off their routes. Plus, with his long, rangy legs, not many teams could get the deep ball by Bobby.

9. Lito Sheppard. So super productive. He was physical and fast as hell. Even when he was out of position, Lito had make-up speed to catch up on the ball. He had great ball skills and the ability to break a return on a kick or an interception. A very dangerous player.

8. Andre Waters. Andre was perfect for Buddy Ryan's 46 Defense. The Eagles needed a guy at safety who could cover tight ends or take on a pulling guard. Andre wasn't big, but he had a huge heart. He was fearless, and boy, could he hit.

7. Troy Vincent. Great ability and great hands. What I always think about with Troy was that even if a guy beat him with the first move, Troy had the speed to catch up and still make the play. No one could bump at the line of scrimmage like him and throw a receiver off his pattern.

6. Asante Samuel. Like Herm Edwards a generation before, Asante could read splits, quarterback drops, and anything the receiver was going to do based on alignment. He was a studier who always understood the possibilities. Sometimes his gambling cost him, but his 51 career interceptions show how he could turn the game around.

5. Wes Hopkins. One of the most feared guys in football. He roamed the secondary, and opponents feared coming into his area. I remember talking to receivers on other teams, like Roy Green of the Cardinals, and they'd say, "How's Wes? Is he healthy? Is he playing?" They were scared. I was glad he was on my team because I never wanted to get hit by him.

4. Roynell Young. I had to go against him every day in practice. As a young guy, it taught me a lot to go against an All-Pro like that. Roynell had great cover skills, he was great with his hands, and he was mean as a snake.

3. Malcolm Jenkins. Tremendous versatility, in that he does so many things so well. Secondly, he's like having a coach on the field. Jim Schwartz trusts him so much that he'll let Malcolm make changes to the defense on his own out there. His football intellect, his leadership, and his range of skills put him near the top.

2. Eric Allen. He was the best cover guy I ever saw on the Eagles. His great ability to stay with guys allowed the defensive coordinator freedom to do a lot of things, because you always knew that Eric could go one-on-one with the other team's best receiver and not get burned. It helped the team in so many ways.

1. Brian Dawkins. He's a Hall of Famer and deserves to be. Brian tops my list because of his overall impact on the defense and the variety of ways you could use him. On one play he would blitz, and on the next he could cover as well as any cornerback. Plus, he was a safety who hit like a linebacker. The best.

By this, we don't mean the Eastern and Western conference. Or the AFC and the NFC. No, we mean the NHL and WHA. Or the NFL or USFL. Baseball never really had two separately run, competitive leagues, although we'll address Phillies who starred in the American League later in this book.

10. "He Hate Me." Remember, "This is the XFL!" Hate's real name is Rod Smart, and he actually played in three different leagues. He began 2001 getting cut by the CFL's Edmonton Eskimos, then played in the XFL's debut game in its only season. Rod came up with "He Hate Me" personally and planned to use a different moniker for every game. But "He Hate Me" became so popular he kept it. He finished 2001 playing six games as a special teamer on the Eagles—and even got two rushing attempts for six yards. Quick, what was the name of the XFL team Hate played for? (Answer: Las Vegas Outlaws.)

9. George McGinnis. I can't verify this story, but it's a doozy. Of all people, it was then–Denver Nuggets coach Larry "Play the Right Way" Brown who traded Bobby Jones to the Sixers for George McGinnis in 1978. After a single practice, Brown attempted to weasel out of the deal, realizing what a boneheaded mistake he'd made. Not that George wasn't a terrific player—he was. But you couldn't come up with a more ideal Brown player than Bobby Jones. Anyway, McGinnis, a two-time champion and one-time MVP in the ABA, never got the respect he deserved with the Sixers after Julius Erving arrived.

8. Bobby Jones. Bobby spent his first two pro years with those ABA Nuggets before coming to Philadelphia. The *Daily News* once published an article asking all the Sixers what their favorite movie was. There were a lot of obvious answers like *The Godfather* and *Scarface*. Bobby's favorite movie? *Mary Poppins.* You can't make this stuff up, folks.

7. Mark Howe. This Hall of Famer began his career in the WHA with the Houston Aeros, where he teamed up with his pop, Gordie, and his brother Marty. The trio then ended up in Connecticut playing for the New England Whalers. When the WHA folded, the Whalers were among four teams gobbled up by the NHL, and they became the Hartford Whalers. In 1982 he began a 10-year run as a talented and popular Flyer. Did you know the Whalers' arena was in a mall? And by the way, what is an "Aero"?

6. Billy Cunningham. The Kangaroo Kid, along with Rick Barry, became one of the NBA's first major stars to jump to the ABA when he left the Sixers to join the Carolina Cougars. This was when the ABA was throwing money around like bounced checks. As a matter of fact, many of them did bounce. We're sure, though, that Billy, a tough Brooklyn kid who ended up a highly successful businessman, got his dough. He won the ABA's MVP in 1973. Like Barry, he hung around that league a few seasons before returning to the NBA.

5. Bernie Parent. Lured by the big bucks of the World Hockey Association, Bernie became the first NHL player to jump leagues. Although he thought he was signing with the Miami Screaming Eagles, he ended up with the Philadelphia Blazers when the Miami franchise never materialized. One can only imagine a young Bernie in South Beach. Actually getting his cash was another matter, however, and Parent, after one season, returned to the NHL in 1973. The rest is Philadelphia sports history. The only player on this list to play for two different leagues in the same city. One of the nicest, down-to-earth professional athletes you'll ever meet. "Only the Lord saves more than Bernie Parent."

4. Moses Malone. One thing for sure is that most of the players on this list loved the money over the status of playing in the better league. There is a story going around that the day Malone's Sixer deal went down, Moses insisted that a ridiculous amount of money—in cash—be laid out on a hotel room bed. He began his career in the ABA with the Utah Stars after skipping college ball altogether.

3. Julius Erving. Many Hall of Famers made the successful jump from the ABA to the NBA (George Gervin, Dan Issel). And the league held on. But the ABA simply could not survive losing the Doctor. While none of the other leagues we discussed here (WHA, XFL, USFL) are still in operation, no one player personally put a dagger in the heart of his deceased league like Dr. J did.

2. Reggie White. Reggie played his first two pro seasons with the USFL's Memphis Showboats because, he claimed, he wanted to play in the same state—Tennessee—where he played college ball. Sure, Reggie, the fact they were offering you gobs more money than the NFL had nothing to do with it. Just like God told you to sign with Green Bay later on in your career. All kidding aside, Reggie's the greatest ever at his position and because of some politically incorrect statements toward the end of his life, we fans sometimes forget just how funny he was. He still might be the quickest man of his size to ever wear an NFL uniform.

1. Wilt Chamberlain. We made Wilt number one because he technically was involved in *five* different leagues. There's the NBA and the ABA, where he never actually played for the San Diego Conquistadors (the NBA successfully prevented him from playing), but he "coached" them for one season. (He once skipped a game to attend an autograph session promoting a book.) Then there's a professional volleyball league (the IVA), and who knows what to make of a sport where chicks play in bikinis and dudes in those skimpy French Canadian speedos? In fact, Chamberlain started the volleyball league himself and owned the team he played for, the Seattle Smashers. They actually had a TV contract because of Wilt—or maybe because of the aforementioned "chicks in bikinis." We remember when sports fans would go out of their way to remind you: "Don't forget, Wilt's one of the greatest volleyball players who ever lived." Like any of us could name another volleyball player. How could you not be awesome in volleyball at 7 feet tall? The Dipper also started a pro track-and-field league. And, technically speaking, the Harlem Globetrotters are in a league (or world) of their own—and Wilt played one year for them. That was in 1958 when he left the University of Kansas a year early and was forbidden to go directly to the NBA. That Globetrotter team visited Russia, where Wilt became an international sensation. He might have also added some babushkas to that other famous stat he was well known for.

Honorable mention: Herschel Walker, John Bunting, Ron Reed (in two sports—baseball and basketball), Sean Landeta, Kelvin Bryant, Doug Favell

The Best Philadelphia Baseball Players to Play in Both Leagues

This is the accompanying list to the Eagles, Flyers, and Sixers who played in two different leagues. Since baseball never had a rival like the ABA or the USFL, this is the best we could do.

To make this list, first and foremost, the player had to have had great, not good, years in Philly, preferably a decent number of them.

10. Jim Bunning. He makes the cut, although of the 10 listed here, he played the fewest games (206) for the Phils. Jim became the first pitcher in MLB history with 100 wins and 1,000 strikeouts in both leagues—all of his AL stats with the Detroit Tigers. Oh, and with that famous Father's Day perfect game he pitched for the Phils in 1964, he became the first hurler to ever throw a no-hitter in both leagues.

9. Greg Luzinski. After 11 power-packed seasons with the Phils, the Bull moved to the White Sox, giving them a couple good seasons with his bat—although he *never* stepped into left field. A pure DH. That certainly strikes a chord with any Phils fan who witnessed Greg butcher a fly ball—particularly any who attended the infamous Black Friday heartbreaker.

8. Dick Allen. He abruptly quit the Chicago White Sox in September of '74 with two weeks left in the season. Controversy followed Richie/Dick (even his first name was up for debate) most of his career, which is odd because in his later years he worked in the Phillies PR department (of all places), and a nicer guy you'll never meet.

7. Curt Schilling. One of the spectacular postseason pitchers in history, and it's not like he didn't try to deliver a ring here for Philly. Unfortunately, his three World Series championships came elsewhere—one with Arizona and two with the American League's Red Sox.

6. Robin Roberts. How weird is this? Robin's career with the Phils ended after 1961. He then signed with the Yankees. What happened next will never happen again for any player with any organization. Realizing that the Yankees were scheduled to play the Phils in a spring training game, the Phils decided to retire Roberts' number *in Clearwater, Florida.* In a 14-year career with some of the lousiest teams in Philadelphia history, Robin managed to win 234 games—and they rewarded him in a *preseason* game ceremony. It's the first number the Phillies ever retired, so maybe they just didn't know how to do it properly. By the way, Roberts got rocked in that game, the Yanks never used him in a regular-season game, and he ended up with the Orioles for four years.

5. Cole Hamels. Our 2008 World Series MVP. He won 114 games for the Phils before being traded to Texas. Look out, he's back in the National League with the Cubs. The only active player as we write this list.

4. Jimmy Rollins. Raise your hand if you remember that the greatest Phils shortstop of all time ended his career playing 41 games for the Chicago White Sox, hitting .221.

3. Steve Carlton. What a shame that Carlton seems to have (unjustly) become the poster child for "players who hang around too long" when he followed up his amazing Phillies career with the White Sox (what's up with all these Phils ending up in the Windy City?), Indians, and Twins. Three dreadful years where he hurled himself to a combined total of 10 wins. Don't worry, Steve, you'll always be the legendary Lefty to us.

> **Glen says:** As a sportswriter for the *Detroit Free Press*, I covered Carlton's first start with the White Sox in 1986. He lasted three innings at Tiger Stadium, giving up six runs, three of them on a titanic homer by Chet Lemon. Carlton declined my request for an interview after the game—no shocker there.

2. Ed Delahanty. Ed started his career in 1888 with the Philadelphia A's. Yes, that's an eternity ago, but the beauty of baseball is its incredible longevity. If you ask around enough, you'll find someone in your family who recalls a conversation with their Uncle Max, whose grandfather took him to an A's game at Baker Bowl. For those of you with a "who cares" attitude toward sports from that long ago, ponder this: Let's say you were 10 years old when the Eagles won Super Bowl LII. Now, let's say you live to be 80. How will you feel if someone in 2088 says to you, "Super Bowl LII? Who remembers that?" Oh, you'll remember it, all right. Every second of it. Ed hit .348 in 13 years with the Phils before joining the Washington Senators, where he hit .376 to lead the AL. He died falling into the Niagara River after being kicked off a train. You could look it up.

1. Jimmy Foxx. Double X! Did you know Tom Hanks's Jimmy Dugan character from *A League of Their Own* is based on Foxx? A colorful character right up Philly's alley. He started his career with the A's and finished it with the Phillies. And get this: he became the second player in history—after Babe Ruth—to hit 500 homers. In fact, he held the record as the youngest slugger to ever reach that plateau (32 years old) until Alex Rodriguez got there quicker 68 years later.

Honorable mention: *Roy Halladay, Del Ennis, Manny Trillo, Scott Rolen, Cliff Lee, Larry Andersen, Bob Boone, Shane Victorino, Bake McBride, Chris Short*

Dan Baker was raised in Southwest Philadelphia and Mount Ephraim, New Jersey. He works in athletic administration with Drexel University and the Big 5. But most fans know him through his moonlighting gig—he has been the on-site public address announcer for the Phillies since 1972. When you cheer—or boo—a player upon introduction, the voice you are responding to is Dan Baker's.

"My favorite names tend to be those with multiple syllables," says Baker. "They just lend themselves to more melodic interpretations."

We asked Dan to give us his 10 favorites, but he couldn't limit himself to that. So here is his Terrific 13. We suspect he'll soon be adding, "Number 3 . . . Bryyycce Harrrper!"

13. Steve Carlton. Lefty and I both started our Phillies careers in 1972, and what an incredible season it was for him. Almost every time he pitched at home that year an additional 10,000 fans attended the game. From then until now, his introduction guarantees a loud ovation: "Number 32 . . . Steve Carlton!" The same is true for . . .

12. Mike Schmidt. His all-around brilliance was unsurpassed—offensively, defensively, there weren't enough superlatives. Like Lefty, his every introduction at the annual Wall of Fame induction ceremony is greeted with thunderous applause: "Number 20 . . . Mike Schmidt!"

11. Ted Sizemore. Ted once came back for an old-timers game and told me that he loved the way I said his name. "Let me hear it just one more time," he said. I was happy to oblige. You know: Siiiiizzzzzzemore!

10. Greg Luzinski. The Bull! Boy, could he energize a crowd with those Bull Blasts in the mid to late '70s. He played on some of the best Phillies teams of all time, and he was one of the most exciting players we ever saw.

9. Lenny Dykstra. He was full of energy. I tried to capture that in announcing him and let the fans know what was coming—"Lenny DYK-stra!" How about the season Lenny had leading off in 1993? Few lead-off hitters have ever performed better than he did that year.

8. Mickey Morandini. He played with flair and always hustled. Philadelphia baseball fans admire guys who work hard, and Mickey sure did. You couldn't help but like him, and his name: "Mickey Morandiiiiinnnnniiiii!"

7. Roy Halladay. A Hall of Famer, wasn't he something special? How about what he accomplished in 2010: NL Cy Young Award winner, regular season perfect game, postseason no-hitter. As with Schmidt and Carlton, there was always a majesty announcing his name: "Number 34 . . . pitcher . . . Roy HALL-a-day!"

6. Carlos Ruiz. How about Doc's wonderful battery-mate? I don't think there was a more beloved player on the team. The fans adored him. When I introduced Chooch, the fans would help me say his name: "Number 51 . . . catcher . . . Carlos Ruuiiz!"

5. Cole Hamels. The 2008 World Series team had a first name I could draw out and get the fans involved. What a postseason he had leading the Phillies to the championship: "Number 35 . . . pitcher . . . Colllllle Hamels!"

4. Charlie Manuel. He's the first manager or coach to make my list. "Charrrrrrrlie Mannn-nuel." Of course, he's the only manager who took the Phillies to back-to-back World Series. Since 2008 the cheers upon his introduction equal or exceed our most popular players.

3. Ryan Howard. He could hit the ball such a long way. What's more, he did it in the clutch. His intro was anticipated by the fans like few other Phillies (to my way of thinking only Dick Allen, Greg Luzinski, Mike Schmidt, and Jim Thome). Also, he carried himself with such a regal presence: "Number 6 . . . first baseman . . . Ryyyyyannnn HOW-ard!"

2. Jimmy Rollins. Mr. Excitement. And what a leader; brilliant in the field and electrifying on the base paths. He proclaimed the Phillies the best team in the NL East, then led us to the title. Sometimes, announcing the starting lineup on the field before the game, I would point to Jimmy when I said his name if he was on the field and visible to the fans—as if to say, "There he is!" Sometimes he would point back: "Number 11 . . . shortstop . . . Jimmy Rollins!"

1. Chase Utley. Perhaps the most popular Phillies player ever. Talk about never giving up. Harry Kalas was so right: "Chase, you are the man!" He helped us appreciate what it meant to win it all. How about his hustle, his postseason home runs! "Number 26 . . . second baseman . . . Chaaase UTTTT-ley!"

Lou Nolan has been the in-house voice of the Flyers since 1972, calling thousands of games, including two Stanley Cup championships. He also served as PA announcer for the 2002 Winter Olympics in Salt Lake City, which he calls "the pinnacle for any broadcaster."

Here are his all-time favorite names:

12. Shayne Gostisbehere. *GOST-is-bear!* I have really enjoyed saying his name, beginning in 2014 with me broadcasting the NCAA Frozen Four when Ghost was plus-7 in the 7–4 win for Union College.

11. Simon Gagne. *See-moooan GANNN-yeaaaa!* A ton of fun to draw the name out. He had terrific hands and scored those great clutch goals.

10. Per Djoos. *Pear Juice.* He had a short career for Detroit and the Rangers, but he was an announcer's dream. How could something from the shelf of your market not be a favorite?

9. Gordie Howe. I only got to say this name once, in an old-timers game, as I recall. But I was very honored just for that opportunity.

8. Rick MacLeish. His goal won the Stanley Cup for the Flyers at home on May 19, 1974. Calling that one was my own personal crowning announcement.

7. Alex Ovechkin. Although Alex is usually a nemesis to the Flyers, it is always a thrill to say his name. And he has always been a real gentleman with me. I just wish I said his name for more penalties.

6. Steve Yzerman. *EYE-zer-mann!* A great player with a name that just rolls off your tongue. One day he scored a hat trick at the Spectrum. As I announced him as the first star, he skated over and handed me his stick. A very classy guy.

5. Bobby Orr. A thrill just to say his name. But much more than that, it was a great thrill to call the penalty against him as he pulled down Bobby Clarke at the end of the first Stanley Cup game and just about assured the Flyers' victory.

4. Vyacheslav Solodukhin. *V-AAH-she-slav So-lo-DUKE-in.* He played for the Soviets in that infamous 4–1 Flyers win back in 1976. The great Gene Hart helped me with Soviet pronunciations. It's really easy once you get it.

3. Yvon Cournoyer. The great Montreal Canadiens scorer. He's top three for sure. *EE-von Corn-y-YAY!* What a great name to get to say.

2. Eric Desjardins. *Dey-zhar-daan!* Just an outstanding player and person who the Flyers were fortunate to have at right defense. Best I ever saw at keeping the puck in the zone on a wrap-around.

1. Bobby Clarke. He has to be number one. Know why? I called this name more than any other Flyer—both for scoring and getting sent to the sin bin.

Are you as tired as us of seeing Jack Nicholson and Spike Lee courtside at Lakers and Knicks games? We thought so.

Well, you know, we have our own collection of Philly celebrities to salute. By the way, you don't have to be from this area to make this list, just a well-known fan of a Philly team. Nicholson, in fact, is not from Los Angeles. He's from Neptune, New Jersey.

10. Teller. This Central High grad is the half of Penn and Teller who never talks, and that's why he's making this list. There are bigger stars in the honorable mention section, but they all have one thing in common. *They speak.* Leave it to us to have a diehard Phillies fan who doesn't boo because, well, he doesn't cheer either. We're kidding of course. His Harpo Marx shtick is just that. Shtick. At least we think it is. Has anyone ever seen him speak off stage?

9. Princess Diana. With all due respect, the late princess didn't know a football from a taco, but Google image "Princess Diana Eagles jacket" and you'll find dozens of photos of her wearing a really sharp kelly green Birds jacket. Eagles statistician Jack Edelstein learned that she dug the eagle-in-flight logo, and he sent her the jacket through Jack Kelly, brother of the late Grace Kelly. She called the logo "beautiful." (It's a good thing she never made it to the 700 level.)

8. Christopher Guest. The creator of *Spinal Tap* and other hilarious mockumentaries, this former *SNL* cast member is a passionate Phillies fan—so much so that whenever the Fightins are in Chavez Ravine, Guest goes to every game. He once talked himself into the broadcast booth and became good friends with former Phils announcer Chris Wheeler. After one game, Guest invited Wheels back to his house. They were sitting in the kitchen shooting some baseball breeze when Jamie Lee Curtis glided in and grabbed a soda out of the refrigerator. We're talking *True Lies*–era Jamie. Neither she nor Guest said a word to each other as she came in and walked out in seconds.

Guest babbled on about ERAs or whatever, but Wheels was blown away. "I'm not listening to one word because my mind is exploding," he recalled. "Am I nuts or did Jamie Lee Curtis just magically appear? Is this common in Hollywood? Then I remembered that Guest is *married* to her."

Needless to say, Chris Wheeler never turned down another invite to what is now known as Jamie Lee Curtis's house.

7. Cindy Margolis. Not only a big-time Birds supporter, she was a huge fan of the Wing Bowl as well. Even if the only area team she supported was the West Catholic Burrs, we would still have her on the list because, well, look at her. We're men. We're shallow.

6. Mike Trout. Technically speaking, this Millville, New Jersey, native is a celebrity because he's a superstar athlete, which makes him an oddity on the list. But his incredible loyalty to the Eagles cannot be denied. He's also pals with Carson Wentz, so c'mon, Carson; get him in a Phillies uniform.

5. M. Night Shyamalan. The director of *The Sixth Sense* is a courtside Sixers season ticket holder. He's not only from the area; he's *still living* here. In fact, his next-door neighbor used to be Allen Iverson. (We wonder if Night ever got any sleep.)

4. Meek Mill. Quick. How many other rappers in the country are bailed out of jail by one of the owners of the Sixers (Michael Rubin) a mere hour before tip-off and still arrive in time to ring the bell? We have a fascination with hip-hop names, and Meek's real name is Robert Williams. Let's pray this South and North Philly native starts hooking up with Nicki Minaj again so we can see her courtside, like we used to.

3. Bradley Cooper. Someone called into WIP once and asked the host if Bradley got that breakout role in *Silver Linings Playbook* because in real life, this Germantown High alum was raised an Eagles fan. Who knows? It couldn't have hurt. This Oscar-nominated actor, writer, and director attended Super Bowl LII and is a true bleed-green fan.

2. Kevin Hart. Talk about a dream come true. Imagine. You're from Philly and you graduate from George Washington High. You become a standup comic and not only do you have courtside Sixer season tickets at Wells Fargo, you also routinely perform and sell out the same arena.

1. Will Smith. The Fresh Prince from Overbrook is not only a rabid Sixer fan, at one point he owned part of the team. Though not seen at as many games as other stars on this list, here's the reason Will is number one. He just might be the biggest star this town has ever produced. Here's a fun question. Who else has conquered these three worlds of entertainment? Music. Smith sold millions of CDs. Television. We will all be on our deathbeds and *Fresh Prince* will still be on the tube. And movies. Sinatra and Streisand never had hit TV shows. Neither did Elvis or Michael Jackson. Will's one of the most bankable entertainers in the world.

> **Big Daddy says:** Sorry to hit you with this visual, but I was once standing next to Will Smith at a urinal outside the Sixers' media room. I say to him, "Will Smith! My kids love you!" and without missing a beat, Will replied, "So do mine."

Honorable mention: Joe Biden, Bryan Cranston, Art Garfunkel, Chuck Barris, David Bore-anaz, Maria Bello, Jim Cramer, Kendall Jenner, Dean Ambrose, The Roots, Kim Delaney, and the band Phish

Matt Cord wears many hats. (He literally has a cool collection of brims.) He's a longtime popular Philadelphia radio DJ and host, and he has been the Sixers PA announcer since 1998.

We asked him to name some of his favorite bell ringers, a tremendous new tradition before Sixer games.

5. Joel Embiid. I'm not sure if current players should even be on the list, but doesn't it seem like everything he touches turns to gold?

4. Kevin Hart. He's our Jack Nicholson. He hit that bell out of the park during the Boston Celtics series, which I can imagine Jack would have done also.

3. Nick Foles. Absolutely brought the house down, but let's face it, the Eagles water boy would have received a standing ovation after they won Super Bowl LII.

2. Meek Mill. Everyone knew he was getting out of jail that day in April 2018, but no one thought he could make it in time to ring the bell. The crowd went wild.

1. Doug Pederson. He came onto the hardwood holding the Lombardi Trophy and wearing a hoodie with the big Sixer snake on it. A few days earlier, he threw out the first pitch at a Phillies game. Both times the good guys won.

WIP program director Spike Eskin doubles as the most vocal advocate of the Process, former GM Sam Hinkie's plan to tear down and then rebuild the Sixers. Eskin hosts The Rights to Ricky Sanchez *radio show and podcast—which continues to celebrate all things Hinkie.*

5. Traded Jrue Holiday and Pierre Jackson to New Orleans for Nerlens Noel and the Pelicans' 2014 first-round pick, July 12, 2013. I'll never forget the sense of shock, excitement, and relief when Hinkie pulled this one off on draft night in 2013. Our small clique of Sixers blog and podcast nerds had always dreamed about tearing the entire thing down and building it up from nothing, and we finally had a general manager who wanted to do the same.

This wasn't an anti–Jrue Holiday stance; we all recognized he was the most valuable player the team had. It was that Hinkie was willing to trade him that made us feel things were really, finally, going to change.

4. Traded a 2014 second-round pick to the Memphis Grizzlies for Tony Wroten, August 22, 2013. This one was great for a couple of reasons:

First, the Sixers acquired one of my three favorite Process Sixers ever in Wroten. Supreme confidence, incredible handle (even though he mostly went left), tons of swagger . . . and couldn't shoot. Wroten's biggest moment on the court would be a game-winning layup to beat the Cavaliers in January 2015. His biggest moment off the court would be his "trust the process" quote in a Pablo Torre *ESPN The Magazine* column that was the first one recognized in relation to the Sixers.

Second, the protections on the second-round pick Hinkie traded away were hilarious. It was top-50 protected, and it also protected 56–60, so it would only actually convey if it fell between 51 and 55. The pick did not convey, so we got Wroten, and "trust the process" for nothing.

3. Traded Michael Carter-Williams to the Bucks in a four-team deal that included the Suns trading a 2018 Lakers first-round draft pick (eventually Mikal Bridges) to the Sixers. Man, this one was glorious. If there were any people sitting on the fence of whether they supported what Hinkie was doing, this move certainly knocked you to either side of it. For some, trading the reigning Rookie of the Year was unforgivable and a disgrace to the game. For me, it meant I would jump in front of a bus for the Process.

The Sixers ended up with an asset (the Lakers' pick!) that would give us a couple of years of drama (when it was top-five protected, and later top-three protected), and finally get us Mikal Bridges, who would get us Zhaire Smith and the 2021 Miami Heat pick, which would net us Tobias Harris. And it all starts with Sam.

2. Traded the rights to Arturas Gudaitis and Luka Mitrović to the Kings in return for Nik Stauskas, Carl Landry, and Jason Thompson, Sacramento's 2018 first-round pick, and the right to swap first-round picks with

Sacramento in 2016 and 2017. His deal would start as the "Nik Stauskas trade," but it quickly shifted to the "Pick Swap trade," in a move that would live in Process and NBA lore as one of the greatest trades of all time.

In exchange for letting the Kings use some of the Sixers' cap space, Hinkie got a flyer on Stauskas, a first-round pick in 2018 (which Bryan Colangelo would later blow in the Fultz trade), and the right to swap first-round picks with Sacramento in 2016 and/or 2017.

It was a great trade and would have been regardless of the result. But the fact that in 2017 the Sixers were able to activate the pick swap, move from number five to number three, create the biggest Lottery Party celebration of all time, only to then have Colangelo blow it by taking that pick and the 2018 first-round pick to move up and take Markelle Fultz at number one . . . that's true legend.

1. Traded Elfrid Payton to the Magic for Dario Šarić, a 2015 second-round draft pick, and a 2018 first-round draft pick. This wasn't the biggest trade (that was probably the MCW trade), and it probably wasn't the best in terms of value (that was the Kings trade), but it just took such guts. This was Hinkie jumping out of a plane without a parachute because he knew he was going to land in a pile of pillows.

Hinkie, who already had a point guard who had just won Rookie of the Year, took Elfrid Payton anyway, because he had a hunch that the Orlando Magic wanted him. There was a great moment during the draft when they showed Carter-Williams's puzzled reaction to the pick. Hinkie was right—the Magic wanted him and ended up getting the player the Magic selected (Dario Šarić) and a 2018 first-round pick that was actually the Sixers' own pick that had been traded away in the Bynum trade and would later become Landry Shamet. So this is the night that would ultimately give the Sixers what they needed to trade for Jimmy Butler and Tobias Harris.

As the adage goes, "You can't win without a Johnson." With all respect to the Birds' Albert, Alonzo, Bill, Chris, Don, Dwight, Eric, Gene, Jay, Kevin, Lee, Maurice (a Temple alum), Norm, Reggie, Ron, the other Ron, and Vaughn, well, sorry you didn't make the cut.

To the Phils' Charles, Darrell, Davey (yes, *that* Davey), Jerry, John (who names their kid John Johnson?), Ken, Si, Syl, and Tom—try again next year.

As for the Sixers' George and Reggie, sorry, you didn't cut the mustard. We didn't focus on the Big 5 or any coaches (all apologies to the great Eagles defensive coordinator, Jim) because, you know, we have lives. There's only so much time you can spend on a list, eh?

And sorry to the Flyers' Jimmy Johnson, who's not even the best in local history with that name.

10. Alvin Johnson. According to many NFL websites, Alvin doesn't even exist. Study the Eagles media guide, however, and it appears that this Hardin-Simmons grad got in one game in the championship year of 1948. He punted once for five yards. Yes, you read that right, five yards. Hmmm, wonder why he never punted again? Let's start an Alvin Johnson fan club.

9. Charles Johnson. The skinny wide receiver arrived from Pittsburgh and caught 45 balls for eight touchdowns in two seasons with the Eagles. Fans never liked him, and he quietly left town. His replacement, James Thrash, did no better, and it's because of these two mediocrities—along with a few others—that the fans started screaming for the Birds to sign "a true number one." This eventually led us to Terrell Owens, which leads us to . . . well, you know how that story ends.

8. Jimmy Johnson. Unless you want to count Kim Johnsson, and frankly we were tempted, Jimmy is the only Johnson to ever play for the Flyers. This center from Winnipeg played the first four seasons of the Flyers' existence from '68 to '72 and put up decent numbers. Damn, how many Jimmy Johnsons are there on this planet?

7. Alex Johnson. He had a fine 13-year career as a big-league outfielder, unfortunately just 140 games of it with the Phils. He broke in here in the infamous 1964 season, hitting .303 in 109 at bats. So he *has* to be included just for being on that team. He was hitting .297 the next year when the Phils sent him to St. Louis in a deal that brought future National League president Bill White and Bob Uecker. R.I.P.

Glen says: In 1986, I played in a men's hardball league in Detroit. One night we played a team featuring Alex Johnson as well as former major leaguer Billy Bruton. Mary Wells (famous for the song "My Guy") sang the national anthem. Their team beat us, about 15–1, and then Johnson grabbed four cases of Stroh's beer from his trunk for everyone to share.

6. Deron Johnson. This first and third baseman put up big home run and RBI numbers for the Phils from 1969 to 1972. In 1971, the first year at the Vet, he slammed 34 homers and had 95 RBIs.

5. Dirk Johnson. Yes, we know, he's a punter. But he punted for the Birds in the Super Bowl, for crying out loud, and that counts for a *lot* in our book. Nothing spectacular, mind you, but no disaster either. And when you do anything at all in that game, it's magnified a hundredfold. Plus, he used to brand cattle in Colorado, so there's extra points for that.

4. Ollie Johnson. We're aware that this former Southern High grad only played 66 games for the Sixers from 1980 to 1982, but he's the only Johnson in the Big 5 Hall of Fame, where he starred for the Temple Owls.

3. Clemon Johnson. This 6-foot-10 backup center arrived just in time from Indiana in 1983 and was a big help to the Sixers as they drove to their last NBA championship. He appeared in 12 playoff games, logging more than 200 minutes. This graduate of—get this—Florida Agricultural and Mechanical University proved a point that, while one Johnson is good, two—Reggie and Clemon—will earn you a parade down Broad Street.

2. Lane Johnson. At the moment, he's the number two Johnson on this list, but it's only a matter of time that this future NFL Hall of Famer moves to number one.

1. Charlie Johnson. Hands down, no Johnson had as great a career with a Philadelphia pro team as did this defensive lineman out of Colorado. (By the way, three of the Eagles Johnsons are out of Colorado.) In a five-year career with the Birds, Charlie went to three Pro Bowls (1979–1981). Here's to you, Charlie. You're still Our Favorite Johnson.

Ten Terrible Commercials Starring Philadelphia Sports Figures

You likely forgot about these ads—or at least tried to. The good news? Most of them live forever on YouTube. So you can give them a view at your own peril.

One ineligible honorable mention: it's a spoof in a movie, but if you want to see the lamest example of an athlete pushing product, search for the scene from *Rocky II* where the Italian Stallion dons a Fred Flintstone outfit and attempts to read copy for Beast aftershave. Sylvester Stallone is either brilliant in his awfulness—or just awful.

10. Darren Sproles, Mike Vick, and Wayne Simmonds for CURE Auto Insurance. The fake news conference setups are as convincing as Bert Reynolds's old toupee. A bunch of third-rate actors who've never set foot in a newsroom ask inane questions like, "Hey, Wayne, they tried to put after-market parts on your car?" Simmonds answers back, "Oh yeah, but I won the fight by switching to CURE Auto Insurance." Further realism points deducted because the media types are both well dressed and know how to comb their hair.

9. Terrell Owens for *Desperate Housewives*. This is a bit of a cheat, because it was a *Monday Night Football* pregame teaser rather than an actual ad. Speaking of teaser, Nicollette Sheridan enters the Eagles' locker room clad only in a towel, finding T.O. alone. "My house burned down, and I need to take a long, hot shower," she flirts. Owens demurs, mumbling something about playing Bill Parcells and the Cowboys, until Sheridan drops her towel and jumps into his arms. "Oh hell, the team's going to have to win this one without me," he says. The sexually suggestive skit drew complaints to the FCC, and ABC later apologized for airing it. Oh, and by the way, the Eagles beat Dallas that night, 49–21.

8. Chip Kelly for Tostitos Chips. The shtick is the Chipper whines that he wants to supplant Tostitos as the "official Chip" of the NFL. Clever enough. But the 2015 series of 15-second spots proved cringeworthy. In one, Kelly stands in a shopping cart while a mom orders her son to put him back on the shelf. In another, tight end Zach Ertz ignores his coach, instead scarfing down the Frito-Lay product. They got a lot more annoying as Kelly's won-lost record went south.

7. Mike Richards (with Al Morganti) for West German BMW. Richards was an astoundingly dull human being (although perhaps not when he was trawling Old City bars at 2:00 a.m.). In this one, he and our WIP pal are in a TV studio. Al, who's a hockey authority, plays the dunce, saying, "Mike, I don't get all the abbreviations. SOG, GWG?" Richards, displaying all the emotion of a doorknob, answers back, "All you need to know is WG." Then he tosses a monotone insult at Morganti, saying that BMW products "are smarter than you look, Al."

6. Phillies players for Citizens Bank Park. In an embarrassing 2004 promo for "real grass" at the new ballpark, Randy Wolf frolics through a pasture and Jason Michaels puts a buttercup under his chin. Judging from their excitement, you'd think the players were smoking grass rather than playing on it. This tacky spot barely edges out the 2005 Phils promo, where a big-nosed teenage girl goes to a Phils game, takes a Bobby Abreu foul in the schnozz, and comes away as a beauty. Yeah, that makes us want to buy tickets.

5. Buddy Ryan for Super Million Hair Color. Here's a fat man trying to convince us bald guys to feel inadequate. Poor Buddy, stuffed like a sausage into an ill-fitting sport jacket, looks baffled as the emcee sprays some sap's head with hair-in-a-can. Near as we could figure, it was Krylon Black No. 1602.

4. Eric Lindros and Bob Clarke for Ellio's frozen pizzas. The acting is so wooden you can almost feel the splinters. At the end, Clarke swipes young Eric's slice fresh from the toaster oven. We thought we caught a glimpse of Bonnie Lindros off camera, shrieking, "He's stealing from my baby!"

3. Hunter Pence for Liscio's rolls. The short-term Phillies outfielder searches for other uses for the bakery's products, as if eating them wasn't enough. So he works a fake rowing machine using two loaves of Italian bread as oars. He performs exercise machine reps, saying, "I like to work my lats and delts with their patented rolls." And he uses a hoagie roll to measure his baseball socks for some reason.

2. Muhammad Ali and Joe Frazier for Vitalis. This ad came out right before the 1971 Thrilla in Manilla, so Ali boasts, "Joe Frazier, you're gonna be so messed up on March the 8th, even Vitalis won't help." We could be wrong here, but did it make sense to have two black fighters promote a product used exclusively by white folks?

1. Pete Rose for Aqua Velva. This 1979 ad is the all-timer champ for its combination of campiness, awkwardness, lack of realism, and star power. Rose dives headfirst into second base, avoiding a tag by the Reds' Joe Morgan. Here's the dialogue:

Morgan: "Hey, it's Pete Rose of the Philadelphia Phillies." (As if he was surprised to learn his opponent.)
Rose, dusting himself off: "That's right."
Morgan: "And what kind of aftershave are you using these days?" (Seems an odd question for the moment.)
Rose: "I'm an Aqua Velva man, Joe."
Morgan: "Oh, that's right, a man wants to smell like a man."
Rose then puts his arm around the 5-foot-7 second baseman and starts to croon. "There's something about an Aqua Velva man." Let's just hope Pete was a better gambler than singer.

We're not advising you to ever take drugs, but doing so would likely make this easier to endure.

Boy, this isn't too daunting of a job, is it? Hundreds have been made over the years, which is weird because sports movies traditionally don't do well at the box office.

But even a mediocre sports movie, or a comedy sports movie, can hit us on some emotional level. Characters like Rocky Balboa and Roy Hobbs left as much of an impression on some of us as Joe Frazier and Mike Schmidt.

We left out documentaries and made-for-TV movies, which eliminates great works like *Brian's Song, Hoop Dreams, When We Were Kings, Four Minutes, *61, Basketball: A Love Story,* and many others. And other flicks—like *Heaven Can Wait*—are left off because there's just not enough sports in them.

In the end, these are the 10 each we like the most.

Big Daddy says:

10. *Invincible*, 2006. I know the real Vince Papale and other characters, like Dick Vermeil, so well that I looked for flaws in the performances, and maybe there were a few. But the true-story aspect of it is so Philly, there's no way to keep it off the list. And Elizabeth Banks has never looked hotter than as Vince's bartender love interest, Janet.

9. *Bang the Drum Slowly*, 1973. It's a wrenching tale of an incredible friendship between a Major League star pitcher (Michael Moriarty) and a green catcher (Robert De Niro) who's desperately trying to make the team even as he's terminally ill. It accurately portrays spring training, which is, for fans, a great season of hope, but for players, often a trying time. Vincent Gardenia is his usual great self as the manager. Look for Danny Aiello in a small role.

8. *A League of Their Own*, 1992. Yeah, it has *three* sappy endings, but it's just so much fun along the way that you forgive that. Tom Hanks, technically miscast as the older and rundown manager Jimmy Dugan (based on Jimmy Foxx), is fantastic. In fact, you could make an argument it's his best performance ever. Geena Davis and Lori Petty make convincing athletes, and Jon Lovitz is hilarious. It was supposed to be a breakout role for Madonna, but she ended up being outshone by Rosie O'Donnell and the rest of the cast.

7. *Caddyshack*, 1980. Bill Murray and Rodney Dangerfield destroy the world of snobbish golf—led by the perfectly cast Ted Knight—and in the process, destroy the audience with laughter. *Caddyshack* would also make our top 10 comedies. A true classic. Did you know that after the filming was over, director Harold Ramis realized that Murray and Chevy Chase didn't play one scene together? So the three of them met for lunch and wrote the classic scene where Ty Webb's ball crashes into Carl Spackler's shack and they end up sharing a bong and some thoughts on life—all filmed in one take. And whatever happened to Lacy Underall?

6. _The Bad News Bears_, 1976. As funny as _Bears_ is, it's not far from the truth of what the world of Little League baseball is all about. The coaches, the kids, the parents—none of us are all that perfect, are we? For a little comedy, we would rank Walter Matthau's performance as grumpy, drinking coach Morris Buttermaker with any performance of his career, which is saying a lot. Tatum O'Neal, Vic Morrow, Jackie Earle Haley, and Chris Barnes lead a strong ensemble cast. Did you know that Buttermaker is never seen drinking the same brand of beer more than once? Next time you watch it, see how many brands you can pick out.

5. _Slapshot_, 1977. Reggie Dunlop, the Hanson brothers, Killer Carlson, Ogie Ogilthorpe, Dr. Hook McCracken, the Sparkle Twins, _old time hockey!_ If Hollywood ever made a movie specifically for one group, it's _Slapshot_ for us Broad Street Bully fans. Paul Newman leads as player/coach of the barely surviving Charlestown Chiefs, a small-town minor league hockey team. Hard to believe that this hilariously vulgar script was written by a woman, Nancy Dowd. When the driver of the Chiefs starts pummeling the team bus "because he's gotta make it look mean," we totally lose it. Al Pacino turned down Newman's role.

4. _Rocky_, 1976. Won the Oscar for picture of the year, and it tells the story of Sly Stallone the struggling actor as much as it tells the story of the down-on-his-luck two-bit fighter Rocky Balboa. Ultimately, however, it tells the story of you and me, doesn't it? Because of the sequels, people forget that Rocky loses the fight, one of many cool touches of the film. It's about just hanging in there, believing in yourself, and getting a chance. Arguably the greatest score in movie history, it's only marred by the completely unbelievable fighting sequences. In real life, a penniless Stallone turned down $150,000 to sell the script because he knew that playing Rocky himself was his only chance of hitting the big time. Way to go, Rock!

3. _The Natural_, 1984. The greatest baseball movie ever made, period. Mythical. Magical. Majestic. "What do you want out of life, Roy?" "I want to walk down the street and have people say, there goes Roy Hobbs, the best there ever was." Do you know who used to say that all the time in real life? Ted Williams. Unlike a lot of other films on this list, this is no small film simply about "competing." This is about Babe Ruth, Michael Jordan, America itself. The best there ever was. Incredible cinematography, a grand score by Randy Newman, and a cast that includes Robert Redford, Robert Duvall, Kim Basinger, Darren McGavin, Glenn Close, Robert Prosky, Wilford Brimley, Barbara Hershey, Richard Farnsworth, Michael Madsen, and Joe Don Baker. Are you kidding me? Would be number one if it were just 10 minutes shorter.

2. *Hoosiers*, 1986. Absolute perfection. A slight rip-off of *The Natural* in tone and style, but years after its release, who remembers that? Based on the 1954 Indiana State high school basketball champs, the Milan Indians. Starring the always-believable Gene Hackman as Coach Norman Dale, this movie is "for all the little schools who never got a chance to win the big one." That about sums it up, doesn't it? Funny how Dennis Hopper's performance as alcoholic assistant coach Shooter is his finest ever, even though he's not blowing up buses or killing anyone. Watch for the scene where Maris Valainis, as Jimmy Chitwood, makes shot after shot on an outdoor hoop while Hackman's talking to him. It was done in one take, and Valainis is the only actor on the Hickory team never to actually play high school basketball.

1. *Raging Bull*, 1980. How else can you say this? Robert De Niro's portrayal of psycho middleweight champion Jake LaMotta just might be the single greatest performance by an actor in the history of movies. They should have given him two Oscars—one for all the weight he put on to show LaMotta's downward spiral and another for the underappreciated boxing shape he whipped himself into. It answered any question of whether an athlete brings his "work" home with him. Joe Pesci comes out of nowhere, and Cathy Moriarty is old-school sexy. Sometimes it takes a real brute to rise to the top. Only *Slapshot* or *Scarface* curse like this baby, so please, *never* watch this on network TV, where too much is edited out. The only black-and-white flick to make this list.

Glen says:

I let Big Daddy handle this list because, quite frankly, he begged. Besides, Ray Didinger and I already covered this ground in our book, *The Ultimate Book of Sports Movies*, which listed not just the top 10—but the top 100. You should buy that book too.

One interesting note is that both Big Daddy and I omit a movie that nearly every critic puts at the top of his list of sports movies—*Field of Dreams*. I always found it too reverential. Plus, it all builds up to the scene where Kevin Costner and his dad play catch—and then the dad throws like an eight-year-old girl. Destroyed it right there.

Big Daddy actually put six of Ray's and my favorites on his list, although not in the right order. So, here are the real top 10 sports movies of all time, and I'll be quicker about it:

10. *Million Dollar Baby*, 2004. It's the most honored sports movie of all time, winning four Academy Awards—Best Picture, Best Director (Clint Eastwood), Best Actress (Hilary Swank), and Best Supporting Actor (Morgan Freeman). A tough watch, because of the tragic ending, but a magnificent film.

9. *Caddyshack*, 1980. For reasons already stated. Rumor has it that 4,381 pounds of pot were smoked by the cast and crew during filming.

8. *The Hustler*, 1961. A largely forgotten film because it's black and white and slow moving by today's standards. Besides, who plays pool anymore? But Paul Newman and Jackie Gleason going back and forth in a marathon game—and really making those shots—is as good as it gets. If you've never seen it, call it up on demand. That'll justify whatever you paid for this book right there.

7. *The Longest Yard,* 1974. The original, of course, not the Adam Sandler rip-off. The 47-minute football scene is the greatest that football has ever been done in a movie. "I think I broke his #@%#*&% neck!"

6. *Slap Shot,* 1977. It originally bombed at the box office but has become a cult classic whose fans see it dozens of times and gleefully recite every line. Hey, I've heard more than a few NHL players quote it verbatim—"putting on the foil" or "old time hockey, like Eddie Shore and Dit Clapper." And real credit to Paul Newman, who did all that skating and fighting at age 51.

5. *Bull Durham,* 1988. Like *Slap Shot*, but about minor league baseball and the life of traveling town to town by bus in hopes of reaching the show. Susan Sarandon at her sexiest. This movie started the "sports-movie/chick-flick" genre (copied by *Jerry Maguire*) that actually produces date films you can enjoy.

4. *The Natural,* 1984. That climactic scene, where Roy Hobbs explodes the lights on that homer, still puts a lump in my throat every time.

Glen says: The film was shot in my hometown of Buffalo, New York. The restaurant where Hobbs (Redford) and Iris (Glenn Close) reconnect was actually the Parkside Candy, an ice cream shop where I took my first date in junior high school. I wonder where Laura Rosenfeld is these days.

---

3. *Raging Bull,* 1980. I probably have it too low. A great, great film—but very tough to watch. This was the first of three films De Niro and Pesci made together, followed by *Good-Fellas* and *Casino*. Which is your favorite?

2. *Hoosiers,* 1986. I've literally seen it hundreds of times and know every single line of dialogue—and yet I never flip the channel when it comes on

1. *Rocky,* 1976. The champ of sports movies, and it gets a special nod for being filmed here. Hundreds of sports movies have told the story of the downtrodden underdog getting his shot at the big time. Rocky did it the best.

My Favorite Sports Movies :: Claude Giroux

Captain Claude has been one of the NHL's most prolific point producers since entering the NHL at age 20 in 2008. The five-time All-Star finds that all those cross-country flights and nights on the road are made easier by watching great sports movies. Here are 10 of his favorites.

10. *Any Given Sunday.* Al Pacino's pregame locker room speech is one of the most inspirational ever in any movie.

9. *The Rookie.* You have to admire the persistence of an athlete who holds on to his dream and finally makes it to the Majors at age 35.

8. *Moneyball.* The movie really shows you how teams are put together and another way of thinking about how to build a franchise.

7. *Mystery, Alaska.* It focuses on regular guys playing pond hockey at a high level at the far end of the Earth. Then they challenge the New York Rangers to a game. Great stuff, funny stuff.

6. *Talladega Nights.* Will Ferrell is a national hero and really funny as Ricky Bobby. You'll laugh through the whole movie.

5. *Bull Durham.* A great look at life in minor league baseball. A great love story, as well. Kevin Costner plays that guy who was always one step away from Big League stardom.

4. *Miracle.* It's dramatic and exciting, and, of course, it's based on the true story of the 1980 US Olympic hockey team beating the Russians and eventually winning the gold medal. Very inspirational.

3. *Invincible.* Another inspirational movie, and also based on a true story. Happened right here in Philadelphia.

2. *Slap Shot.* Oh man, the minor league game was really something back then. Such great characters in this one.

1. *Tin Cup.* This has been my all-time favorite sports movie since the first time I saw it. I watch it all the time. Roy McAvoy (Kevin Costner) plays a headstrong golfer with a stubborn attitude who decides to make the PGA Tour. He and Dr. Molly Griswold (Rene Russo) work really well together and have great chemistry. She's a psychiatrist who happens to be dating his rival, David Simms (Don Johnson). The story is great. The movie is kind of a comedy, but not really, because it does have some serious moments. I love this movie.

Best Performances by an Actress in a Sports Movie

We love movies and look for any opportunity to bring them up. And while sports movies usually focus on male athletes, more than a few great actresses have stolen the show—or at least made it better.

As far back as 1942, in *The Pride of the Yankees*, Gary Cooper (as Lou Gehrig) had Teresa Wright (as his wife, Eleanor) to play off of. Though we haven't seen a ballplayer talk to his spouse while she was sitting in the stands since we saw this film, it was established that if you are going to produce a sports film, there better be a strong female character to persuade women to buy tickets.

This is *not* a list strictly of actresses who played athletes, although some of those made the final grade.

10. Allison Janney as LaVona Golden in *I, Tonya*. An Oscar-winning performance in a brutal film that shows you the devastating hurdle Tonya Harding had to leap to get to the Olympics—not that she was an innocent bystander. We're not talking about her dirt-bag husband, Jeff Gillooly, but her abusive mother, portrayed by Janney.

When the casting of this film was announced, we thought there was no way the drop-dead gorgeous Margot Robbie could pull off the built-like-a-truck-driver Tonya Harding, but Robbie does. (By the way, Big Daddy once appeared on a TV show with Harding, and she scared the crap out of him.) But it's Janney, as the tyrannical Mommy Dearest, who steals this film. Not that we ever want to watch it again.

9. Melissa Leo as Alice Ward in *The Fighter*. If you didn't know *The Fighter* is based on the true story of boxer Micky Ward, you would think the whole thing is just too outrageous. The seven sisters, the crackhead brother, the mother who oversees it all as Micky's manager—quite a load of characters. Leo portrays the mom in an Oscar-winning performance. (Geez, the first two are Oscar winners and we're only just starting.)

8. Keira Knightley and Parminder Nagra in *Bend It Like Beckham*. Knightley (who you've heard of) and Nagra (who you haven't) play London teens who idolize David Beckham and play soccer well enough to win scholarships in the USA. If you've got a daughter who loves sports, watch the movie with her. If not, you'll enjoy it anyway.

7. Sanaa Lathan as Monica Wright in *Love and Basketball*. Next time you watch this excellent romantic-sports movie, pinch your keister to remind yourself that Sanaa Lathan never picked up a basketball until four months before she landed this plum role.

6. Geena Davis as Dottie Hinson in *A League of Their Own*. Davis handles comedy, romance, being an older sister, and playing a catcher—one of the more physically demanding positions in team sports. And she's completely believable in this Golden Globe–nominated portrayal.

5. Tatum O'Neal as Amanda Whurlitzer in *The Bad News Bears* (1976). We list the year here, so no one gets confused with any inferior remakes or sequels, which

O'Neal and the legendary Walter Matthau avoided. O'Neal's real life, it turned out, was as rough as Amanda's. O'Neal plays this role hard and wise-crackingly funny. But what makes this performance special is Amanda crying on the mound when she realizes Matthau is just going to be her beer-guzzling coach—and not the stepdad she longs for.

4. Susan Sarandon as Annie Savoy in *Bull Durham*. Why can't sports book writers have an "Annie" that "meets" them when they come to town? It's not fair. By the way, are we nuts or does Susan still look pretty damn good at 72? And she's a sports freak in real life.

3. Hilary Swank as Maggie Fitzgerald in *Million Dollar Baby*. It's like watching two entirely different films for the price of one. The first half is a fun fairytale of a poor, determined woman who convinces the craggy old boxing trainer (is there any other kind?) played by Clint Eastwood (who else?) into training her. It's full of clichés, but it still hooks you in. When disaster strikes in the second half of the film, it's heartbreaking. Swank won the Oscar for Best Actress for the role. If you're keeping score, that's three Oscar winners on the list so far.

2. Cathy Moriarty as Vikki LaMotta in *Raging Bull*. Not only is she incredibly sexy, she's tough as nails. Robert De Niro won the Oscar as the violent, loner, wife-abusing boxer in the performance of *his* lifetime. But it's Moriarty who must not only stand there and take it but dish it out as well. All while looking like a million bucks. Moriarty was 17 and had never acted in her life when she won a beauty contest at her favorite bar that ultimately got her into this movie, directed by Martin Scorsese, and nabbed her an Oscar nomination. *That's* a debut.

1. Talia Shire as Adrian Pennino in *Rocky*. Shire is not someone you think of immediately when you consider big-time movie actresses. But with *Rocky* and *Godfather*, she is in two of the most popular franchises ever.

Her portrayal of Adrian gives Sylvester Stallone's character a believable neighborhood girlfriend, and Shire draws out the sweet side of Rocky Balboa, which makes the film for us. Also nominated for an Oscar. I heard Shire say in an interview that to this day, more than four decades later, fans still yell out "Yo! Adrian!" when they see her walking down the street. Oh, and we bet you didn't know Adrian's last name was Pennino.

Philadelphia's Ultimate Pickup Team :: Sonny Hill

Sonny Hill has been Mr. Basketball in Philadelphia as long as anyone can remember. He is the executive advisor to the 76ers and founder and director of the Sonny Hill Community Involvement Basketball League. He is also a respected broadcaster who has called NBA games on CBS, and he currently hosts a popular Sunday morning show on WIP. In 2003, Sports Illustrated ranked Hill among the 101 most influential minorities in sports.

This is my all-time Philadelphia high school team of players from the Public and Catholic Leagues, most from back in the heyday. I picked the players based on these criteria: you're in the schoolyard, and if you lose, you have to wait a long time before your next game. With these players, I don't plan to lose.

Forward—Tom Gola, La Salle High. You're talking about a player who was way ahead of his time. Tom was a big man for his era, and he did things in the 1950s that people just started doing in the past 10 years—put the ball on the floor, rebound, play defense. A great team player as well.

Forward—Ray "Chink" Scott, West Philadelphia High. Another quintessential player who was ahead of his time. He was one year behind Wilt in high school and was Wilt's best competition back then. At 6-foot-9, he could dribble, shoot the long jumper, play the post; he could do it all.

Center—Wilt Chamberlain, Overbrook High. You don't need any comments from me here. If you don't know, you don't know basketball.

Guard—Guy Rodgers, Northeast High. So many light-years ahead that the game still hasn't caught up. Just 6 feet tall, but he was Magic Johnson long before there was Magic Johnson. Averaged 35 points per game in high school and went on to become one of the best-ever players at Temple. He could shoot both left- and right-handed hook shots. Imagine that.

Guard—John Chaney, Ben Franklin High. A folk hero in city basketball. John played at a time when not everything was on TV or radio, but word still got out on the street about how great he was. John would dribble the ball and five guys couldn't get it away from him. His best skill was his tenacity. The same drive you saw in him as a coach at Temple, he had as a player. As close as John and I were—and still are—he used to say to me, "I don't come to play against you, I come to kill you."

My other top players include:

Overbrook High: Wayne Hightower, Jackie Moore, Walt Hazzard, Andre McCarter, Wali Jones, Lewis Lloyd, Hal Lear

West Catholic High: Michael Brooks, Gene Banks, Ernie Beck

Northeast High: Joe Belmont, James "Tee" Parham

Ben Franklin High: Claude Gross

Gratz High: Rasheed Wallace

Lincoln High: Larry Cannon

Olney High: Jimmy Baker

South Philadelphia High: Lionel Simmons

"Ready to play?"

10. Wayne Cashman, Flyers. He was a competent assistant who got the big job in 1997. Demonstrated all the leadership skills of the high school principal in *Ferris Bueller.* You could actually *see* sweat drenching through his shirt on your TV. He stepped down on his own to become an assistant again. Give Cashman this; unlike many of us, he knew his limitations.

9. Terry Francona, Phillies. What bothered us most is that Francona spent his four seasons here constantly trying to lower expectations. Actually, what bothered us most is that after he left, he made it to the World Series three times and won it twice. He could get to the Hall of Fame—and our city served as his training wheels.

8. Eddie Jordan, Sixers. A dim-witted, overmatched joyless coach with all the personality of a blank piece of paper. Jordan wanted to bring the Princeton offense to the Sixers, who clearly didn't have the talent to fit that system. Ended up at Rutgers, where it was soon discovered he did not have a degree, as was claimed on his transcript. He got fired from there after putting together a 32-game losing streak. The first of four Sixers coaches on this list.

7. Joe Kuharich, Eagles. Not the only "worst" list he makes in this book. Before coming to the Eagles, Kuharich was most known for being the only losing coach in the history of Notre Dame. Between 1961 and 1975, the Eagles' head coaches were Nick Skorich, Kuharich, Jerry Williams, hailstorms, poisoned cattle, Ed Khayat, Mike McCormack, locusts, and raining frogs. Fortunately, Dick Vermeil got here before the plagues took each Philadelphian's firstborn son.

6. Johnny Davis, Sixers. Trusting him with a $200 million NBA franchise was like trusting a pimply 15-year-old with the family sedan. What Pat Croce and Ed Snider saw in him defies description.

> **Glen says:** The day he was named, I was on WIP blasting the choice. A furious Snider called me and compared Davis to Fred Shero in terms of being an unknown who would come in and prove his genius. "The name of the game is to win," screamed Snider. "W-I-N."

Not in Davis's case. Enduring memory: Davis calling a timeout in the final seconds of a blowout loss so that rookie Allen Iverson could continue his late-season streak of 40-plus-point games.

5. Art Fletcher, Phillies. Yeah, we never heard of him either, so go ask your great-grandfather about the guy who ran the Phils for four dreadful seasons in the 1920s. Here's what our research found: There are 187 guys in history who managed as many Major League games (623) as Fletcher. Just one ever did worse than Fletcher's .382 winning percentage. You could look it up.

4. Rich Kotite, Eagles. The only guy on this list who actually won a postseason game—but who's kidding, that was Buddy Ryan's team and Bud Carson's defense. Kotite was perceived by fans as a confused buffoon, by players as a puppet of ownership, by media as a flop-sweating ignoramus. After losing the final seven games of 1994, Kotite was fired by Jeff Lurie. He was quickly hired by the Jets, and many in the New York media suggested that Kotite had gotten a raw deal in Philadelphia. Kotite rewarded their faith by going 4–28 over two seasons.

3. Ryne Sandberg, Phillies. The Cubs Hall of Famer inherited a declining team in 2013 and made things worse—alienating exalted veterans like Jimmy Rollins while also gaining no respect from upcoming youngsters like Ken Giles. Sandberg displayed the strategic acumen of Homer Simpson. The final straw came when Chase Utley loudly told off pitching coach Bob McClure on the mound during a hot summer 2015 game, after outfielder Jeff Francoeur was left in to throw 40 pitches in a blowout. A few days later, Sandberg resigned, saying that "all the losses weighed on me." There were 159 of them, compared to 119 wins—a .428 winning percentage.

2. Doug Moe, Sixers. At one point he was considered a competent—even innovative—NBA coach. That wasn't in Philadelphia. Moe had the work ethic of a Florida retiree—he just neglected to tell that to Harold Katz before signing a five-year contract in 1992. And, yes, it really is true that Moe sometimes whistled an early end to practice so he could get to a movie matinee at the Bala Theatre.

But, rather than us rip the guy, we'll give you two of Moe's own quotes to sum him up:

"The passing game is basically doing whatever the hell you want. But what coach is going to say, 'We're a freelance team?' It sounds like you're not coaching. Hey, if a coach gets some sort of thrill when the team runs a play right, that's good. I just happen to think differently."

"Somebody said to me, 'It's Friday the 13th, are you going to be jinxed?' I said, 'Bleep, you can't jinx us. We stink.'"

1. Roy Rubin, Sixers. When he was hired to coach the Sixers in 1972, Rubin was asked how he felt about coaching Hal Greer, a future Hall of Famer entering his 15th season.

"Who?" he responded.

Rubin came to the Sixers from Long Island University, which, near as we can tell, has never seriously challenged for the NCAA title. He predicted the Sixers would be "neck-and-neck" with the Celtics in 1972–1973. They fell just 57 games short. He got fired with a 4–47 record. By then, the Sixers had acquired the nickname "the Universal Health Spa," because they made all the other sick teams well.

Michael Barkann has asked his share of questions in his longtime role on NBC Sports Philadelphia, where he has served as host of the station's postgame show for all four pro sports teams. He has also worked for WIP, CBS Sports, and the USA Network covering the Olympics and US Open Tennis Tournament. He does not discuss his brief time broadcasting the XFL.

6. Bryce is nice (who knew?)—Bryce Harper, March 2, 2019.
A few days after signing a record 13-year, $330 million contract, Bryce Harper put on the red pinstripes for the first time in Clearwater. He hit every right note with Phillies management, with new teammates who'd come to watch, and—especially—with fans.

"I want to put down my roots," the new right fielder says. "At the end of this, I could have a couple of kids, and they could be able to say they're from Philly."

Every new star enters town with a honeymoon, but Harper—a player we'd booed during his years in Washington—went out of his way to say he liked us. Hey, he really liked us.

During a half-hour newser, he praised the Flyers, Sixers, teammate Aaron Nola, Philly's blue-collar fans, our cuisine, neighborhoods, even Gritty the mascot.

How much of a hit did he make? Harper's number 3 jersey then broke the 24-hour sales record for a launch in any sport. A few days later, the Phillies merchandise store ran out of *R*s because so many people wanted H-A-R-P-E-R on their back.

5. Who let the dogs out?—Mike McCormack, Veterans Stadium, September 29, 1975.
McCormack was in his third season as coach of the Eagles. The Birds lost their first two games of 1975, and at the regular Monday news conference, reporter Tom Brookshier asked the coach, "Mike, how many dogs do you have on the roster?"

To everyone's surprise, McCormack answered: "If you're talking about real mutts, I'd say two."

The next week, as the Eagles lost to the Rams, 42–3, fans at the vet tossed a huge inflatable dog bone around the stands and chanted, "Al-po, Al-po."

Then, at season's end, they waved goodbye to Mike McCormack and hello to . . . Dick Vermeil.

4. Deep Schmidt—Mike Schmidt, Jack Murphy Stadium, San Diego, May 29, 1989.
For 17-plus seasons, Mike Schmidt played third base for the Phillies. He was the town's greatest enigma. Fans loved him. They hated him. They stood for him. They booed him. He won it all. He couldn't catch a break. He once said Philadelphia was the only town where a player could "experience the thrill of victory, and the agony of reading about it the next day."

At age 39, Schmidt knew his skills were abandoning him. He had allowed a costly error the night before at San Francisco. So, on a Monday afternoon at Jack Murphy Stadium, just two hours before the Phils were to play the Padres, he said goodbye to baseball. Actually, he cried goodbye to baseball. It was a site to behold coming from a man who almost never displayed any public emotion at all.

"Some 18 years ago, I left Dayton, Ohio, with two very bad knees and a dream to become a Major League baseball player . . . and . . . uh . . ."

He began to cry.

"I thank God the dream came true . . ."

Sobbing, he stopped speaking. After Schmidt was unable to compose himself for about a minute, Phillies president Bill Giles took over the microphone. He eloquently thanked Schmidt for "over 7,000 hours of baseball in a Phillies uniform" and for the work ethic that never accepted mediocrity.

At his most vulnerable moment, Schmidt was the man. He truly was.

3. "I'll kick your ass!"—John Chaney, Amherst, Massachusetts, February 13, 1994.

After Temple's one-point loss at UMass, head coach John Chaney interrupted Minuteman coach John Calipari's news conference, pointing a finger and shouting, "Next time I see you, I'll kick your ass!"

Calipari had confronted two of the referees following the game. Chaney thought he should have been present during any postgame meeting with the refs and blew the roof off Calipari's newser. Beautiful. Come on now, didn't you want to see what would have happened had Coach reached his destination and gotten his hands on a little Calipari booty?

2. "Next question!"—Terrell Owens/Drew Rosenhaus, Moorestown, New Jersey, November 8, 2005.

One sunny day in South Jersey, Terrell Owens vainly tried to save his Eagles career. He had been suspended for remarks he made about quarterback Donovan McNabb in a nationally telecast interview on ESPN. He opined that had Brett Favre been quarterbacking the Eagles, the team would be undefeated.

Owens had already been given two chances to apologize and failed to do so. Coach Andy Reid suspended Owens for the Eagles' Sunday-night game at Washington, which the Birds lost 17–10. Following the game, the Eagles lengthened Owens's suspension to four weeks, which had him singing a different tune—in front of his house.

So that Tuesday, T.O. declared his respect for his quarterback—oh, it was beautiful—and apologized up and down and back and forth. The pièce de résistance, however, came from his agent, Drew Rosenhaus—who undid any chance Owens had of reinstatement by acting like a buffoon.

Rosenhaus read a statement calling Owens a "great person" and said, "He is here again today to make sure that everyone understands that he is making an apology."

But when asked specifically about his client's plight, Rosenhaus could only reply, "Next question!" Thirteen times.

1. Practice makes perfect—Allen Iverson, Wachovia Center, May 7, 2002.

This has to be the all-timer. Allen Iverson—tortured by his coach, the media, and the Sixers' first-round playoff loss to the Celtics—was incredulous that anyone would wonder about his workout habits. When asked about how much time he actually put in practicing, AI couldn't take it anymore and delivered this soliloquy:

"I'm supposed to be the franchise player, and we're in here talking about practice. I mean, listen, we're talking about practice. Not a game. Not a game. Not a game. We're talking about practice. Not a game. Not the game that I go out there and die for and play every game like it's my last. Not the game. We're talking about practice, man. I mean how silly is that? And we're talking about practice."

I don't think any player ever put his insides on the outside like AI.

Ten Philly Athletes Who Jumped to Broadcasting

It's not an easy transition. Many have tried and failed. The greatest team athlete of all time, Bill Russell, couldn't get it. In fact, he ruins our VHS tape (anyone have a VHS player?) of Game 4 of the Sixers' championship win over the Lakers in 1983, as Russell did color with our least favorite play-by-play announcer of all time, Dick Stockton.

You also have the type like Tim McCarver, who just overanalyzed everything to the point you just wanted him to shut up.

On the local level it's even more difficult because you listen to them constantly. If they don't grow, they will eventually get on your nerves. And God forbid if they are replacing a legend; it can take you more than a season to get adjusted—if you ever do at all.

To be a fantastic color analyst, one must bring three qualities to the table:

One, you must know your Xs and Os. Most ex-players get this one because they performed at the highest level.

Two, bring a little humor. We're not asking you to be Carrot Top, but levity goes a long way.

Three is the toughest, and only a few have succeeded. That's the challenge of making you wish you were at the game. You know the broadcaster is doing a superlative job if you're lying on the couch thinking, "Damn, I should be there!" Dick Vitale (ex-coach, but not an ex-pro player) was excellent at this—at least before he became a caricature of himself.

The greatest color analyst of all time was John Madden. He excelled at all three like no other analyst ever. Unfortunately, though drafted by the Eagles, he never played in a single game due to injury, so he's not making the list. Rules are rules.

We did not include on this list ex-players who do just talk radio or pre- and postgame shows—like our pal and colleague Ike Reese. We love those guys as well.

10. Vai Sikahema. Played 32 memorable games for the Birds, and although his sports broadcasting was fine (we particularly loved him hosting *Sports Final*), he's the one person on this list who graduated into doing "real" news. One of the nicest guys you'll ever meet. Unless you're a goalpost.

9. Heather Mitts. You have to be a soccer freak to remember the Philadelphia professional soccer team, the Charge, that Mitts played for. But she's a three-time Olympic gold medalist, collegiate All-American, and was an in-studio analyst for ABC and ESPN. Did sideline college football work as well.

8. Mike Golic. This Notre Dame grad played 82 games with the Eagles and has been a cohost of some version of a morning show on ESPN for over 18 years. That's a very long time in this business.

7. Ron Jaworski. Started 137 games for the Eagles and took them to Super Bowl XV. Who hasn't at some point met Jaws and come away saying, "What a nice guy!"? Ron did an excellent job on *Monday Night Football* from 2007 to 2011 and an even better job on *NFL*

Matchup. One thing we love about Ron is if he's a guest at 94-WIP before an Eagles-Bears game, he will pick the Birds. If you catch him on a Chicago radio station later in the day? He just might pick the Bears. It was Doug Collins who dubbed him "Jaws." One of us, by the way, is thrilled he was raised in the Buffalo area.

6. Howie Long. Okay, he never played professionally in Philly, having spent 13 Hall of Fame seasons with the Raiders. But he suited up collegiately at Villanova and was a bouncer at Kelly's on Lancaster Avenue, so that has to count for something, right? He's had such a long career as an analyst and commercial pitch man, you might have forgotten his terrific performance as a thespian in the action flick *Broken Arrow*. Unfortunately, we still remember it, and, well, Leonardo DiCaprio is not losing any sleep.

5. Tom Brookshier. This Pro Bowler played 76 games for the Eagles before an injury cut his career short. A great career as a color analyst with Pat Summerall, you also could say that Tom had more to do with the success of WIP than anyone with his *Brookie and the Rookie* morning show—the "rookie" being Angelo Cataldi. I guess because Tom hails from the UFO-famous Roswell, New Mexico, he was used to working with aliens.

4. Keith Jones. A national hockey analyst and local color guy for the Flyers, Keith is also part of 94-WIP's morning show where, simply put, we find him at his hilarious best. He was a trash-talking fight starter with the Flyers, but off the ice he's the nicest guy. Just don't get caught in an elevator with him if he decides to, uh, "cut the cheese." You might not make it out alive.

3. Larry Andersen. Everyone loves Larry. No one, and we mean no one, combines humor and anger like Andersen does as a radio color guy. One second he'll make you laugh, and the next he's fuming at an ump's bad call. The former Phils reliever's take on the *Daily News*'s Home Run Payoff inning is always hilarious. "Scott and Larry" is as good as it gets, and we'll always remember Scott Franzke letting Phils fans know that Larry was making an appearance at a Home Depot and you could pose for a photo with Larry. "It might be the only photo you'll ever get of Larry where he's not coming out of a bar," mused Franzke.

2. Charles Barkley. There are many funny people on this list, but in our opinion there's no one as honest and hilarious as Sir Charles. It's like he has no governor on that motor mouth of his and says whatever comes to his mind. And by the way, he's not only in the Hall of Fame, the Chuckster is in any conversation as the greatest power forward of all time.

1. Richie Ashburn. "His Whiteness," as Harry Kalas loved to call him. Those two are, in our opinion, the greatest Philly broadcasting team of all time. Richie invented his own laid-back style of color. If he had nothing to say at a particular moment, guess what he said? Nothing. He was unique. Between playing in 1,794 games as a Phillie, starting in 1948, and then calling well over 5,000 games from 1963 to 1997, you see why this Hall of Famer is number one on this list.

Honorable mention: Steve Coates, Steve Mix, John Kruk, Chris Therien, Malik Rose, Mike Quick, Gary Dornhoefer, Bill Clement, Doug Collins, Stan Walters, Bobby "The Chief" Taylor

Larry Andersen pitched 17 seasons in the Major Leagues, including six for the Phils over two stints. He has been a broadcaster for the team since 1999. This list is in alphabetical order.

Darren Daulton. Dutch's goal was to wake up and see how he could make everyone else's day better. He was a selfless guy and a loving human being. That 1993 team doesn't win the pennant without him, and I'm not talking about how great he was on the field. Jim Fregosi had to appreciate how Dutch did half the manager's job for him—he controlled the clubhouse. One game in 1994, he broke his collarbone on a foul tip early in the game. He didn't know it was broken and stayed in the game. Then he got hit by another foul tip in the eighth inning and broke another bone. Man, he was tough.

Scott Franzke. Salt of the earth. Well rounded, even keel. Full of great ideas and advice. One reason we click on the air is the rapport we have off the field as friends. Our families, too. When we started working together regularly in 2007, I took it as a demotion because they moved me off TV to radio. But the Phils thought Scott would help bring out my personality. Well, whatever it was, it's worked out for us and, I think, the fans.

Dallas Green. With that booming voice, there was never a more intimidating coach or manager to be around. I loved talking the game with him, especially pitching, of course. A real old-school guy. Of course, I liked him best around September when he'd bring in bushels of corn and tomatoes from his farm in Delaware. You always wanted to be on Dallas's good side in the fall.

Harry Kalas. He loved the Phillies and loved doing the games. Harry was a naturally funny man who didn't have to force it. One time, we were in a plane in Denver, stuck at the airport. We drank up all the beer, and Harry fell asleep. He wakes up three hours later, and we're still on the runway. Harry looks over at me and says in that great voice, "Pretty smooth ride so far, LA." I said, "Harry, we haven't moved yet." Harry looks out the window and, cool as can be, says, "Well, I'll be."

John Kruk. He and I were teammates in 1993 and 1994. People love his shtick. But the thing is, he's not a very sociable guy. He's funny in front of a group, but it's hard for Krukker to talk to people he doesn't know. I'll tell you this: with kids or someone in need, his heart is as big as it gets. He's very gracious and appreciative of what he's been able to do.

Garry Matthews. Sarge has charisma. People gravitate to him because he's always smiling and you never see him mad. He's comfortable talking to everyone, from players to the Amtrak conductor. He also believes that he's mastered the English language. He hasn't; he just knows a few big words that he uses again and again. He'll tell a story and make sure he gets the word *peripheral* in it, and add, "That means to the side." I've never heard him talk for five minutes without using the word *peripheral*. Also, you don't know if he's talking to you because he forgets your name. He called Jim Jackson "John" for years.

Johnny Podres. It would be a contest to see who's more positive, him or Gabe Kapler. As our pitching coach, Johnny always had the back of all of his pitchers. And he'd make you feel like Cy Young. Once, back in 1993, Mark Davis had to pitch four games in a row, and he got pounded in that last one for four runs. Podres goes to the mound and says, "Hey, kid, you're looking good; keep battling." MD looks back at him and says, "Pods, what bleeping game are you watching?"

Juan Samuel. Sammy has that infectious smile. Playing with him—and even against him—he was so fun to watch. I've never enjoyed watching anyone hit triples as much as him—flying around the bases, always a smile. He appreciated the talent and ability he had and the life it allowed him to have. He showed that in how nicely he treated everyone, right down to the clubhouse kids.

Dan Stevenson. Video Dan and I started with the Phils at the same time—back in 1983— and we stayed together in spring training. I got him hooked on Nintendo. I'd get up at 6:30 to go to the ballpark, and he'd still be up from the night before playing video games. He blames me for his addiction. I'm godfather to his two kids, who he adopted from Russia.

David West. One of my favorite teammates, and a riot. And, yeah, he could eat. In 1993, we had adjoining rooms on the road, and we never locked the door in between. Every night that season, around 2:30 a.m., he'd shout from his side, "Hey, you want a cheeseburger?" I'd say, "No, I'm trying to sleep." He'd say, "You want french fries?" and then, into the phone, "Make that two." And then, "Hey, Larry, forest cake or carrot cake?" I think he went from 250 to 275 that season. I put on 20 pounds myself. He was always jovial, especially around dinner time.

Honorable mention: Frankie "Two Scoops" Mazzuca. Frankie gives out the ice cream in the media dining room. A big, loud, gregarious guy. His goal in life is to get people to eat ice cream. Ask for one scoop, and he'll give you three.

Philadelphia sports fans are often left to wonder, "What if we had drafted this guy over that guy?" Or, "What if our superstar hadn't been injured that season?" Or, "What if our clubs' owners weren't such a band of blithering idiots?"

We are left with too few championships. Instead, we live in the Land of What Might Have Been.

We've assembled a list here of 20 of the biggest "what ifs" in Philadelphia sports history—each of which would have dramatically affected our sports lives.

What if . . .

20. The Phillies—and not the A's—packed up and left town back in 1954?
For the first half of this century, this was a two-team city. Both losers, by the way. The A's went on to 19 postseason appearances and four world championships since moving on. The Phils . . . well, two titles. Not that the A's would have enjoyed all that success if they'd stayed here. We're just wondering.

19. Vince Lombardi had taken the Eagles head coaching job when it was offered in 1958?
Lombardi was a New York assistant at the time, and Giants owner Wellington Mara talked him out of coming here by saying the Eagles were a second-rate organization. The irony is that the Eagles hired Buck Shaw, who—two years later—beat Lombardi's Green Bay Packers in the NFL title game. Still, for the long term, who wouldn't want Lombardi?

18. The Cuban Missile Crisis had never occurred?
Huh? What's the sports connection, you ask? Well, here's the story. In October 1962, the three Kennedy brothers— President John, Attorney General Bobby, and Senator Teddy—were chatting about what they might do after Jack was finished in the White House. Teddy noted that Eagles owner Jim Clark had just died and the team was up for sale. The president ordered his youngest brother to meet with team management. Alas, the next day—moments before Ted Kennedy was to board a train for Philadelphia—American spy planes revealed the presence of Soviet missiles in Cuba. The football plan got sidetracked and never was revisited.

17. The 1968–1969 La Salle basketball team hadn't been on probation and, thus, ineligible to play in the NCAA Tournament?
The Explorers finished 23–1 that season under new coach Tom Gola but had to stay home because of violations under former coach Jim Harding. They were ranked second at the end of the regular season. Could they have challenged Lew Alcindor and his undefeated UCLA squad?

16. The Phillies recognized that Dallas Green knew their farm system pretty damn well when—as the Cubs' new general manager in 1982—he insisted that the Larry Bowa-for-Ivan DeJesus trade be sweetened by inclusion of a minor-league third baseman whose path here was blocked

by Mike Schmidt? Green moved the kid to second base, and Ryne Sandberg went on to have a Hall of Fame career in Chicago.

15. The NCAA Men's Basketball Tournament had started using the shot clock one year earlier? The Villanova Wildcats took just 11 second-half shots in their brilliant win over Georgetown in 1985. It was the last season without the clock, and there's no way Nova could have frozen the ball under the new rules. Taking things one step further: 1985 was also the *first* year the tournament expanded from 48 to 64 teams. Nova—an eight seed—probably would have been left out under the old setup. Sometimes, timing is everything.

14. Leonard Tose had actually moved the Eagles to Phoenix in 1985? Would we have quickly gotten a replacement team? Would it have been called the Eagles? Could we have ever gotten used to dressing in different colors, say powder blue and canary yellow, and heading down to the Vet to chant out P-R-E-T-Z-E-L-S . . . Pretzels!?!?

13. Someone had the common sense to take away Pelle Lindbergh's car keys that night back in 1985?

12. Harold Katz hadn't concluded that Brad Daugherty was "soft" after working him out at Katz's Villanova home back in 1986? Katz's not-so-temporary insanity led to two of the all-time worst trades, both on draft day that year: sending the first-overall pick (which became Daugherty) to Cleveland for journeyman Roy Hinson, and—even worse—trading Moses Malone, Terry Catledge, and two first-rounders to Washington for Cliff Robinson (who spent the next three seasons being intimidated by Charles Barkley) and Jeff Ruland (whose lower leg fell off every time he got up from a chair).

11. Cris Carter had been able to get clean before Buddy Ryan had to cut him in 1989? Carter caught 89 passes as an Eagle—and 1,012 after Ryan released him, Carter sobered up, and the Vikings signed him. Shouldn't we have benefited from that greatness?

10. The Phils had recognized Jeff Jackson as nothing more than a good high school player on draft day in 1989? They picked Jackson with the fourth overall pick, passing up an Auburn first baseman named Frank Thomas. Jackson never reached the bigs; Thomas went on to have 10 seasons with 100-plus RBIs and make the Hall of Fame.

9. The Flyers had believed in scouting Eastern Europe a little earlier—say, 1990? That's the year they spent the fourth overall pick of the draft on an Ontario plugger named Mike Ricci, bypassing Czech sensation Jaromír Jágr.

8. NHL arbitrator Larry Bertuzzi had ruled Eric Lindros property of the Rangers—not the Flyers—back in 1992? Peter Forsberg (part of the deal that brought number 88 here) would have played out his brilliant career in Philadelphia. The Flyers also would have kept Ron Hextall, two first-round draft picks, Chris Simon, Ricci, and a few other muckers. Would the two Stanley Cups Forsberg won in Colorado instead have been paraded down Broad Street?

7. Jim Fregosi had left Larry Andersen in to pitch the ninth inning of Game 6 in the 1993 World Series? Hell, the fans all knew that Mitch Williams was shot—how come Fregosi didn't see it? "Touch 'em all, Joe. You'll never hit a bigger home run in your life."

6. Matt Geiger had waived his no-trade clause back in the summer of 2000? A complicated four-team trade that July would have sent Geiger—and Allen Iverson (!)—to Detroit, bringing Glen Rice and Eddie Jones to the Sixers. But Geiger refused to give up a $5 million trade kicker, and the Pistons, unable to add that much to their salary cap, backed out. Given a reprieve, Iverson won the scoring title in 2000–2001, leading the Sixers to the NBA Finals. Iverson won the MVP that season, although, looking back, maybe the true MVP was Geiger—just for his selfishness.

5. The Eagles had offered Terrell Owens a new contract after Super Bowl XXXIX? We all know the story: Owens played through injury to star in the Super Bowl. His agent asked for a new contract, and the Eagles said no. Owens went cuckoo and turned on Donovan McNabb, who offered no support. Fast forward to sit-ups on the driveway and D-I-V-O-R-C-E. But, let's say the Eagles had renegotiated his deal and made Owens happy. Would it have worked out long term? Would there have been more Super Bowls? Years of peace, harmony, and glory for the franchise? Nah, probably not.

4. The Flyers had won the 2007 draft lottery? The Orange and Black had the NHL's worst record by far that season and the best odds to win the top pick. But the ping-pong balls fell another way, and the Flyers settled for the second pick, which became James van Riemsdyk. The Chicago Blackhawks landed junior sensation and future Hall of Famer Patrick Kane. Two seasons later Kane scored the Stanley Cup–winning goal in overtime to beat the Flyers right here in Philadelphia.

3. The Phils had lost their last regular-season game in 2011? Charlie Manuel's squad was facing the collapsing Braves, who were 10–21 down the stretch. Good news: if the Phils managed to lose to the Braves, they'd have the pleasure of facing that easy opponent in the playoffs. Instead, the Phils won their franchise-record 102nd game in 13 innings that afternoon, earning the honor of facing red-hot St. Louis in the NLDS. The Phils lost to the Cards in five games, marking the end of our great era of baseball.

2. The Eagles had moved quicker to hire a coach in 2016? First, owner Jeff Lurie and GM Howie Roseman chased former Giants coach Tom Coughlin, but Old Red Face took himself out of the running. Then they interviewed Giants assistant Ben McAdoo and, by all accounts, planned to offer him the job. Before the Eagles could close the deal, the Giants swooped in and promoted McAdoo to be *their* head coach. McAdoo went 13–15 and got canned after two seasons. The Eagles, meanwhile, fell back on some guy named Pederson.

1. Sixers president Bryan Colangelo hadn't persuaded Danny Ainge of the Celtics to swap first-round picks in 2017? The Sixers leapt to the top of the draft and grabbed point guard Markelle Fultz, who Colangelo expected to direct the offense for a decade. The Celtics dropped to Pick Three (getting a future Sixers' first-rounder as part of the deal) and "settled" for taking Jayson Tatum.

Need a bonus one? What if Eagles receiver Alshon Jeffery hadn't let that last-minute pass slip between his hands for an interception in that 2018 playoff game against the Saints? Could the Eagles have won, then beat the Rams the following week, and returned to the Super Bowl against the Patriots?

Ahh, we'll never know. We live in a world of what ifs . . .

Since the day Joey Caveman threw a rock farther than Felix Caveman, it was Joey who was gonna score the awesome-looking babes. Chicks dig the "long ball." They dig the uniform, the money, the fame, the whole nine yards. You think Marilyn Monroe would have looked at Joe DiMaggio if he was just another San Francisco fisherman like his dad? We think not. Here are some local jocks you won't see perusing the classifieds the next time they need a date—along with their women.

10. Kris and Anna Benson. Okay, so Kris never actually pitched for the Phillies, but he did pitch for the Lehigh Valley Iron Pigs, and that's close enough. His wife, Anna, was bats. (Pun intended.) A former gun-toting stripper, Anna once told Howard Stern that if Kris cheated on her she "would sleep with the entire roster of the New York Mets," who Kris was pitching with at the time. Believe us, when that news got around, Kris's teammates started paying awesome-looking women to hit on Kris.

9. Charles Barkley and Madonna. It was Madonna's legendary appearance on the Letterman show in 1994, when she strongly hinted that she had "known" Sir Charles intimately. It's the same Letterman show where Madonna dropped the F-bomb 13 times in a 20-minute appearance, a network television record at the time.

8. A. J. Feeley and Heather Mitts. We can't help it. We're old school. When we see a beautiful woman, we expect her to be dating the absolute cream of the crop. It kills us when we see a great-looking dish on the arm of some dork. And when you're as spectacular looking as Heather *and* one of the world's premiere female athletes, former Eagles quarterback A. J. qualifies as a dork. He's barely a backup, for crying out loud. We were backups!

7. Rodney Peete and Holly Robinson. If you were married to this gorgeous TV star, you'd be smiling all the time too.

6. Cole Hamels and Heidi Strobel. When Cole was promoted to the majors, he called Heidi first, then his parents. We certainly understand that. This beauty was a contestant on *Survivor: The Amazon* and lasted 33 days—partly by stripping in return for some Oreos. (Who wouldn't?) This led to a cover shot for *Playboy*.

5A. Andrew McManus and Salma Hayek. Who the heck is Andrew McManus? Well, he was a 22-year-old WIP producer on vacation in Vegas, at a dance club, when he spotted Salma Hayek. He strutted over and asked Salma to dance. It's irrelevant to us that she looked at him with the same degree of revolt that Angelo Cataldi looks at a restaurant check. Bottom line: Andrew went for it, and for that, he's our hero.

5. Kobe and Vanessa Bryant. Of course we need to mention Kobe's $4 million rock-wearing girl. Kobe discovered her while she was dancing in a video for Snoop Dogg (she was 17), and you know the Dogg just doesn't use Alpo for his videos.

4. Chris Webber and Tyra Banks. Maybe Chris's game wasn't quite what it once was when he came to the Sixers, but Tyra's was.

3. Ben Simmons and Kendall Jenner. And you ever notice how the Sixers lose every time Kendall shows up at the arena?

2. Jeff Garcia and Carmella DeCesare. What could be better than dating a former Playmate of the Year? How about if that certain playmate is prone to getting in bar brawls with *other* gorgeous babes? *Catfight!*

1. Alexandre Daigle and Pamela Anderson. We don't care if it was only one date. This is Pamela Anderson we're talking about. How did this underachieving hockey player do it? We wish the Flyers had realized this right winger was a dud as quickly as Pam did.

Once-in-a-Lifetime Weirdness

We can be sports fans for the next 50 years, and here are 10 things we're certain that we'll never see again.

10. The likes of Karl Wallenda's high-wire stunts at the Vet. Given the cost of liability insurance these days, no team would take the chance of allowing a 68-year-old circus act to perform headstands 200 feet above the paying customers on a tightrope. By the way, has anyone seen Kiteman lately?

9. An arena closed because the roof blew off. It happened at the Spectrum in February 1968, during a matinee performance of the Ice Capades. The Sixers finished their season at Convention Hall; the Flyers moved their home games to Quebec City.

8. A 30-year-old Eagles season-ticket holder make the team as a walk-on. Vince Papale—who never even played college football—did it in 1976. He stayed with the club for three years as a hard-nosed special-teams player. Disney ended up making a movie of his life, called *Invincible*.

7. A hockey game canceled for a president's speech. Nine days after September 11, 2001, a preseason contest between the Flyers and New York Rangers was delayed before the third period so that President George W. Bush's address to the nation could be broadcast on the Wachovia Center's Jumbotron screen. When it came time to resume the game, players on both sides agreed that—given the magnitude of the president's words—it would be inappropriate to resume playing hockey. They shook hands and skated off as 14,000 fans applauded in agreement.

6. A goalie lose sight of a puck in the sun. It happened the last game of the 1969–1970 season, when the glare coming through an open window at the Spectrum caused Bernie Parent to lose track of a fluttering shot from center ice and give up a rare cheap goal. The 1–0 loss cost the Flyers a playoff berth.

5. A barefoot kicker. By most accounts, there have been just four in the history of the NFL. Two of them—Tony Franklin and Paul McFadden—played for the Eagles in the 1980s. There hasn't been another since 1990, so we're pretty sure we've seen the last of the shoeless ones.

4. A baseball game that ends at 4:45 a.m. or starts at 1:25 a.m. On July 3, 1993, six hours of rain delays turned a two-night doubleheader between the Phils and San Diego Padres into an all-night event at the Vet. When Mitch Williams finally ended the marathon with a run-scoring single, it was the *morning* rush hour that fans had to worry about.

3. A middle-aged physician picked in the NBA draft. Sixers owner Harold Katz was pretty bored toward the end of the 1983 draft. When the 10th round finally rolled around, he used the team's choice to select Norman Horvitz from Philadelphia Pharmaceutical College. Horvitz happened to be a 50-ish doctor who worked for Katz's Nutrisystem, Inc.

2. A World Series game played over three days. The Phils and Tampa Bay Rays started Game 5 of the 2008 Series on October 27 in a light drizzle. The drizzle turned into steady rain—and then sleet. With the score tied, 3–3, in the sixth, Commissioner Bud Selig called it for the night. The next evening was no better. So the game resumed on October 29 after a 46-hour delay. It ended at 9:58 p.m. when Brad Lidge's slider buckled under Eric Hinske's bat for strike three. Our city's 25-year championship drought ended that night.

1. Players switch teams in the middle of an NBA game. It started on November 8, 1978, and ended four months later, as the Sixers beat the New Jersey Nets in a contest that featured three players suiting up for both sides.

Here's the story behind the story. The game initially ended with the Sixers winning in double-overtime and the Nets protesting some highly questionable calls by the refs. Commissioner Larry O'Brien upheld the Nets' protest and ordered the game resumed with six minutes left in the third quarter—the time of the refs' mistakes. The teams were told to finish the game March 23, 1979, before another scheduled Sixers-Nets contest at the Spectrum.

Except there was one further complication. On February 7, 1979, the Sixers traded Harvey Catchings and Ralph Simpson to the Nets for Eric Money. The league ruminated, then decided to let all the players participate in the game for their new teams. So the three men appear on both sides of the box score.

Oh, and the Sixers won the suspended game. Again. They also took the second game of the faux doubleheader.

They come, they go, they come back again—as players, coaches, broadcasters, or executives. Here are some of the best—and worst—second acts in Philadelphia sports history.

The Best

10. Mark Recchi. Set a Flyers record with 123 points in 1992–1993. Got swapped to Montreal two seasons later, and then back to Philadelphia four years after that. He led the NHL with 63 assists in 1999–2000—seemingly all of them nifty power play feeds to Lindros and LeClair. A true class act who endured 22 years in the NHL.

9. Howie Roseman. You're going to see a theme to this list. In 2010, he became the NFL's youngest general manager at age 35. Three years later, Roseman helped Eagles owner Jeff Lurie lure coach Chip Kelly—who pushed Roseman aside in a power struggle on New Year's Day 2015. Roseman bided his time in a broom closet until Kelly self-immolated; then he got his old office back. He was named NFL Executive of the Year in 2017 for his role in helping construct the Super Bowl championship team.

8. Cliff Lee. We never forgave GM Ruben Amaro for swapping Lee to Seattle for three dubious prospects (remember Phillippe Aumont?) just two months after he embarrassed the Yankees in the 2009 World Series. A year later, Lee returned under a free agent mega-contract. Injuries ended Lee's career early, but he still got Cy Young votes in two of the three full seasons he pitched here after his return.

7. Dallas Green. He was a hard-living relief pitcher who went 20–22 for the Phillies in four seasons in the early 1960s. He came back to manage in 1979 and, the following year, led the Phils to the first championship in their 125-plus-year history. They say that mediocre players make the best managers. Mr. Green was walking proof.

6. Wilt Chamberlain. There's simply no way that Act II with the Sixers could match Act I with the Warriors (or even, to those who may remember, the prequel career at Overbrook High). Still, Wilt averaged 27.6 points per game during his four-year return, and we needn't remind you of his role on the 1966–1967 team that went 68–13 and cruised to an NBA title.

5. Billy Cunningham. A three-act play, actually. In the first scene, the Kangaroo Kid plays sixth-man and rising star on that great Sixers team centered by Chamberlain. Then he departs for the ABA's Carolina Cougars. In the second scene, Cunningham returns to Philadelphia in 1974, only to have his career end two years later with a serious knee injury. Scene three—the finale—has Billy C. as the greatest coach in Sixers history, winning 510 games and the 1982–1983 NBA Title.

4. Bernie Parent. What, you didn't know? Yes, Bernie did two tours of duty—the so-so and the outstanding. The first time around, from 1967 to 1971, he was decent, nothing more.

The Flyers traded him to Toronto for some scoring punch (getting Rick MacLeish), and Parent eventually ended up in the fledgling WHA. In 1973 he returned to the Flyers. When he did, Bernie became the most important cog on the team that won two Stanley Cups. In 1984 he became the first Flyer elected to the Hockey Hall of Fame.

3. Richie Ashburn. There are two groups of "Whitey" fans. The Old Heads who recall him as a fleet-as-a-deer center fielder, and the Almost-as-Old Heads who grew up listening to him marvelously describe Phillies games on radio and TV. Both groups are privileged. Ashburn spent 12 years roaming Shibe Park and slapping his way to a .311 career batting average. He left for three seasons to play out the string before returning in 1963 to try his hand in broadcasting. The second career lasted 35 years—including 27 in which he and partner Harry Kalas made up the most beloved broadcasting team in city history.

2. Doug Pederson. We'll admit we heckled him as Andy Reid's bridge-to-McNabb starter in 1999, when he went 2–7 and put up a lousy 62.9 QB rating. We'll also admit that we scoffed when Lurie made him head coach in 2016, which seemed mostly like an overcompensation to bring in a nice guy after Kelly had alienated everyone in town. Yeah, we had our doubts right up to that moment when Pederson was brushing championship confetti off his visor at the Super Bowl. Sometimes we're happy to be wrong.

1. Nick Foles. Has anyone in these parts ever had a stranger career? Nicky Six accomplished that amazing 27-TD, two-interception season at age 24 and then quickly fell to Earth—or below Earth—losing his gig here, bouncing around the NFL, and nearly retiring. He returned to back up Carson Wentz and wound up MVP of the Super Bowl, basking in the glow of it all with the Lombardi Trophy on one arm and his infant daughter on the other. We were sad to see him leave in 2019, and we've reserved a spot for Foles in the Eagles Hall of Fame.

The Worst

10. Pete Retzlaff. As a player, the Baron was probably the most popular Eagle in the early and mid-'60s. He was the prototype of today's pass-catching NFL tight ends—blocking down on a defensive end on one play and snatching a long gainer on the next. His 1965 stats (66 receptions, 1,190 yards, 10 TDs) were astounding for the era. Not so astounding was Retzlaff's work as Eagles general manager from 1969 to 1972. He resigned after a four-year record of 15–37–4. By then, the fans who cheered Retzlaff the player were booing Retzlaff the GM.

9. Jim Bunning. A Hall of Famer who won 74 games in four seasons (1964–1967) for the Phils, each year finishing in the top five on the National League ERA list. And of course, there was that perfect game. He moved on to Pittsburgh and Los Angeles before coming back in 1970 at the tender age of 38. In two more seasons, on two hideous Phils squads, he went 15–27. A frustrating end to a great career.

8. Kenny Jackson. The Eagles selected this Penn State star with the fourth pick in the 1984 NFL draft (to be fair, it was a stinker of a class), and he averaged just 27 catches and three TDs in four seasons. So we all said goodbye. Somehow he ended up returning in 1990 to serve no apparent role beyond being Randall Cunningham's personal Mini-Me. Rumor had it that Buddy Ryan kept him around because the coach so enjoyed the honey-baked chicken from Jackson's Camden restaurant.

7. Moses Malone. If you look back at their history, the Sixers made a habit of bringing back once-great players long after their productive days were gone. Remember Wali Jones? Certainly, Malone's first four years here were brilliant and led the Sixers to their last title. But when he wandered back in 1993, he was just some fat old CYO League refugee stuffed into that number 2 jersey pretending to be the Great Moses. Kind of sad.

6. Pete Peeters. In his first tenure with the Flyers, Peeters was a miserable guy, but a pretty good goalie, who was a big part of that 35-game unbeaten streak in 1979–1980. In his second term, which ran from 1989 to 1991, he was still a miserable guy—and a miserable goalie. One season he played in 24 games for the Flyers and won exactly one.

5. Marion Campbell. He was an All-Pro defensive end who was critical to the Eagles' 1960 NFL Championship. And he was a clever coordinator who ran the defense for Dick Vermeil's 1980 NFC Championship team. Too bad it didn't end there. Campbell became coach when Vermeil left in 1983. He rang up a three-year record of 17–29–1. To be fair, a lot of it wasn't Campbell's fault. But when you hear Eagles fans wax about the good old days of Vermeil or Buddy, they rarely recall that golden era of the Swamp Fox.

4. Allen Iverson. The decade-long first run earned Al a permanent spot in our hearts and the Hall of Fame. By 2006, we all knew the ride had ended, so he was traded to the Nuggets to help push that team past the first round of the playoffs (it didn't work). Iverson meandered around the NBA for three seasons, looking misplaced in other teams' uniforms. It seemed the end of the road when he was waived by Memphis in November 2009—until Sixers GM Ed Stefanski brought him back to jog around on an Eddie Jordan–coached team headed for oblivion. That was merely a cynical move designed to put a few bucks in Iverson's pocket and a few fans in the seats. The 25 games he played were a hollow reminder of past glory.

3. Andy Ashby. One of those highly regarded prospects whom the local franchise always seems to let go, Ashby was twice an All-Star after being drafted away from the Phils in '93. "What if he had stayed?" we always asked. We found out when he came back in 2000 (in a trade for Adam Eaton, another bad penny who found his way back). Ashby combined a rotten demeanor with lousy performance, running up a 5.68 ERA by mid-season and going 1–6 at the Vet. He punctuated his final appearance by grabbing his crotch and inviting the local fans to get to know him more personally.

2. Doug Collins, Mo Cheeks, Jim O'Brien, Chris Ford. Take your choice on this quartet of one-time local hoops heroes who tried their hand coaching the Sixers as the franchise tumbled toward irrelevance in the post–Larry Brown, pre–Brett Brown era. Combined, they went 287–324. We'll give top (bottom?) honors to Collins, a one-time great player and broadcaster who could never acknowledge our frustration. Remember his directive to fans on Andrew Bynum, who collected $17 million in 2012–2013, only to injure himself bowling?

"I hope we all keep Andrew in prayer," said Collins. "He's not played for us this year, but he's still a 76er."

1. Ryne Sandberg. We spent 32 years mourning him as the Hall of Fame second baseman who got away. He finally returned—as manager—and proceeded to alienate veteran players and do nothing to improve the young ones. For parts of three seasons, Sandberg racked up a .428 winning percentage and was a black cloud in the clubhouse until, in June 2015, he just suddenly quit the job and left town. The second time we didn't mourn.

Thanks to listener Jim Phillips for coming up with this idea. Sure, our teams have acquired terrific athletes at the end of their careers. Or at the very beginning, before they broke out with another squad. But when we researched, we found more than 30 stars who were inducted into their respective Halls of Fame who fit this criterion. It was tough narrowing this one down to 10. These are ones who got away, and the ones we got too late.

10. Ty Cobb. After a spectacular 22-year career with Detroit, Cobb played his final two seasons with the Philadelphia A's. It's not like he went out with a whimper. He hit .357 in 1927 and .323 in his final year at age 41. Cobb had the reputation of being an ornery bastard. When Pete Rose was chasing his all-time hits record, a reporter asked Rose if he ever felt Cobb looking down on him when Rose would step up to the plate. Rose responded, "Well, from what I hear, he ain't up there."

9. Julius Erving. This selection caused Big Daddy a lot of on-air grief. Fans were beside themselves. "How dare you suggest we did not get the best of Dr. J," they demanded. "He's one of the spectacular players of all time, and he never played for anyone else!"

Wrong, horsebreath.

Doc spent his first five years defying the laws of gravity in the legendary ABA, and while the NBA attempted to paint that as a minor league, it was anything but. Julius was an ABA All-Star all five seasons. He won championships and was a three-time MVP.

If we had a dollar for every time we watched a documentary or read anything about the ABA and noted this comment, "You think the Doc was a legendary player for the Sixers? Well, you should have seen him in the ABA!" Well, we'd be richer than Angelo Cataldi.

When Erving came to the Sixers, he decided to become a "team" player. While we admire that, we still wish we had seen one season where he decided to shoot the ball 25 times a game, like he did in the ABA. In his 11 Sixer campaigns, he only once reached an average of even 20 shot attempts. Great as he was here, we did not get his best.

8. Paul Coffey. A four-time Stanley Cup winner. Four Cups. Not only did we get this Hall of Fame defenseman at the end of his career, but he played terribly in his one Stanley Cup Finals for the Flyers. It's just not fair.

7. Pedro Martinez. One of Don Zimmer's favorite pitchers and wearer of cool hats, Martinez produced a remarkable Hall of Fame career (his years with Boston are amazing), and then arrived in Philly for—you guessed it—his final season in 2009. He gave the Phils nine good starts, going 5–1. Then, of course, he fell apart in Game 6 of the 2009 World Series.

6. Joe Morgan. He's arguably the greatest second baseman in the history of baseball and a legendary member of Cincinnati's Big Red Machine. Some fans forget he spent 10 seasons with Houston before he even got to Cincy. But, alas, the Phils didn't get him until he was 39, and he hit .230 in his one season with the "Wheeze Kids." At least that team did get to the World Series before losing to the O's.

5. Pete Rose. I get it. The Phils won their first-ever World Series with Pete, so it's not like we got chopped liver when he arrived in 1979. But look at the numbers he put up in 16 years with the Reds. They're staggering. They don't call him the Hit King for nothing.

When the Phils were courting Rose as a free agent, he arrived at the now-closed Philadelphia Sheraton at 17th and JFK. Big Daddy was a doorman at the time and opened the cab door for him, to see Rose step out wearing a three-quarter-length black fur coat.

Probably won it in a bet.

4. Jaromír Jágr. He's still probably playing as you read this. A 24-season career and we got him for one stinkin' year. He had to be talked into coming back to the NHL at age 39 after a three-year hiatus. Who knew he would skate for five more teams after the Flyers? What an amazing athlete. Big Daddy rode an elevator with him once in a Pittsburgh hotel and he was huge, even in street clothes. He's a sure bet to get into the Hall of Fame as soon as he's eligible.

3. Terrell Owens. We're not quite sure who really did get the best of Owens. San Francisco? Dallas? It would have been the Eagles, had T.O. played more than 21 games wearing the green and silver. Oh yeah, his performance in the Super Bowl wasn't that shabby either. Break out the popcorn. Do some sit-ups in your driveway. He sure was fun while he was here.

2. Cris Carter. Carter has thanked Buddy Ryan for cutting him as a young player when Carter was on the verge of failing his second drug test—which would have gotten him tossed from the NFL. To Carter's credit, this proved a wake-up call, and he cleaned himself up. Well, good for him, bad for Eagles fans, because he went on to have a Hall of Fame career, making the Pro Bowl eight times with the Vikings.

Our take on it has always been, why couldn't Ryan figure out a way to rehab Carter while keeping him here? Not that we expected Buddy to get in the rehab business. Just saying.

1. Bob McAdoo. One of the first outside-shooting big men in NBA history, Bob led the NBA in scoring three straight years with Glen's Buffalo Braves (his number 11 jersey was the first sports jersey Glen ever owned), averaging over 30 points a game each of those years. By the way, it's really hard to lead the NBA in scoring when your head coach is Philly's own team-oriented Dr. Jack Ramsay. In a 17-year career, McAdoo averaged a remarkable 22 points per game.

Unfortunately, the Sixers got McAdoo for the final 29 games of his career. He still managed to score 10 points a game. You could probably wake up Bob in the middle of the night and he'd still nail a jumper.

Honorable mention: Ferguson Jenkins, Jim Ringo, Peter Forsberg, James Lofton, Richard Dent, Ryne Sandberg, Adam Oates, Claude Humphrey, Dale Hawerchuk, Hack Wilson

Mike Angelina is the head studio producer for all Eagles games on 94-WIP as well as the producer of The Big Daddy Graham Show.

10. *Winging It/The J. J. Redick Podcast.* These are technically separate podcasts, but they're both Ringer productions and have the same gist to them: current NBA players talking about being in the NBA. *Winging It* features future Hall of Famer Vince Carter and his Atlanta teammate Kent Bazemore, while Redick obviously is the host of his, and they talk to current and former players and executives. In both, you get tales about trash talkers, big-game moments, and if there's a guest who spent a night out with Allen Iverson, you will surely be entertained by hearing what that was like.

9. *Pardon My Take.* If you're into this podcast, you know you are going there not for sophisticated breakdowns but rather to enjoy the banter. A Barstool production, *PMT* is just a giant parody of sports talk—but also ably touches on current topics. Barstool in general does a good job talking about sports in a fun, amusing way.

8. *Phillies Today.* Over the past eight seasons, the show has had a few lead hosts, but James Seltzer has held things down in recent seasons. Published early mornings on week-days, there is almost always a new 30 minutes of content for fans on their daily commute. It's challenging to come up with nearly three hours of Phillies talk weekly, but Seltzer has a solid format that allows him to react to each night's previous game while also touching on long-term trends and developments. This podcast is tailored for die-hard fans looking to hear about each game but also allows casual fans to just play catch-up.

7. *Pro Football Talk.* Who would have thought being a (former) lawyer, or at least thinking like one, would make someone a great football podcast host? You'd be surprised how much that former line of work for Mike Florio comes into play when it comes to talking football. What makes this podcast interesting and a fresh perspective on tackling football topics is that Florio often looks at things the way a lawyer, judge, or arbitrator would, and often he is the first to point out contract language, loopholes, and rules.

6. *Pardon the Interruption.* It's not technically a true podcast—it's simply the ESPN show in audio form—but if you missed the TV show, it serves as a podcast. There's nothing too crazy going on here, just two guys debating topics of the day. It does a good job catching you up on the previous 24 hours of sports news. Michael Wilbon and Tony Kornheiser won't give the most accurate or most entertaining sports takes ever, but they do a good job covering the big points in each two-minute topic.

5. *NBA Group Chat.* The coolest thing about this one is it reminds me of so many group chats you have in real life. Anyone who gets into regular group text exchanges with a collec-tion of friends can relate to this style of discussion: everyone just chimes in with what they have to say on any particular subject. I like it because it allows me to surround myself with different perspectives.

4. GM Street. Former NFL executive Mike Lombardi sits down a few times a week with the Ringer's Tate Frazier, first to review the previous week's games and storylines and then later in the week to preview the upcoming card. Instead of talking about individual performance, they steer more toward Lombardi's expertise, looking at scheme and game plan. I admire the way Frazier is able to integrate himself into the discussion. It's hard to talk to an expert about the subject he knows more than you. While Frazier doesn't try to match Lombardi, he does a great job of blending in his observations.

3. One Shining Podcast. This is the college basketball authority. Featuring Mark Titus, a former Ohio State walk-on who played with Mike Conley and Greg Oden, and Tate Frazier, a North Carolina grad/fan, the two blend their expertise of the college hoops scene. The enjoyable aspect of this one is their recurring bits. They often poke fun at the incredibly corrupt industry that is college recruiting while also noting the serious nature of it. It would be foolish to fill out a bracket in March without hearing these guys' thoughts.

2. The Rights to Ricky Sanchez. Anyone who thinks being right doesn't count for anything should look no further than this podcast. The hosts took a firm position that the 76ers needed to rebuild the Evan Turner and Spencer Hawes teams to get blue-chip talents like Joel Embiid and Ben Simmons. They were right (probably), and the podcast has blossomed into playing a critical role in the mind-set of the fan base. The Sixers went as far as taking their slogan "Trust the Process," perhaps the biggest validation of the podcast. The format is biweekly analysis of the Sixers' recent play and their overall standing as the team tries to mold a title contender.

1. The Bill Simmons Podcast. Most weeks Simmons puts out a gambling podcast with Sal Iacono, a pure sports-talk one with a writer, and a Friday movie/TV/pop culture episode with someone in that business. He's measured and passionate in his sports points, delivering them with conviction. His Boston fandom makes the shows more enjoyable because for as long as the podcast has been out, the Celtics, Patriots, and Red Sox have been pretty relevant in their respective sports.

The ABCs of Philly Pro Sports—Part 2

Here are our choices for the best athlete—for each team and each letter. See if your answers from page 154 match ours:

A

Eagles　**David Akers.** Eric Allen was considered, but no one played more games in an Eagle uniform, and David was a kicker who tackled!

Phillies　**Grover Cleveland Alexander.** This Hall of Fame hurler won 190 games in his eight seasons back in the early 1900s, leading the league in wins five times.

Sixers　**Paul Arizin (Warriors).** Wilt referred to him as the greatest shooter he ever played with. 'Nuf said.

Flyers　**Barry Ashbee.** This was not a sentimental choice. This defenseman earned this letter.

B

Eagles　**Chuck Bednarik.** Was Concrete Charlie the greatest Eagle ever?

Phillies　**Larry Bowa.** Extremely hard not to select Jim Bunning, but Jim's six years of service pales to Bowa's 12 seasons, 1,739 games, and World Series ring.

Sixers　**Charles Barkley.** Top-five power forward ever.

Flyers　**Bill Barber.** You were expecting Mike Boland, who played two games for the Flyers in 1974?

C

Eagles　**Harold Carmichael.** Caught at least one pass in 127 consecutive games, an NFL record for many years.

Phillies　**Steve Carlton.** You could make a case that Lefty's 1972 season was the single most remarkable season any MLB pitcher ever had.

Sixers　**Wilt Chamberlain.** Best player on this entire list.

Flyers　**Bobby Clarke.** Thanks, Bobby, for the two greatest Philly parades ever.

D

Eagles　**Brian Dawkins.** This Hall of Famer might be the most popular Eagle ever.

Phillies　**Ed Delahanty.** The Hall of Fame left fielder played in 1,557 games for the Phils with a career average of .348. He hit four HRs in one game in 1897 when the HR leader that year hit all of 11.

Sixers　**Samuel Dalembert.** Okay, this D seems lame compared to B-Dawk. And it is. But he played eight Sixer seasons, and his numbers are decent if you check them out.

Flyers　**Gary Dornhoefer.** Eleven seasons, 825 games, and two Stanley Cups.

E

Eagles   **Zach Ertz.** It seems a little premature, but he already holds several impressive Eagle records.

Phillies   **Del Ennis.** This slugging outfielder was a perennial MVP candidate, but what we remember about Del the most was that he owned bowling alleys. Huh?

Sixers   **Julius Erving.** The Doctor!

Flyers   **Pelle Eklund.** The Swede's amazing performance against Edmonton in the 1987 Stanley Cup Finals was only topped by a guy named Gretzky.

F

Eagles   **Nick Foles.** Do we really have to tell you why?

Athletics   **Jimmy Foxx.** This Hall of Fame Athletic hit 534 homers by the time he retired in 1945.

Sixers   **World B. Free.** Here's a cool oddity. His first name was Lloyd his first three years as a Sixer. He left for 10 years and returned with a new first name—World. How often does that happen?

Flyers   **Peter Forsberg.** Only played 100 games for the Orange and Black, but he's Peter Forsberg. Expecting someone else?

G

Eagles   **Brandon Graham.** Every championship team needs a good player who keeps the team loose, and this strip-sacker did exactly that.

Phillies   **Lefty Grove.** This left-handed Hall of Famer fireballer led the league in strikeouts his first seven years.

Sixers   **Hal Greer.** Quiet and reserved, he flew under the radar, but he's in the Hall for one big reason: he never missed. Plus, he shot his free throws like his jump shot, and we've never seen another player do that.

Flyers   **Claude Giroux.** As of this writing, he's in his 12th season for the Flyers, and he's only 31.

H

Eagles   **Wes Hopkins.** Spent his entire 10-year career as an Eagle. RIP, Wes; you left us way too soon.

Phillies   **Ryan Howard.** Will any Phillie ever hit 220 HRs in his first five seasons again?

Sixers   **Hersey Hawkins.** That's Hersey, not Hershey. Keep an eye on Tobias Harris.

Flyers   **Mark Howe.** Hard to follow in your dad's footsteps when your dad is Gordie Howe, but Mark's a Hall of Famer himself.

I

Eagles   **Mark Ingram Sr.** Maybe this selection will bring a smile to Mark's face since he's been in and out of prison since he caught all of two balls for the Birds in 1996.

Phillies **Raúl Ibañez.** Clutch.

Sixers **Allen Iverson.** You were expecting Royal Ivey?

Flyers **Gary Inness.** A goaltender who was in net a grand total of eight games, but he's the only Flyer ever whose last name begins with *I*.

J

Eagles **Seth Joyner.** Ron Jaworski obviously came to mind, but he only made one Pro Bowl while Seth made three. Who knows? Someday Lane Johnson may represent this letter. Keith Jackson should be mentioned as well.

Phillies **Willie "Puddin' Head" Jones.** We know what you're thinking: he made this list simply because of his name. But he played in over 1,500 games at third base in 13 years.

Warriors **Neil Johnston.** Geez, it hurts to leave Bobby Jones off, but Neil's in the Hall of Fame.

Flyers **Keith Jones.** Tough call between Jonesy and Kim Johnsson, but Keith's much funnier.

K

Eagles **Jason Kelce.** Thanks, Jason, not only for your outstanding play but also for the greatest speech of all time.

Phillies **Chuck Klein.** This Hall of Fame right fielder played 1,405 games for the Phils and led the league in HRs, RBIs, and hits many times.

Sixers **Red Kerr.** Played most of his career in Syracuse but did make an All-Star team when the franchise moved to Philly.

Flyers **Tim Kerr.** A no-brainer. And what's the chance of two straight Kerrs?

L

Eagles **Chad Lewis.** Sorry to Frank LeMaster and apologies to Randy Logan, but Chad's three Pro Bowls (all as an Eagle) give the tight end the nod.

Phillies **Greg Luzinski.** The Bull is what a power hitter should look like.

Sixers **George Lynch.** His lone trip to the NBA Finals puts him over a weak selection of *L*s.

Flyers **Eric Lindros.** One of the most famous (or infamous) names in Philly history.

M

Eagles **Tommy McDonald.** This could easily have gone to Shady McCoy, but Tommy's NFL Championship and five Pro Bowls (all as an Eagle) give him the nod. Don't forget Donovan McNabb and Wilbert Montgomery. What a letter.

Phillies **Garry Maddox.** The Secretary of Defense. But do us a favor and look up Sherry Magee's stats as a Phil and you'll see this wasn't such an easy pick.

Sixers **Moses Malone.** So he didn't play here for long, but his "Fo-Fi-Fo" led us to the last championship this franchise has seen.

Flyers **Rick MacLeish.** Oh, to see Rick's hair flowing down that ice again.

N

Eagles **Al Nelson.** Slim pickings, but this DB suited up 105 games for the Birds in the late '60s and early '70s.

Phillies **Aaron Nola.** Barring injury, Aaron's Hall of Fame bound.

Sixers **Nerlens Noel.** Really?!

Flyers **Simon Nolet.** This right winger has a Stanley Cup ring.

O

Eagles **Terrell Owens.** We know he was here for barely more than a year, but oh, what a year it was. Sorry, John Outlaw.

Phillies **Lefty O'Doul.** Check out this season: in 1929, Lefty hit .398 with 254 hits, 32 HRs, 122 RBIs—and he lost the MVP race to Rogers Hornsby. (What's with the *s* on the end of your first name, Rog?)

Sixers **Kevin Ollie.** The Sixers signed this solid guard on three different occasions.

Flyers **Joel Otto.** The Rangers originally tried to sign him to help defend Eric Lindros, but Otto wisely said to himself, "You know, I think I'd rather play *with* Eric."

P

Eagles **Pete Pihos.** This end (he played both ways) won back-to-back championships with the Birds and is in the Hall of Fame.

Phillies **Jonathan Papelpon.** We would have rather chosen the Phillie Phanatic over this knucklehead, but he is the Phils' all-time saves leader.

Sixers **Tim Perry.** Or Eddie Pinckney? Kenny Payne? It doesn't seem to make much difference.

Flyers **Bernie Parent.** You have to feel sorry for the other legit *P*s like Dave Poulin, Brian Propp, Keith Primeau, and Chris Pronger. You didn't stand a chance.

Q

Eagles **Mike Quick.** If not for injuries, he's in the Hall.

Phillies **Paul Quantrill.** Go ahead. Find a Phils' *Q* more deserving.

Sixers **Quint.** You remember him, right? He gets eaten by Jaws? Just making sure you're still reading. The Sixers have never had a *Q*.

Flyers **Dan Quinn.** Used to be John Daly's caddie, which is certainly more memorable than the one season he played here.

R

Eagles   **Pete Retzlaff.** We so respect Jon Runyan and love Ike Reese, but five Pro Bowls and an NFL championship in '60 gives Pete the nod.

Phillies   **Robin Roberts.** Another difficult letter. Jimmy Rollins, Carlos Ruiz, Pete Rose, and a pretty good fielding third baseman in Scott Rolen just don't cut it when you're going up against Robin.

Sixers   **Theo Ratliff.** We thought long over super-sub Clint Richardson, but Theo gets the nod. We still wonder what would have happened in 2000–2001 if he didn't get hurt?

Flyers   **Mark Recchi.** If only he could have won one of his three Stanley Cups for us.

S

Eagles   **Clyde Simmons.** We could have flipped a coin between Clyde and Jerry Sisemore.

Phillies   **Mike Schmidt.** Or as Harry used to call him, Michael Jack Schmidt!

Sixers   **Ben Simmons.** Boy, this pick is going to piss off a lot of fans, but do you really want to go with Eric Snow?

Flyers   **Dave Schultz.** We know what you're thinking. Wayne Simmonds (for example) is much more talented. But the way the NHL was played in Hammer's era, the Flyers might have never won those Cups without him.

T

Eagles   **Tra Thomas.** Extremely difficult to pick Tra over Jeremiah Trotter and Willie Thomas, but Tra started 166 games with the Birds.

Phillies   **Tony Taylor.** This second baseman and leadoff hitter played in an incredible 1,669 games for the Phils and always blessed himself at the plate. (Not sure why we mentioned that.) It hurts us to leave off another second baseman, Manny Trillo.

Sixers   **Andrew Toney.** A Hall of Famer if he wasn't so often injured. What a killer first step.

Flyers   **Rick Tocchet.** To quote Bono introducing Sinatra, "I wouldn't mess with him; would you?"

U

Eagles   **Morris Unutoa.** Who?

Phillies   **Chase Utley.** Uh, like you thought it was going to be someone else? Del Unser also gave the team some quality bats and Bob Uecker some quality laughs in his one year with the squad.

Sixers   **Lacey Underall**

Flyers   **R. J. Umberger.** His '08 playoff performance and 334 games as a Flyer gives him the nod over Scottie Upshall.

V

Eagles **Steve Van Buren.** Who would have thunk that the Birds would have so many quality *V*s? Sorry, Norm Van Brocklin and Troy Vincent.

Phillies **Shane Victorino.** The Flyin' Hawaiian outruns his competition because, well, there isn't any.

Sixers **Tom Van Arsdale.** You were expecting Danny Vranes?

Flyers **Ed Van Impe.** Start with two Stanley Cups, three All-Star nods, and that famous hit on the Soviets' Valeri Kharlamov.

W

Eagles **Reggie White.** Sorry, Brian Westbook and Hall of Famer Alex Wojciecho- wicz. It's Reggie.

Phillies **Cy Williams.** Cy played in 1463 games for the Phils in the '20s and was a career .307 hitter. He's also the first major leaguer to hit 200 HRs.

Sixers **Chet Walker.** No NBA player (maybe Charles Barkley) ever used his keister to back down an opponent like this Hall of Famer.

Flyers **Jimmy Watson.** Barely gets the nod over his brother Joe.

X

No *X* for any team

Y

Eagles **Roynell Young.** This Birds DB played in 117 games. If Charle Young had played just a couple more seasons, he would have been selected.

Phillies **Bert Yeabsley.** Gets one at bat and walks! That's it. But he's not the inspira- tion for Doc in *Field of Dreams*—that was Archibald "Moonlight" Graham of the Giants. Look it up. It easily could have been Bert.

Sixers **Thaddeus Young.** Hall of Famer George Yardley played for Syracuse but never in a Philadelphia uniform. We liked Thaddeus.

Flyers **Dmitri Yushkevich.** Tougher-than-nails Russian played 215 games for the Flyers.

Z

Eagles **Michael Zordich.** Did you know the Birds have had 11 *Z*s?

Phils **Todd Zeile.** Played for the Fightin's in '96 and hit 20 HRs.

Warriors **Zeke Zawoluk.** A double *Z*! What are the chances?

Flyers **Peter Zezel.** One of Mike Keenan's favorite players and certainly one of the Flyers' all-time heartthrobs with the ladies. Died too young at the age of 44 of a rare blood disorder. A real shame.

We think this is the greatest sports city in America. Still, there are entities that Philadelphia is missing that would make our fandom even better. We realize some items on this wish list are unlikely or impossible. We're just saying . . .

10. Better participatory sports. Take some of those fields in Fairmount Park and let's build a world-class toboggan run. Or how about a body-surfing-friendly wave pool? Hell, there are 9,200 acres in America's largest intra-city public park. Let's use a few of them for something different.

9. A Grand Prix event. We'll be honest and tell you that we're not fans of auto racing. Still, there's something about Formula One cars driven by guys with names like Nigel, Alain, and Keke zipping around actual city streets that draws in even us. Imagine them trying to negotiate past the fountains on the Ben Franklin Parkway. Cities like Detroit, Cleveland, and Indianapolis have hosted American Grand Prix races. We want to be next.

8. An annual stop on the PGA Tour. The Delaware Valley has some of the greatest golf courses in America. So how come dippy towns like Milwaukee and Grand Rapids get annual visits and we don't?

7. Summer Olympics. Yes, it's the ultimate pipe dream. But there once were local chamber of commerce and tourism types studying bringing the Games here. Crew on the Schuylkill. A marathon that circles Kelly and West River Drives. Hey, if we can host the major party conventions and Live Aid, we can host anything. Let's show the world how world-class this city can be. Seriously, who loves synchronized swimming more than Philly?

6. A local college basketball tourney. Run it at the start of the season. Invite the Big 5 schools, plus Drexel, plus, perhaps, Pitt and Penn State. Call it the Liberty Bell Challenge, and play it at the beginning of the season. If you played the games at the Palestra, we *guarantee* it would become a tough ticket.

5. A world-class beach volleyball tourney. Preferably a female one. With all due respect to #metoo, what did you expect us to say? We're men.

4. A college football fanbase. Temple has done well in recent years, even making a few bowl games. But the city has never rallied behind the program—some team named the Eagles draws all the attention. Back in the day—and we're talking 70 years ago—the University of Pennsylvania drew 60,000 every game. That would be absolutely dynamite.

3. A Final Four. Isn't there any way we can put a temporary dome on the Linc? If we can put a man on the moon and invent the pushup bra, this problem shouldn't be insurmountable. WrestleMania and many other cool events would follow.

2. A marbles tournament. Whoops, Wildwood already has one that's been going on since 1922. Imagine—we don't have any of these other cool events, yet we have a stinkin' marbles tournament?!

1. A Super Bowl. We don't think there's anything wrong with a Super Bowl played in the real elements. The Meadowlands got one, and they were blessed with a temperature of 48 degrees when they kicked off. Our take on it? Either rotate *every* Super Bowl between New Orleans and Miami, or else rotate among every NFL city. One or the other.

From 1971 until his passing in 2009, Harry Kalas was the voice of the Phillies. In 2002, he was inducted into the Baseball Hall of Fame in Cooperstown, New York. He wrote this list for us in 2006.

10. Start with the opening of Citizens Bank Park in 2004. It was my third stadium opening—I started with the Astros in '65, the same year they opened the Astrodome. Then I started with the Phils in 1971, the same year the Vet opened. Citizens Bank Park is a beautiful place and a great place to work. And I was truly honored to have a restaurant named after me. I'm thinking this is the last stadium opening I'll be a part of.

9. It isn't a Phils memory, but it was a thrill to meet my boyhood hero, Mickey Vernon, who lives in Delaware County. I was 10 years old when my dad took me to my first game, in Chicago, to see the White Sox against the Washington Senators. We sat behind the Washington dugout. During a rain delay, Vernon picked me out of the stands and sat me on the Senators' bench. He talked to me and even gave me a ball. I became a fan for life, so it was great to meet him again all those years later.

8. Any game Steve Carlton pitched was special. I always had an extra bounce in my step when Lefty had the ball. He was a joy to watch at work. You knew the games were going to be quicker—he didn't waste a lot of time or pitches. I got along famously with Lefty. He was a good friend and would talk baseball with me until the cows came home. It helped that I didn't carry a notebook.

7. The closing of the Vet was, of course, a special day for me. I was there from the beginning to the end in 2003. Sure, it had seen better days, but I have so many fond memories of the old place. It was special to be honored as the person they asked to pull down the final number counting down the days on the outfield wall.

6. Rick Wise pitched a no-hitter against the Reds in 1971. I was 35 years old, and it was the first Major League no-hitter I got to call, in my first year with the Phils. Wise also hit two home runs in that game—can you believe that? What a fun way for me to break in.

5. I didn't get to call it, but Tug McGraw's final pitch to strike out Willie Wilson in the 1980 World Series was so special. Back then, the hometown announcers didn't get to be part of the World Series. After 1980, Phils fans made such a fuss about it that baseball changed the rule, so I got to call the '83 Series. Tug was such a positive guy, always smiling, always appreciative of the fact that he had a chance to do what he did. I loved him.

4. Michael Jack Schmidt's 500th home run, April 18, 1987, against Don Robinson of the Pirates at Three River Stadium in Pittsburgh. Out of Michael Jack's 548 homers, I probably called all but a handful. What a privilege to call his Hall of Fame career. I was told that they played my call for Mike after the game and he choked up. I'm flattered.

3. The 1993 club, from Day One, has to be next. Not much was expected from that crew, and yet they took us to the World Series. What a cast of characters—Krukker, the Dude, my current partner, Larry Andersen, and the best team leader ever, Dutch Daulton. What a fun bunch to be around. And what a great team, in the real sense of team. So many come-from-behind wins.

2. The 1980 National League Championship Series against the Houston Astros was unforgettable. Remember, it was a best-of-five series, and four of those games went into extra innings. Imagine being down 5–2 to Nolan Ryan in Game 5 and coming back to win against a Hall of Fame pitcher. When we won that one, I knew we'd win the World Series.

1. Undoubtedly, the top is my 22 years alongside Whitey Ashburn. There was a combination of things making it special—his friendship, his expertise, his sense of humor. We spent every night together in the booth and on the road, and it never stopped being fun. I still think about His Whiteness every single day.

If I can add one more, it was a special moment for me, of course, when I was inducted into the Baseball Hall of Fame in 2002. It was just a breathtaking weekend, the ultimate honor from the game I love. You know what was most special about it? The huge number of Phillies fans who came to Cooperstown for the weekend. It was a sea of red hats.

Scott Franzke joined the Phillies broadcast team in 2006. He has been the primary radio play-by-play announcer since 2008, partnering with Larry Andersen and, since 2018, Kevin Frandsen.

10. Let's start with Ryan Howard's three-homer game in September 2006, when he hit numbers 50 through 52 off the Braves' Tim Hudson. That was the summer Ryan emerged as a star and also my first season here, so it was special to watch that story unfold. Also, my dad, who instilled my love of baseball, was in town from Texas that weekend, so being able to call that amazing game with my dad in the stadium was special.

9. Chase Utley's walk-off hit in August 2007 capped a four-game sweep of the Mets. The Phils were down in that Sunday game, 10–9 in the ninth, when they rallied off of Billy Wagner. Chase ended it with a big single to right as the fans went crazy. When that happened, and the Phils closed the gap to two games, it gave me the realization that this team might actually win the division and be what Jimmy Rollins had said they were—the team to beat.

8. The last day of that 2007 season, which began with the Phils and Mets in a dead heat. The Mets played the Marlins at home that day, and they started a half hour before us, so the fans filling Citizens Bank Park were watching the out-of-town scoreboard. The Marlins went out and thumped Tom Glavine. I was standing in the booth, exchanging looks with the fans, and their sense of joy was incredible. This buzz came through the stadium—"We're going to win it." Of course, the Phillies had to hold up their end, which they did with a 6–1 win over the Nationals, as J-Roll hit his 20th double of the season.

7. I've got to put in Game 4 of the 2008 NLCS in Dodger Stadium, where Shane Victorino hit that two-run homer in the eighth inning to tie it, and then Matt Stairs won it with his two-run homer off Jonathan Broxton. It was a real folk-hero moment for Stairsy, who I came to know as a great guy when he was part of our broadcast team. Those days, Harry (Kalas) and Wheels (Chris Wheeler) broadcast the middle innings—and they were on the air when the Dodgers took a lead. So LA and I came back on for the late innings pretty dejected. But things turned around, and it was one of those moments where you really start to believe great things could happen.

6. The postgame celebration with the team at an emptied-out Dodger Stadium after we won the NLCS in 2008. The fans left the stadium, but our whole traveling team—broadcasters, office people, ownership, even my wife—were on the field because we had to walk through the centerfield exit to leave. It was just my third year, and it struck me how so many of the people with the team had waited so long for this moment. We got out a bottle of champagne, and there was no way to take the smile off everyone's face.

The second half of that was standing on the mound at Citizens Bank Park interviewing players after the final out of the '08 World Series. I grabbed Victorino and caught the joy and disbelief in his eyes as 45,000 fans cheered and enveloped the field in joy. It was a very powerful moment for me, seeing it on the field from the players' perspective.

5. The parade, of course, was awesome. The broadcasters were all on one float, along with the Phanatic, and the thing I'll never forget is Harry and the way he and the fans showed their love for each other. I knew how much it meant to him to call that final out a few days before, because the local announcers hadn't gotten that chance in 1980. He was overcome with joy, and I just loved soaking it all in. I have a home video of it, where you can hear Harry under his breath say, "Oh, my goodness." It was very special.

4. Eric Bruntlett's game-ending unassisted triple play in August 2009 against the Mets. This is a professional highlight for me in this sense: everyone wants to have a good home run call. Young announcers practice those. As someone calling games, I pride myself on accurately describing the play. But, you never expect a triple play, let alone to end a game. You can't rehearse those. Once before, the Phils had pulled off a triple play and I bungled the call. So I was excited when I heard myself afterward that I not only got all three outs, but I called them in order.

3. Let's go back to October 19, 2009, Game 4 of the NLCS, when Rollins hit that walk-off two-run double against Broxton. That may be the call of mine that people comment on most, and you know why? It's because of that YouTube clip from *GoodFellas*, where Ray Liotta is listening to the radio in the shower, screaming, "Jimmy! Jimmy!" Some very creative person—I don't know who—inserted my call of the play into that clip, and that has become the lasting memory of it for me.

2. When Roy Halladay threw that perfect game in May 2010, it was obvious early on that he was locked in. By the seventh inning, my biggest fear was making a mistake with a detail. Misstating a fact like, how many perfect games have been thrown in Major League history? Larry and I didn't have a producer, so I was frantically scrambling between innings to Google the right info. There was no one to fact-check; if Wikipedia was wrong, I'd be wrong forever. I remember Larry being nervous next to me and thinking to myself, why would he be nervous? He's pitched in the World Series. But it was such a big moment that we wanted to make sure we were doing it justice on the air.

1. That leads to Roy's World Series no-hitter. After watching him for the year, I knew how hard he worked and wanted to win, and I felt great seeing him get that opportunity. The home crowd was tremendous that night, building in anticipation as he got closer. I also remember not wanting to blow the roof off as an announcer at the end but to let the crowd carry the moment. And we had the perfect crowd to do that.

I need to add one more. Working with Larry Andersen has been special. When I interviewed for the job in 2006, they said, "We have this pretty entertaining guy, and we want to bring in someone who will recognize and bring out his humor." Well, we hung out that first spring and instantly connected. I can't sell short what he's done for my career. I'm a voice and he's the personality. It was just my dumb luck to end up with such a great partner and a great friend.

No book like this is complete without our take on the greatest athletes. We started with a list of 10, expanded it to 25, and then, well, kept asking ourselves, "How can we leave off *this guy?*" In the end, we couldn't even stop at 100.

Obviously, it's tough to compare the magnitude of Eagles and Phillies with that of boxers and Olympians. But we tried to spread the wealth. You'll find a golfer, tennis player, and soccer star represented.

We started our list in 1970 because, well, wizened as these two authors may be, we couldn't fairly assess Lefty Grove vs. Steve Van Buren. So don't think we set out to snub Wilt Chamberlain. His career with the Sixers ended in 1968—before our start date.

We required that team-sports athletes played college or pro ball here—not just high school—so all apologies to Mike Trout (for now). And the individual-sport athletes also had to hang around a little during their competitive years. See you later, Carl Lewis.

You'll find current stars on this list. It's toughest to assess those young guys based on what we hope and expect them to do in future years. We did our best to place them, hoping that when we next rewrite this book they crack the top 10.

One more guideline: only those years in a local uniform count. So Curt Schilling's World Series moments in Arizona and Boston? They never happened. At least not for our purposes.

Like many lists in this book, this one will promote debate. If you think we shortchanged Randall Cunningham or overrated Allen Iverson—well, that's your opinion. Here's our opinion, and we don't mind if it gets you all riled up. In fact, we hope it does.

101. Andre Iguodala. Start with a player this town never liked. Iggy averaged 15.3 points per game over eight seasons as a Sixer but never won over the fan base. He later became an integral part of the Warriors dynasty and was named the MVP of the 2015 Finals.

100. Keith Jackson. A rookie sensation who snagged 81 catches in 1998. The focal point of a power struggle between ownership and coach Buddy Ryan, which led to Jackson leaving after four seasons. We'd rank him higher had he not dropped an easy touchdown in the Fog Bowl.

99. George McGinnis. He played just three seasons with the Sixers (1976–1978) but averaged 21.6 points per game and gave this city's hoops fans someone worth watching until Doc showed up.

98. Jonathan Papelbon. A bad teammate, a spoiled brat, a selfish player. On the other hand, his 123 saves top any Phillie closer. Struck out 9.5 hitters per game, made two All-Star teams, and alienated this city.

97. Brent Celek. Tough, hard worker who had soft hands and learned to become a solid blocker. His 398 catches are fifth in franchise history. Ended 11-year Eagles career on top, walking off the field a Super Bowl winner.

98. Tug McGraw. Leaped off the mound as the Phils won their first World Series in 1980. Five postseason saves in the red pinstripes.

95. Lisa Raymond. The Wayne native was an 11-time grand slam doubles tennis champion and ranked as the number one woman's doubles player for more than two years. Won an Olympic bronze as well as more than $10 million over her career.

94. Jim Thome. His free-agent signing in 2003, coupled with the opening of Citizens Bank Park the following year, signaled a new era of Phillies baseball. In 2003–2004, he had 89 homers and 236 RBIs while we waited for Ryan Howard to arrive.

93. Carlos Ruiz. This undersized Panamanian one-time infield prospect crouched down and became an All-Star catcher, the heart of a five-time NL East champ, and a brilliant handler of the pitching staff. Chooch was a terrific clutch performer. Received votes in the MVP race three straight seasons.

92. Brandon Graham. A late bloomer who never put up great stats (42.5 sacks in his first nine seasons) but became an integral part of a solid defensive line. His late-game strip sack of Tom Brady in Super Bowl LII is one of the most important plays in our city's history.

91. Jayson Werth. This scrapheap pickup grew into the dangerous five-hole hitter protecting Howard for four seasons. His .885 OPS is the fifth-best among Phillies who started their career after 1940. Departed for a huge free-agent contract; got booed each time he returned.

90. Ricky Watters. Forget the "For who? For what?" The guy was a fearless workhorse who always wanted the ball (just ask Jon Gruden). His 975 carries and 3,794 rushing yards from 1995 to 1997 are the most by any Eagles back over a three-year period.

89. Jerome Brown. In just five seasons he established himself as an all-time favorite of Eagles fans. Big defensive tackle was the soul of the Eagles' Gang Green defense. Made two Pro Bowls before dying in a car accident at age 27.

88. Rick Tocchet. A triple threat who could score, pass, and fight for the Flyers. Scored as many as 45 goals in a season and registered as many as 299 penalty minutes. A fun and unique player.

87. Pelle Lindbergh. The NHL's first great European goalie, he won the 1985 Vezina Trophy and established himself as a fan favorite in his three-plus seasons. Everyone's heart was broken on November 11, 1985.

86. Pat Burrell. Pat the Bat was, perhaps, more legendary in Old City clubs than Citizens Bank Park, but his numbers cannot be ignored: 251 HR, 827 RBIS, .851 OPS. Do you recall the name of his English bulldog who rode atop the 2008 parade float? Why, it was Elvis, of course.

85. William Thomas. A versatile playmaking outside linebacker, "Willie T" finished his career with 37 sacks and 27 interceptions, including seven pickoffs in his Pro Bowl 1995 season. He was durable too, playing in 142 of a possible 144 games during a nine-year Eagles career.

84. Doug Collins. A four-time All-Star whose Sixers career was cut short by injury. His career field-goal percentage (.501) and free-throw percentage (.833) both rank near the top in franchise history. Not quite as successful years later as the team's coach.

83. Shane Victorino. Among nine from the '08 Phils you'll find here. They got him for $25,000 in the Rule 5 draft; he went on to average 92 runs, 30 steals, and a .348 OBP during the 2007–2011 playoff run. Won Gold Gloves, provided postseason heroics.

82. DeSean Jackson. This 175-pounder owns the career record for TD catches of 60-plus yards. He drove opposition DBs and his own coaches crazy. Averaged 17.5 yards per catch and more than 10 TDs a season in his first tenure as an Eagle. His Miracle at the Meadowlands game-winning punt return may have been the most exciting play in Eagles history before the Philly Special. We were excited to see him return in 2019.

81. Danny Briere. A free agent who the Flyers signed to an eight-year, $52 million deal in 2007. He was solid in the regular season, but spectacular in the playoffs—notching a league-leading 30 points in the 2010 run to the Finals. A class act with fans, media, and local charities.

80. Lane Johnson. The fourth-overall pick in 2013 overcame early-career injuries and PED suspensions to become the NFL's top right tackle by 2017. He was an all-state high school QB in Texas but grew to 6-foot-6, 310 pounds. One of seven Super Bowl champion Eagles here—others may earn their way on the next time we do this list.

79. Lenny Dykstra. The offensive sparkplug behind the '93 Phils. He got on base 325 times that season and scored 143 runs. He deserved the 1993 NL MVP Award that went to Barry Bonds. Had six homers and 10 RBIs in the Phils' 12 postseason games that season.

78. Bill Bradley. Holds the Eagles records for interceptions in a season (11) and career (34, tied with Eric Allen and Brian Dawkins). An outstanding safety who never played for a winning team during his eight seasons here. A versatile player who both punted and returned punts.

77. Jim Furyk. West Chester native had 17 PGA Tournament wins through 2018, including the 2003 US Open. Holds the tour record for lowest round, with a 58 at the 2016 Travelers Championship. Glen once tied that score in the front nine at Cobbs Creek. Fourth-highest all-time money winner with more than $68 million.

76. Trent Cole. This unheralded fifth-round pick started a decade's worth of games for the Eagles. His 75.5 sacks rank second in franchise history, behind someone whose name will show up toward the top of this list.

75. Tra Thomas. Sturdy-as-a-rock left tackle who, along with Jon Runyan, anchored the Eagles offensive line and kept Donovan McNabb upright for years. A huge man at 6-foot-7 and 349 pounds. (What, he was too embarrassed to be listed at 350?) Got flagged for holding just 16 times in an 11-year career.

74. Ben Simmons. The highlight-film Aussie was the first pick of the 2016 draft, won Rookie of the Year in 2018, and made the All-Star Game his second season. The first of three guys named Simmons on this list. Also the first of three rising stars we put in a row here—all with the potential to zoom up this list in coming years.

73. Carson Wentz. He was the favorite for the NFL MVP Award in 2017 when a torn knee ended his season. Playing just 13 games that year, he broke the franchise record for TD passes, with 33. Here's hoping he can avoid injuries and achieve the greatness he's capable of.

72. Aaron Nola. The Phils' first-round pick in 2014 was projected as a middle-rotation starter. He became so much more. In 2018, at age 25, Nola went 17–6 with 224 strikeouts and a 2.37 ERA. A smart, fundamentally sound pitcher who would fit right in with the Phils' great rotations of a decade earlier.

71. Clyde Simmons. The "other" defensive end in Buddy Ryan's system. He led the NFL with 19 sacks in 1992. Once scored a miracle overtime touchdown at the Meadowlands by picking up teammate Luis Zendejas's blocked field goal and lumbering into the end zone.

70. Jason Kelce. He'll be immortalized for the greatest victory parade speech ever delivered in sports. The two-time first-team All-Pro is also the top center in franchise history. A bit undersized, Kelce's strength came from his cunning and the speed to make him an effective downfield blocker.

69. Simon Gagne. The catalyst for the Flyers' historic comeback in the 2010 playoffs, after they lost the first three games to the Bruins. He scored an overtime goal in Game 4 and the series winner in Game 7. Scored 264 goals in orange and black, peaking at 47 in 2005–2006.

68. Hugh Douglas. The Eagles stole him from Bill Parcells's Jets in '98, and Big Hugh went on to register double-digit sacks three times and twice lead the NFL in tackles for losses. One of Jim Johnson's favorite players and a big part of the clubhouse chemistry in the early 2000s.

67. Dawn Staley. Dobbins Tech star was two-time USA Basketball Female Athlete of the Year. A fixture on national teams from 1989 to 2004. She played in three Olympics, winning two golds. Chosen to carry the American flag at the opening ceremonies of the '04 games in Athens.

66. Zach Ertz. Set the NFL record for tight ends with 116 catches in 2018. With 437 through age 28, he has a great chance to wind up the Eagles' all-time receptions leader and one of the NFL's most productive TEs ever. His 11-yard TD with 2:21 left in Super Bowl LII gave the Eagles the lead for good.

65. Reggie Leach. The Rifle combined a 115-mile-per-hour shot with a quick release to rack up 306 goals for the Flyers. His 19 in the 1976 playoffs earned him the Conn Smythe Trophy. His career was shortened by alcoholism, which he later overcame.

64. Bobby Jones. Six-time NBA all-defense first-teamer as a Sixer. Others scored; he did the dirty work. When he did shoot, he did it well—note the .550 field-goal percentage. Said Julius Erving: "He's totally selfless, runs like a deer, jumps like a gazelle, and plays with his head and heart each night."

63. Curt Schilling. Another name that makes you wonder what might have been had he stayed. Most valuable player of the 1993 NLCS, in which he bewitched the Braves. Five times during his Phils career he finished in the NL top 10 in ERA. Achieved even greater stardom in Arizona and Boston.

62. Pete Rose. His best years were spent elsewhere, but it's fair to say the Phillies *never* would have won a World Series without his contributions. Still had enough after arriving here (at age 38) to twice lead the NL in times-on-base. Four-time All-Star as a Phil.

61. Troy Vincent. Played in five straight Pro Bowls for the Eagles; only Reggie White and Pete Pihos topped that streak. What a great secondary the Eagles had in the early 2000s, with Vincent, Bobby Taylor, Brian Dawkins, and, uh . . . Damon Moore.

60. Mark Recchi. Bet you didn't remember that he holds the Flyers record for points in a season—123—in 1992–1993. In two tours of duty, he totaled 232 goals and 395 assists. Hall of Famer survived 22 seasons in the NHL, including 10 with the Flyers.

59. Malcolm Jenkins. Between 2014 and 2018, Jenkins played in 98.3 percent of all Eagles' defensive snaps, in addition to a significant role on special teams. The unofficial captain of the Super Bowl defense. A three-time Pro Bowl safety who could also help at corner and linebacker.

58. Leroy Burrell. Set the world 100-meter dash record in 1994 at 9.85 seconds. Big Daddy can't cross the kitchen that fast. As a student at Penn Wood High in 1985, he single-handedly won the state championship by taking four events. Won Olympic gold in Barcelona in 1992.

57. Jon Runyan. One of Andy Reid's first free-agent signings, the massive right tackle was a cornerstone for nine seasons, never missing a game. Made only one Pro Bowl because players around the league hated his, shall we say, chippy style of play. His head-to-head battles with Michael Strahan were classic.

56. Andrew Toney. The Boston Strangler tormented the Celtics and thrilled Sixers fans through the 1980s. Shot exactly .500 for his career. Very few guards today ever approach that percentage.

55. Jeremiah Trotter. The Axe Man was the middle linebacker in Jim Johnson's scheme who blew up plays on run blitzes. He made two Pro Bowls early, left in a contract dispute, and came back two years later to make two more Pro Bowls. His postsack celebration honored his father, who had a wood-cutting business in Texas.

54. Scott Rolen. Ah, what might have been. Rookie of the Year in 1997. Four-time Gold Glover as a Phillie. Left town with an .877 OPS and 150 homers in seven seasons. A first-class jerk, but a great player.

53. Matthew Saad Muhammad. South Philly native won the light heavyweight belt in 1979 and defended it eight times during a Hall of Fame career. Twenty-nine KOs among his 36 pro wins. Nicknamed Matthew Miracle for his ability to take punishment and mount comeback victories.

52. Rod Brind'Amour. Teen heartthrob could kill penalties, shadow other teams' scorers, and run a power play. Scored 235 goals in eight-plus years as a Flyer. He was the team's top playoff performer (13 goals) in the 1997 run to the Stanley Cup Finals.

51. Carli Lloyd. Two-time Olympic gold medalist and two-time FIFA Player of the Year. The Delran, New Jersey, native is best remembered for becoming the first woman ever to score a hat trick in a Women's World Cup Final in 2015. She scored 105 goals (and counting) for the US national team.

50. Larry Bowa. Slap hitter who parlayed a fiery temper and great hands into five All-Star appearances. Just three players—Mike Schmidt, Jimmy Rollins, and Richie Ashburn—played more games in a Phillies uniform.

49. Fletcher Cox. Affable defensive tackle had 44.5 sacks and forced 18 turnovers in his first seven seasons. He starred in the run to the Super Bowl, recording 20 tackles in playoff games against Atlanta and Minnesota. Signed a six-year, $103-million deal in 2016, making him the highest-paid defender in franchise history.

48. Greg Luzinski. Finished second in NL MVP voting in both 1975 and 1977. Averaged 32 homers and 112 RBIs per season between 1975 and 1978. His 223 parabolic "Bull Blasts" thrilled Phils fans. Also adept at manning the BBQ.

47. Seth Joyner. A terrific playmaking linebacker who deserved to make more than the two Pro Bowls in which he represented the Eagles. Leader on the field and in the locker room. Intimidating in his play and his facial expressions.

46. Bill Bergey. Rough, big (250 pounds) middle linebacker who, unfortunately, spent most of his career on those bad Eagles teams of the mid-'70s. Final game of his career was the 1980 Super Bowl. Three-time Eagles MVP, he registered 1,200 tackles in his seven seasons here.

45. Brad Lidge. We'll remember the perfect season, 48 for 48 in saves in 2008. And we'll remember the image of Lidge falling to his knees, looking to the heavens and embracing

Chooch after he put a slider past Eric Hinske to win the Series. Finished fourth in Cy Young voting and eighth in MVP that great year.

44. Jameer Nelson. St. Joe's point guard put up lofty career stats—2,094 points and 713 assists. He was the 2004 NCAA National Player of the Year when he and Delonte West led the Hawks to a 28–0 regular-season record. Went on to a 14-year NBA career.

43. Ron Hextall. The ultimate Flyer, he guarded the nets with anger and bravado. His 240 regular-season wins are a franchise record, and his Conn Smythe performance against Gretzky's Oilers in the 1987 Finals was one of the greatest ever. First goalie in NHL history to directly score a goal. Not as successful as Flyers GM in the 2010s.

42. Ron Jaworski. A blue-collar quarterback who withstood the fans' booing to break most of the Eagles' career passing records. NFL's Player of the Year in 1980, when he took the Birds to the Super Bowl. From 1978 to 1981, he won 42 regular-season games, second to Terry Bradshaw among NFL QBs.

41. John LeClair. Scored 50-plus goals in three straight seasons as left winger on the Legion of Doom. Twice led the NHL in plus/minus, and twice was named first-team All-Star. He'd rank higher on this list but for his mediocre postseason performances.

40. Eric Allen. Intercepted 34 passes in his seven Eagles seasons, returning five for touchdowns. His 94-yard TD return against the Jets in 1993 is among the most exciting plays in franchise history. Five-time Pro Bowler in Philadelphia. Top-notch cornerback for 14 seasons in NFL.

39. Bobby Abreu. Not exactly Pete Rose in the hustle department, or Reggie Jackson in the clutch. Still, Mr. Stats has to be respected for his .416 on-base percentage in nine seasons here. He is fourth all-time in doubles for the Phils, second to Mike Schmidt in walks.

38. Cliff Lee. Signature moment: Game 1 shutdown of Yankees in 2009 World Series, when he speared groundballs behind his back and nonchalantly snagged pop-ups. He was 4–0 that postseason, with a 1.56 ERA. In 2012–2013, he had 429 strikeouts to 60 walks—an astounding 7.15-to-1 ratio.

37. Joel Embiid. Difficult figuring where to rank him, and he has the chance to move into the top 10 of this list. He sat hurt for two seasons before developing into one of the NBA's most dominant big men at age 22. The face of the franchise favors the nickname the Process to honor the dream of former GM Sam Hinkie.

36. Roy Halladay. The 2019 first-ballot Hall of Famer graced Philadelphia with the final four seasons of his career. Won the Cy Young in 2010, going 21–10 with a 2.44 ERA. Threw a perfect game against Miami as well as a no-hitter against Cincinnati in his first postseason start. RIP, Doc.

35. Eric Desjardins. Rico arrived with John LeClair in a franchise-changing 1995 trade. A reliable blueliner who could also quarterback the power play. Second among defensemen (to a guy yet to come on this list) in career goals, assists, and points for the Orange and Black.

34. Rick MacLeish. Graceful, occasionally lackadaisical winger amassed the sixth-most goals (328) and fifth-most points (697) in Flyers history. He was the NHL's leading playoff scorer in both of the title years of 1974–1975. Scored the lone goal in the 1–0 Cup-clinching victory over the Bruins in 1974.

33. Lionel Simmons. The Big 5's all-time scoring leader with 3,217 points in four seasons at La Salle. The Explorers finished 30–2 his senior season and was a number four seed (their highest ever) in the NCAA Tournament. National Player of the Year in 1990. His seven-year NBA career was hindered by injuries.

32. Tim Kerr. Only Flyer to top 50 goals four times. Scored 34 power play goals in 1985–1986. Tough as nails and a class act, he played through personal setbacks and serious injuries, which ultimately shortened his career.

31. Wilbert Montgomery. Sixth-round pick ran for 4,912 yards and scored 44 TDs between 1978 and 1981. First player in team history to rush for more than 1,000 yards three different times. No one will forget his 42-yard TD sprint to open the 1980 NFC title game against Dallas.

30. Claude Giroux. Over five seasons, ending in 2016, no NHL player scored more than his 367 points. Arguably deserved the 2017–2018 MVP Award (he finished fourth) when he topped 100 points for the first time. Tied for league lead with eight postseason goals in 2012—the last season the Flyers actually won a playoff round.

29. Brian Propp. Second all-time in goals (369) and assists (480) for the Flyers. Scored winning goal in his first NHL game. Registered 28 points in 1987 playoffs. Always a bridesmaid, he played in five Cup Finals—three with the Flyers—without ever winning. His "geefaw" postgoal salute was a fan favorite.

28. Nick Foles. Where to put the man so responsible for our last parade? Foles's career is among the NFL's oddest. Start with the 27-TD-to-2-INTs in 2013. Seven touchdowns in one game, tying a league record. He left, faltered badly, came back, and stepped up to . . . well, you know. Threw for 373 yards and three TDs in the Super Bowl and, of course, caught a TD pass of his own. Nick, we forever salute you.

27. LeSean McCoy. Shady led the NFL in rushing (1,607 yards) in 2013, the first Eagle to do so in 64 seasons. The franchise's career leader with 6,672 rushing yards. He had a brilliant 217-yard game dancing through eight inches of snow against the Lions. Chip Kelly traded him in 2015 for Kiko Alonso and a bag of beans.

26. Mark Howe. More goals (138) and assists (342) than any defenseman in Flyers history. His plus/minus was an amazing plus-85 in 1985–1986. An underrated Hall of Fame talent who was overshadowed by exciting teammates and his own bloodlines.

25. Mike Quick. Graceful, disciplined receiver made five straight Pro Bowls. Caught more TDs than anyone in NFL from 1984 to 1988—one of them a 99 yarder. Broken leg at age 29 stole his career. He's done pretty well in his second job as Eagles radio color man.

24. Brian Westbrook. He amassed 10,710 rushing and receiving yards (including playoffs) plus 74 TDs in eight seasons with the Eagles. Created some of the franchise's most memorable highlights. Also set five NCAA records at Nova, including 9,885 career all-purpose yards.

23. Randall Cunningham. The Ultimate Weapon. An electric, sometimes infuriating QB who could pass, run, and—yes—even kick. In 11 seasons as an Eagle, he emerged as the third leading all-time passer and sixth leading all-time rusher. NFL Player of the Year in 1990.

22. Harold Carmichael. Eagles' all-time leader in receptions (589), yards (8,978), and TDs (79). A 6-foot-8 target with good hands. Once held the NFL record by catching a pass in 127 straight games. It's a sin that he's not in the Pro Football Hall of Fame.

21. Ryan Howard. Baseball's most feared slugger from 2006 to 2009, averaging 50 homers and 143 RBIs a year. He was second-quickest player ever to 300 HRs (to Ralph Kiner), reaching that mark in 1,093 games. Only Phillie to win awards as Rookie of the Year, MVP, *and* postseason MVP (for the 2007 NLCS). "Just get me to the plate, boys." Injuries, particularly torn Achilles, stole his talents.

20. Maurice Cheeks. Mo holds Sixers records for steals (1,942) and assists (6,212). Spent his career making many others on this list look good. Hallmark moment was his exclamation-point slam-dunk against the Lakers in the 1983 Finals. Finally elected to the Naismith Memorial Basketball Hall of Fame in 2018.

19. Donovan McNabb. Had a .652 winning percentage as an Eagle—92 wins, 49 losses, and one infamous tie. The first QB in NFL history to throw more than 30 TDs and fewer than 10 interceptions in the same season. He was known to disappoint in big games. "Number 5 will always love you!"

18. Cole Hamels. His 2008 postseason was among the best ever: five starts, 4–0 record, 1.29 ERA, MVP of both the NLC *and* the World Series. His 114 wins as a Phillie rank first among any homegrown pitcher since 1959. A consistent and durable lefty who made between 30 and 33 starts nine straight years. Tossed a no-hitter in his final Phillies start, July 25, 2015.

17. Moses Malone. Arrived in 1982 to help a team that owed us one and delivered the NBA title. In 1982–1983, he was league MVP for the regular season and Finals, all-NBA first-team, and all-defensive team. Played only five seasons in Philly, but what an impact— three times led league in rebounding, four times averaged more than 22 points per game. "Fo', fo', fo'."

16. Eric Lindros. MVP in 1995, a year he tied for the NHL scoring title. Totaled 659 points in 486 games, the best point-per-game ratio in Flyers history. Elected to the NHL Hall of Fame. Injuries and a nasty divorce from the Flyers keep number 88 from moved further up toward the top of this list.

15. Billy Cunningham. The only guy who makes the lists of top players *and* top coaches in this book. The sixth man on the 1966–1967 title team, he averaged 20.8 points and 10.1 rebounds over nine Sixers seasons. Three-time all-NBA first team. Named to league's 50th Anniversary All-Time Team.

14. Bill Barber. Hockey Hall of Famer was the left winger on Broad Street Bullies' high-scoring LCB Line. Ranks first in goals (420) in franchise history. Often overshadowed by more colorful teammates, he was the hallmark of consistency—his nine 30-goal seasons are the most of any Flyer. Scored 31 shorthanded goals and triggered Flyers power play from the point.

13. Bernard Hopkins. The Executioner won his first middleweight title in 1993 and his last light heavyweight title in 2008. Made more than two dozen successful title defenses, destroying Trinidad and De La Hoya along the way. Career record: 55–8–2, with 32 KOs. A genuine Philadelphia guy. Outspoken and strategically brilliant.

12. Jimmy Rollins. Captain and sparkplug of the great Phillies teams, and the guy who started it in '07 by declaring, "We're the team to beat." Won MVP that season when he joined Willie Mays as the only two men in history to surpass 20 doubles, 20 triples, 30 homers, and 30 steals in the same year. Phils' all-time leader in hits. Winner of four Gold Gloves playing shortstop, playing alongside . . .

11. Chase Utley. From 2005 to 2009, he averaged 111 runs, 101 RBIs, 78 extra-base hits, and a .922 OPS. A terrific clutch hitter whose five homers in the 2009 World Series tied the MLB record. For all of Utley's offensive prowess, the second baseman's greatest moment may have come in the '08 Series when he faked a throw to first and pegged Tampa's Jason Bartlett scampering home. "World F#%@ing champions!"

10. Charles Barkley. Tenacious, entertaining Sir Charles led the NBA in rebounds in 1986–1987, despite standing just 6-foot-5. Four-time first-team all-NBA and six-time All-Star in his eight seasons here. Averaged 23.3 points and 11.6 rebounds as a Sixer. His .576 field goal percentage ranks second only to Wilt Chamberlain. A tremendous offensive force and maybe the most fun athlete ever to play in our city.

9. Allen Iverson. Certainly the most controversial man on this list. First pick of 1997 draft won four scoring titles and the 2001 league MVP Award. Two-time All-Star Game MVP. Took Sixers to 2001 Finals, averaging 32.9 points in 22 playoff games. At under 6 feet and 165 pounds, he regularly topped NBA charts in minutes, shots, steals, and tumbling to the hardwood. Only six players in history top the Answer's career 26.7 per-game scoring average.

8. Brian Dawkins. Greatest safety in Eagles history played more games (183) than any nonkicker to wear the uniform. A nine-time Pro Bowler and five-time first-team All-Pro.

He remains the only player in NFL history with more than 25 sacks, forced fumbles, and interceptions. We raged in 2009 when Joe Banner let him escape. Wolverine was named to the Pro Football Hall of Fame on February 3, 2018, the eve of the Eagles' win in Super Bowl LII.

7. Reggie White. Minister of Defense was Birds' greatest lineman, registering 124 sacks in eight seasons. First game as an Eagle: 10 tackles, 2½ sacks. Had 21 sacks (one short of the NFL record) in strike-shortened 1987. Cornerstone of Gang Green defense. At 295 pounds, he could outrun many running backs. His departure in 1993 started the downfall of the Braman-Kotite Eagles and led to a Packers Super Bowl win. Died at age 43, made Hall of Fame two years later.

6. Bernie Parent. "Only God saves more." Top goalie of his era posted shutouts in both Cup-clinching games. Backbone of those title teams, winning back-to-back Vezina Trophies (top goalie) and Conn Smythes (playoff MVP) in 1974 and '75. His combined goals-against average those years—1.95 for regular season, 1.96 for playoffs. Fifty shutouts as a Flyer, plus six more in postseason. First Flyer in the Hall of Fame. Eye injury ended his career at age 34. Nicest superstar you'll ever meet.

5. Julius Erving. Changed the game of basketball before he got here and Sixers' fate after arriving in 1976. MVP in 1981, All-Star each of his 11 seasons. Five-time all-NBA first-teamer. "We owe you one." Despite highlight-film status, was an amazingly consistent player, averaging over 20 points per game nine straight seasons. Doctor J's gravity-defying, floating baseline scoop against the Lakers in the 1980 Finals may be the most spectacular shot in NBA history.

4. Joe Frazier. Smokin' Joe won Olympic gold in 1964 and the world heavyweight title six years later. His 1971 Madison Square Garden defense over Muhammad Ali established his status as a Hall of Famer; indeed, his trilogy of fights against Ali are regarded as boxing's greatest-ever spectacles. Career record of 32–4–1, losing twice each to Ali and George Foreman. His 27 KO victims include solid fighters Jimmy Ellis, Bob Foster, George Chuvalo, and Jerry Quarry.

3. Bobby Clarke. Did more to define his franchise than any player on this list by instilling a work ethic and nastiness in Flyers. Three-time MVP, two-time Stanley Cup champion. Twice led NHL in assists, three times topped 100 points. Overtime goal vs. Bruins in Game 2 of '74 Finals turned the series to the Flyers. Holds all franchise career scoring records. Great passer, face-off man, always came out of the corner with the puck. Plus/minus for career an amazing plus-506. Never got booed (at least as a player).

2. Steve Carlton. Won four Cy Young Awards; no NL pitcher won more. Lefty's 1972 season—27 wins, 1.97 ERA for a 59-win team—is one of the best in baseball history. A horse, he topped 250 innings 12 times for the Phils. Holds franchise records for wins (241), starts (499), and strikeouts (3,031). First-ballot Hall of Famer. Started and won two games—including clincher—in 1980 World Series. Said Willie Stargell: "Hitting him is like trying to drink coffee with a fork."

1. Mike Schmidt. Without question the best third baseman ever. Led NL in homers eight times. His 548 HRs rank seventh among presteroid players. A warehouse full of awards: three-time MVP, 10 Gold Gloves, 12 All-Star appearances. Played 18 seasons in Philadelphia, most of any athlete. In his best season, 1980, he had 48 homers, 121 RBIs, and won the World Series MVP. Elected to the Hall of Fame in 1995 with 96 percent of the vote. Cool, aloof, always professional.

Photo Credits

Index

Seumalo, Isaac, 77
1776, 31
Shake Shack, 113
Shamet, Landry, 214
Shantz, Bobby, 172
Sharp, Patrick, 125
Shaw, Buck, 237
Sheppard, Lito, 200
Sheppard, Mel, 6
Shero, Fred, 44, 136, 162, 228
Shire, Talia, 225
Shockey, Jeremy, 144
Shoemaker, Craig, 87
Shorr-Parks, Eliot, 119
Short, Chris, 9, 36, 165, 205
Shyamalan, M. Night, 31, 211
Sielski, Mike, 27
Siemiontkowski, Hank, 48
Sigel, Jay, 1
Sikahema, Vai, 12, 233
Silver, Adam, 150
Silver Linings Playbook, 30
Simmonds, Wayne, 217, 258
Simmons, Ben, 11, 15, 36, 127, 242, 253, 258, 270
Simmons, Clyde, 26, 37, 258, 270
Simmons, Curt, 128
Simmons, Lionel, 81, 227, 274
Simon, Chris, 238
Simon, Paul, 193
Simpson, O. J., 34
Simpson, Ralph, 244
Sinatra, Frank, 32–33, 62
Sisemore, Clyde, 258
Sisemore, Jerry, 37, 96, 258
Sixth Sense, The, 31
Sizemore, Jerry, 19
Sizemore, Ted, 206
Skorich, Nick, 228
Slap Shot, 220, 222, 223
Smallwood, Wendell, 45
Smart, Rod, 202
Smith, Ben, 82
Smith, Billy, 148
Smith, Claire, 29
Smith, Emmitt, 8, 83
Smith, John, 80
Smith, Kate, 195
Smith, Lamont, 6
Smith, Lonnie, 23, 177
Smith, Marcus, 26, 34
Smith, Stephen A., 27
Smith, Steve, 183
Smith, Torrey, 119, 185
Smith, Will, 88, 211
Smith, Zhaire, 213
Snead, Norm, 197
Snider, Ed, 123, 158, 183, 228
Snipes, Wesley, 62
Snoop Dogg, 63
Snow, Eric, 185
Snow, Garth, 165

Söderström, Tommy, 68
Solodukhin, Vyacheslav, 208
Solomon, Freddie, 96
Soul Survivors, 98
Space Jams, 60
Spahn, Warren, 139
Spinners, 98
Spot Gourmet Burger, 113–114
Springsteen, Bruce, 30, 100
Sproles, Darren, 24, 172, 217
St. Joseph's University, 80
Stacy, Siran, 34
Stairs, Matt, 133, 163
Staley, Dawn, 3, 52, 270
Stallone, Sylvester, 31, 217, 220, 225
Stansbury, Terence, 156
Stargell, Willie, 277
Stark, Jayson, 28
Starr, Bart, 93–94
Starr, Ringo, 192
State Property 2, 62
Staubach, Roger, 144
Stauskas, Nik, 50, 213–214
Stefanski, Ed, 109, 185, 247
Steinbreneer sons, 146
Stern, David, 149
Stevens, Scott, 148
Stevenson, Dan, 236
Stickle, Leon, 124, 151
Still, Art, 6
Sting, 192
Stockton, Dick, 233
Stockton, John, 64, 92
Stone, Jeff, 24
Stoner, Lil, 46
Strahan, Michael, 144, 168
Stringer, C. Vivian, 52
Stuart, Dick, 43
Stubblefield, Clyde, 192
Stylistics, 98
SugarHouse, 112
Summer Catch, 62
Summerall, Pat, 234
Superman, 60–61
Superman II, 60
Swank, Hilary, 221, 225
Switzer, Barry, 83
Sykes, Terry, 25

T
Tait, Sean, 56
Talbot, Max, 126
Taliaferro, Adam, 101–102
Talladega Nights, 223
Tartabull, Danny, 182
Tatum, Jayson, 240
Tautalatasi, Junior, 48
Taylor, Bobby, 68, 168, 181, 200, 234, 271
Taylor, Jim, 94
Taylor, Michael, 138

Taylor, Tony, 11, 143, 170, 258
Teller, 210
Temple University, 80
Te'o-Nesheim, Daniel, 48
Thai Burger, 114
Theismann, Joe, 35
Therien, Chris, 50, 169, 234
This Is 40, 60
This Is Us, 62
Thomas, Frank, 90, 238
Thomas, Isiah, 64
Thomas, Kenny, 183
Thomas, Lee, 199, 207
Thomas, Tra, 37, 258, 270
Thomas, William, 196, 258, 269
Thome, Jim, 20, 37, 92, 181, 268
Thompson, Billy, 6
Thompson, Jason, 213
Thompson, Tessa, 30
Thompson, Tommy, 197
Timonen, Kimmo, 11, 97
Tin Cup, 223
Tinker, Mark, 63
Titus, Mark, 253
Tocchet, Rick, 65, 72, 76, 198, 258, 268
Tommy and Me, 88
Toney, Andrew, 13, 19, 42, 168, 258, 271
Tose, Leonard, 238
Trading Places, 31
Trammps, 98
Travolta, John, 30
Trillo, Manny, 143, 205
Tropic Thunder, 32
Trotter, Jeremiah, 50, 157, 185, 258, 272
Trout, Mike, 7, 23, 158, 210, 267
Trump, Donald, 86
Tucker, Darcy, 125, 148
Tugnutt, Ron, 94
Tunnell, Emlen, 1
Turner, Evan, 253

U
Uecker, Bob, 61, 215, 258
Umberger, R. J., 258
Unbreakable, 31
Uncommon Valor, 72
Undefeated, The, 60
Underall, Lacey, 258
Unger, Garry, 147
University of Pennsylvania, 79–80
Unser, Del, 258
Unutoa, Morris, 96, 258
Uosikkinen, David, 192
Upshall, Scottie, 258
Urbina, Ugueth, 59
Utley, Chase, 21, 38, 41, 69, 95, 132, 133, 164, 207, 229, 258, 264, 276